MIDDLE EASTERN MONOGRAPHS 11

POLITICS AND CHANGE
IN
AL-KARAK, JORDAN

MIDDLE EASTERN MONOGRAPHS

Advisory Editor: Albert Hourani, *St Antony's College, Oxford*

The first eight titles in the series, listed below, were issued under the auspices of the Royal Institute of International Affairs.

1. The Labour Movement in the Sudan, 1946–1955. *By* SAAD ED DIN FAWZI (*1957, out of print*)
2. Egypt in the Sudan, 1820–1881. *By* RICHADR HILL (*1959*)
3. The Intellectual Origins of Egyptian Nationalism. *By* JAMAL MOHAMMED AHMED (*1960*)
4. A History of Landownership in Modern Egypt, 1880–1950. *By* GABRIEL BAER (*1962*)
5. The Kurdish Republic of 1946. *By* WILLIAM EAGLETON, JR. (*1963*)
6. The National Income of Iraq, 1953–61. *By* K. HASEEB (*1964*)
7. The Tijaniyya: A Sufi Order in the Modern World. *By* JAMIL M. ABUN-NASR (*1965*)
8. The Egyptian Agrarian Reform, 1952–1962. *By* GABRIEL S. SAAB (*1967*)

---

9. The Society of the Muslim Brothers. *By* RICHARD P. MITCHELL (*1969*)

10. Heaven at Bay. The Jewish Kulturkampf in the Holy Land. *By* EMILE MARMORSTEIN (*1969*)

OXFORD
BOOKS

37 Dover Street London WIX 4AH   629 8494

POLITICS AND CHANGE IN AL-KARAK, JORDAN:
A Study of a Small Arab Town
and its District
by Peter Gubser.
(Middle Eastern Monographs)

£4.50 net

26 July, 1973

The source of the book should be stated as follows

OXFORD UNIVERSITY PRESS

POLITICS AND CHANGE IN AL-KARAK, JORDAN

A Study of a Small Arab Town and its District

BY

PETER GUBSER

LONDON

OXFORD UNIVERSITY PRESS

NEW YORK   TORONTO

1973

Oxford University Press, Ely House, London W. 1

GLASGOW NEW YORK TORONTO MELBOURNE WELLINGTON
CAPE TOWN IBADAN NAIROBI DAR ES SALAAM ADDIS ABABA
DELHI BOMBAY CALCUTTA MADRAS KARACHI LAHORE DACCA
KUALA LUMPUR SINGAPORE HONG KONG TOKYO

ISBN 0 19 215805 8

Printed in Great Britain
at the University Press, Oxford
by Vivian Ridler
Printer to the University

TO MY PARENTS

ACKNOWLEDGEMENTS

MY greatest debt is to my supervisor, Mr. Albert Hourani, of St. Antony's College, Oxford, for his always kind and excellent advice and direction. I also wish to extend my thanks to Miss Elizabeth Monroe and Dr. Roger Owen for helping me to obtain material and arrange interviews; to Lieut.-Gen. Sir John Glubb, Sir Alec Kirkbride, and the late Col. Frederick Peake for kindly answering many questions in the spring of 1969; and to Mr. Frank Stoakes of the University of Manchester for reading the manuscript and making many valuable comments and criticisms. At the American University of Beirut I especially wish to express my gratitude to the late Dr. Nabih Faris, Dr. Yusif Ibish, and Dr. Joseph Malone. In Amman I extend my thanks to Mazen Dajani, Adnan Bakhit, Sulayman Musa, Wasif Azar, and the Rifai family for their hospitality and assistance in helping me to obtain material. Miss Haifa Selman of Beirut deserves special mention for her long, painstaking work in preparing the maps. In addition, I owe considerable gratitude to Miss Katharine Duff for her assistance in editing the manuscript.

My warmest thanks go to the people of Al-Karak. Individuals of all tribes, minority groups, and strata were always kind and hospitable. They patiently answered my questions and opened their town and district to me for a year in 1968.

To my parents I am most grateful for support in all forms and at all times, especially in the trying period after the Arab-Israeli war in June 1967.

To my wife, Annie, I extend my profound thanks for her many and wise comments on the study, her judicious help in editing it, and her gracious and continual encouragement in its preparation.

P. G.

June 1972

ABBREVIATIONS

IBRD	International Bank for Reconstruction and Development. *The Economic Development of Jordan* (1957).
JD	Jordanian dinars (dinar = $2·80).
Q., Al-	'Uda Al-Qasus. 'Memoirs'. MS. written in mid-1920s.
Stat. Yb.	Dept. of Statistics. *Statistical Yearbook* (1950–67).

CONTENTS

DIAGRAMS

TABLES

INTRODUCTION

THE town of Al-Karak is situated on top of a small mountain in the centre of the district of that name in southern Jordan. Although this study is focused on the town, it also involves the district because of the integral relationship between the two. Most of the town's population is drawn from the tribes of the district; its economy is based on the latter's agriculture; and the history of the one is inseparable from that of the other. In the past there was very little difference between the life of the town and that of the district. Today, however, the social and political gap between them is widening. The traditional methods still exist, function, and are dominant in both, but the town has been subject to considerable change, while only a modicum has taken place among the villages and encampments of the district. The latter reinforce the traditional norms of the town, for the people are of the same tribes, political tradition, history, and economy. Conversely, the changed and modernized elements of the town slowly influence the life of the district in their direction.

This study of power and politics in a small Arab town was undertaken for a variety of reasons. Al-Karak was not chosen as a political or historical subject which should be recorded and analysed for its own sake, but as an example of one type of small town and its district in the Arab Middle East which may help to fill the present lack of material on this subject. Because of the political climate in the Middle East during the period of field research in 1968, the choice lay only between Lebanon and Jordan. The latter was chosen as being more typical of the Arab Middle East than Lebanon, where politics are dominated by the religious split between Islam and Christianity. And, among the many small towns in Jordan, the most typical would be one with the least number of Palestinian refugees. A town with deep historical roots and with a small, but significant, Christian minority was sought in order to ensure some continuity and standing tradition and to introduce a feature common to many of the Arab countries. Finally, one with a population small enough to be studied by a single individual was desirable. Al-Karak fulfilled these requirements.

Politics is the art of gathering and exercising power and authority in a human society. From an internal viewpoint, the size of the society may vary from an extended family to the entire world. Externally, as well, each society has different relationships to others. The given society may be an international system, a nation-state, or an integral part of a larger unit, e.g. a district, a village, a tribal segment. In a historical perspective, Al-Karak, the town and district, fits into two categories both internally and externally. Before the late Ottoman reoccupation of the area in 1893, it was an independent unit; no larger force continually exercised power or authority over it. From 1893 to the present time it has formed part of a larger unit, first the Ottoman Empire, then Transjordan/Kingdom of Jordan. In the earlier period, power and authority stemmed entirely from a local base; in the later, they are shared with a larger political system.

Certain limits in scope are therefore imposed in this study. The politics of the area may be considered as part of a continuum in which the extended family, tribal section, tribe, and village are at one end, the provincial capital and district in the middle, the nation-state towards the other end, and the international political system at the extreme. As the focus of this work is on the politics of the district and of the town, kinship structure, villages, and tribes are not investigated for their own sake, but only as they relate to the gathering and exercising of power and authority in the whole area. At the other end of the continuum, the central government and the international system are dealt with only in so far as they influence the area's politics.

Method of Analysis

The purpose of this study is to describe the structure, functions, and dynamics of the political society, to discuss the persistence of traditional forces and practices within the system thanks to the continuing power and authority of the tribe, and to indicate the change within the political system. A description of the area set in a historical perspective will therefore lead directly into the other two themes: continuity with the past and change.

In the field of political science, many theoretical frameworks for the study of any given political system have been formulated. The method of presentation and analysis employed here is dependent upon these theoretical developments. It is simply the investigation of political and politically related groups and roles and the use of selected examples for the purpose of establishing the structure, functions, and dynamics of the political society. Before studying each of these groups certain questions must be posed. Specifically, is it a kin, territorial, or 'cross-cutting' group? Is it corporate (i.e. does it have continuity, identity, organization, exclusive affairs), or non-corporate? Is its structure horizontal, vertical, pyramidal, segmentary, or a combination of these? How does one become a member of it? Finally, what outside influences affect the group

and, what is the nature of its own external influence? It is necessary to note that each group is taken for what it is and is described
in the terms most appropriate to it; it is not just put into an
artificial category. Thus for a given group some of these questions
may not apply and are passed over.

Questions about political roles are the next stage of inquiry. How
are these acquired, maintained, and exercised? To which group or
groups is each of these activities related? What activity does the
political role involve: settling disputes, making and executing
rules, or a combination of these? What is the significance of the
personality of the political leader? What are the limits on his ability
to act? What power and authority does he have? These questions
and others are answered in descriptive passages as well as by the
use of selected examples, which also have other functions. It is
hoped that they will throw additional light on the groups, indicate
the relationships between them and their roles in dynamic terms,
and show how the individual fits into the system. Finally, the
examples are not intended to form a history of the area, but are
rather chosen to analyse and demonstrate the kinds of problem
that the society faces and resolves.

In this consideration of groups and roles, socio-economic strata
require some added discussion. Following in the tradition of Weber
and Parsons, it is socio-economic stratification rather than class
structure that is being investigated. Weber defines classes in
economic terms,[1] while stratification takes on a much broader
definition, of which material possessions or one's relation to the
means of production are only a part.[2] In Al-Karak, as in virtually
any society, economic classes may be defined, but because they
would be artificial abstractions, they would be of little help towards
an understanding of the society. In contrast, socio-economic
strata do have importance, especially in the last two decades.
Although many gradations or levels may be discerned, for the sake
of simplicity (and at the risk of over-generalization) only three
broad strata, lower, middle, and upper, are distinguished in the
traditional system. In studying the contemporary period, the

---

[1] Max Weber states: 'We may speak of a "class" when (1) a number of people
have in common a specific causal component of their life chances, in so far as
(2) this component is represented exclusively by economic interests in the
possession of goods and opportunities for income, and (3) is represented under
the conditions of the commodity or labor markets.' (*From Max Weber*, ed. and
tr. H. H. Gerth and C. Wright Mills (1948), p. 181; see also pp. 180–95.)

[2] Talcott Parsons states that a man's position in a stratification ranking should
be analysed in terms of: (1) membership in a kinship unit; (2) personal qualities,
e.g. sex, age, beauty, intelligence, and strength; (3) achievements; (4) possessions;
(5) authority; and (6) power. ('An Analytical Approach to the Theory of Social
Stratification', *American J. of Sociology*, 45 (May 1940), pp. 848–9.)

educated middle stratum is added; and this group becomes in turn a valuable indicator of the process of change.

In this study, although the functional requisites of the political, system are not always discussed in functional terms, they may be readily discerned. Political socialization is not specifically mentioned, but the roles of the family, tribe, informal groupings, schools, and other formal institutions in this process are easily understood. Interest articulation and political communication as they are manifested in Al-Karak are brought out in the description of the political structure and its dynamics. Patterns of settling disputes, making and executing rules, and political integration are directly involved in the discussion of the groups, roles, and dynamics of the political system.

Through the above method of analysis, the themes of the persistence of tradition and the introduction of change are also present. The groups and roles, and their interaction, are traced through a 100-year historical perspective. Where traditional norms and practices are still operative, they are noted; where change in the system and its parts has occurred, it is recorded.

Although there is substantial literature on change and modernization,[1] no one has yet devised a method for measuring it. Parallels to what was found in Al-Karak, and valuable suggestions as to what to look for and what it means, are present in the works of the students of social and political change, but none has contributed a workable framework for analysis. As a result, for want of a better method, change and modernization must be presented in an entirely descriptive form.

In Al-Karak one of the essential new developments of the changing political system is the growth of an educated middle stratum. Under many names, this feature has been recognized and investigated by students of the developing countries. Each has given it an important, often crucial or key position in the transitional societies. There is, however, no agreement as to what it consists of, or the relative significance of its various segments. (1) Kautsky[2] writes about a new middle class composed of white-collar workers, professional people, and intellectuals. The white-collar workers do not become important until the advanced stages of industrialization, while the intellectuals are the key group in the transformation of the lesser-developed political systems.

---

[1] See, e.g., D. E. Apter, *The politics of modernization* (1965); S. N. Eisenstadt, *Modernization: protest and change* (1966); C. Geertz, *Old societies and new states* (1963); M. J. Levy, Jr., *Modernization and the structure of societies* (1966); and E. Shils, *Political development in the new states* (1968).

[2] 'An Essay in the Politics of Development', in his *Political change in underdeveloped countries: nationalism and communism* (1962), pp. 22, 24.

(2) Hodgkin,[1] in his discussion of the middle class in Africa, distinguishes between the bourgeoisie who have wealth on a substantial scale, or are in the professions, and the *classe moyenne* of small entrepreneurs, traders, and low-level salaried men. Although he gives some general characteristics of the latter group he does not delve further into its origins or its relationships with the other classes. (3) Polk[2] notes the importance of the new men at all levels of society, but contributes little, saying that insufficient information about them is available. (4) Halpern (*The politics of social change in the Middle East and North Africa* (1963), pp. 51–78), devotes a chapter to the new middle class. He attributes paramount importance to the leaders of this group, but virtually passes over the modern lower-middle class. (5) Apter (pp. 138–78) assesses at length the significance of all levels of educated men from the civil servants to the top élites, but offers no systematic method of analysing their role in society. (6) Shils (pp. 15–24, 87–9) sees the higher educated élites as playing a key role in the new states. Although he mentions in passing 'the more or less educated urban middle classes' (p. 15), he does not investigate the group at any length. In a concluding passage, however, he states that, in a modernizing society, the higher élite must, among other requirements, recruit 'a stratum of intellectuals of intermediate level who can reinterpret traditional beliefs, adapt them to modern needs, and translate them into a modern idiom' (p. 89). (7) Binder[3] takes Shils's argument a step further. He stresses that, in order to realize national integration, the gap between élites and non-élites must be closed (p. 627). The middle-level élites are the key to this process, for the nature of government and polity depends on how the gap is eliminated,

that is, upon the performance of the mediating elites. Modernity may not be achieved without mobilizing the support of the human resources of the new states. These resources will not be mobilized unless the goals of modernization are made meaningful to those now beyond the gap, in terms of their own beliefs and experiences (p. 630).

The crucial role of the upper levels of the educated élite for political integration and modernization in Jordan is not denied in this study, but because the subject is a rural district and a small town, this group is only indirectly relevant to it. As it is a lower-level educated middle class that exists and operates in Al-Karak,

[1] T. Hodgkin, 'The African Middle Class', in I. Wallerstein, ed., *Social change, the colonial situation* (1966), pp. 359–62.
[2] W. R. Polk, *The United States and the Arab world* (Cambridge, Mass. 1965), pp. 215–88.
[3] L. Binder, 'National Integration and Political Development', *American Political Science R.* 58 (Sept. 1964), pp. 627–31.

the observations of Shils and Binder that the modernization of a society must affect all levels, just as the political system involves them all, are much more relevant to this study. Teachers and civil servants, then, are the key men in this process, for it is they who deal with the mass of the population on a daily basis.

Any schema for the analysis of a political system necessarily distorts it, because, essentially, the author is merely cutting the society up and putting it back together again. By the examination of one element before another, both somewhat lose their perspective. Any political system is a living, dynamic unity with individuals relating to one another at all levels at all times. It is hoped that the use of examples plus the order of presentation of the groups and roles will demonstrate the life of the system as a whole.

Order of Presentation

It is also desirable briefly to explore the order of presentation. Chapter 1 is devoted to the general background of the area: environment, history, demography, and economics. In the historical section 3,000 years of Al-Karak's past are briefly traced, the emphasis being on the past hundred years. In the other two sections the environment and the local demography and economy are described in order to lay a broad basis for a full understanding of the political system. To bring out the continuity and change in Al-Karak's society, the remainder of the work is divided into two major parts. Although the first involves only the traditional groups, roles, and dynamics, it holds great significance for the next section, for many aspects of these are still operative. The second part is concerned with the changes in the district and town. The continuing traditional features are noted in order to maintain an over-all perspective, but the emphasis is on the new developments in the groups, roles, and dynamics of the political system.

Following the method of analysis outlined in the previous section, Chapter 2 is devoted to the political and politically related groups in the 'traditional' society, and Chapter 3 to the political roles and examples which demonstrate the dynamics of that society. Chapters 4 and 5 correspond to the previous two for the 'contemporary' political system. Legitimacy, authority, and power are given special consideration for both periods, because they reveal some of the limits and possibilities of action on the part of the society's leaders. In addition, because of their crucial role in fostering change, an outline of the growth of communications and education in the last two decades is given in the introduction to Chapter 4.

Source Material

A limited amount of published material on Al-Karak exists in various forms: commentaries and memoirs by travellers, missionaries, colonial officials, and Arab administrators. Some unpublished memoirs, records of the town's Municipal Council, and Foreign and Colonial Office reports are also available. The industrious Department of Statistics of Jordan has published a variety of data which, though often unfortunately of doubtful accuracy, are at the least valuable indicators. By far the greater part of the material, however, was gained through field research by the author, who lived in Al-Karak from January to November 1968.

Transliteration

Arabic words and names are transliterated with no diacritical marks but ' (*'ain*) and ' (*hamza*). This system could be criticized for not changing the classical Arabic 'q' to the predominantly locally used 'g' as in 'game' and the 'k' to the less predominantly used 'ch'. However, a few of the Karakis do not follow the first variation and many do not use the second. The pronunciation of vowels is also subject to considerable variation. A simple transliterated form of the classical Arabic which an increasingly large proportion of the population knows and writes has therefore been adopted.

1

ENVIRONMENT, HISTORY, AND ECONOMICS

Environment[1]

THE governorate of Al-Karak, of which the district forms part, lies east of the southern half of the Dead Sea in the East Bank of the Kingdom of Jordan. Conveniently, the historical area of Al-Karak, as a political entity, is very much the same as the present district.

Map 1, p. 9, indicates Al-Karak's geographical position in relation to the rest of Jordan. The Balqa', which includes the town of Madaba, borders it on the north; and to the south lie the district of Tafila and the governorate of Ma'an. The Dead Sea lies on the west and the Syrian (or North Arabian) Desert to the east. Each of the borders forms a formidable, but not impassable, barrier. The Wady Al-Mujib and Wady Al-Hasa, both dropping from heights of 900 m to well below sea-level, are the northern and southern boundaries. The excessively saline water of the Dead Sea cuts off the west, and the east fades into a virtually rainless desert.

The district of Al-Karak covers approximately 2,850 square km, with an average elevation of about 770 m. From the east the Syrian Desert rises to form high limestone plateaux, with an average elevation of 1,100 m, and hills which reach 1,300 m, forming the backbone of the area. Then the terrain drops precipitously to the Dead Sea, 395 m below sea-level.

As a result of its varied geography, Al-Karak has three distinct types of climate. The region next to the Dead Sea is characterized by warm, short winters, with rainfall varying from 5 to 15 cm, and extremely hot, dry summers. There is no spring or autumn. The central part of the area averages 35 cm of rain from November to April, but in erratic yearly amounts, 10 cm, for example, in 1962/3 but 50 cm in 1963/4. In the winter the temperature often drops below freezing; the summers are mild with a few hot days. The eastern edge of the district receives much less rain, 10–20 cm, and its temperature variation is much like that of the central area.

[1] This section, including the maps, is based on observations by the author and on the following publications: G. L. Harris and others, *Jordan* (1958), pp. 19–27; R. Patai, *The Kingdom of Jordan* (1958), pp. 3–9, 119–21; IBRD; and *Stat. Yb.*, *1950–67.*

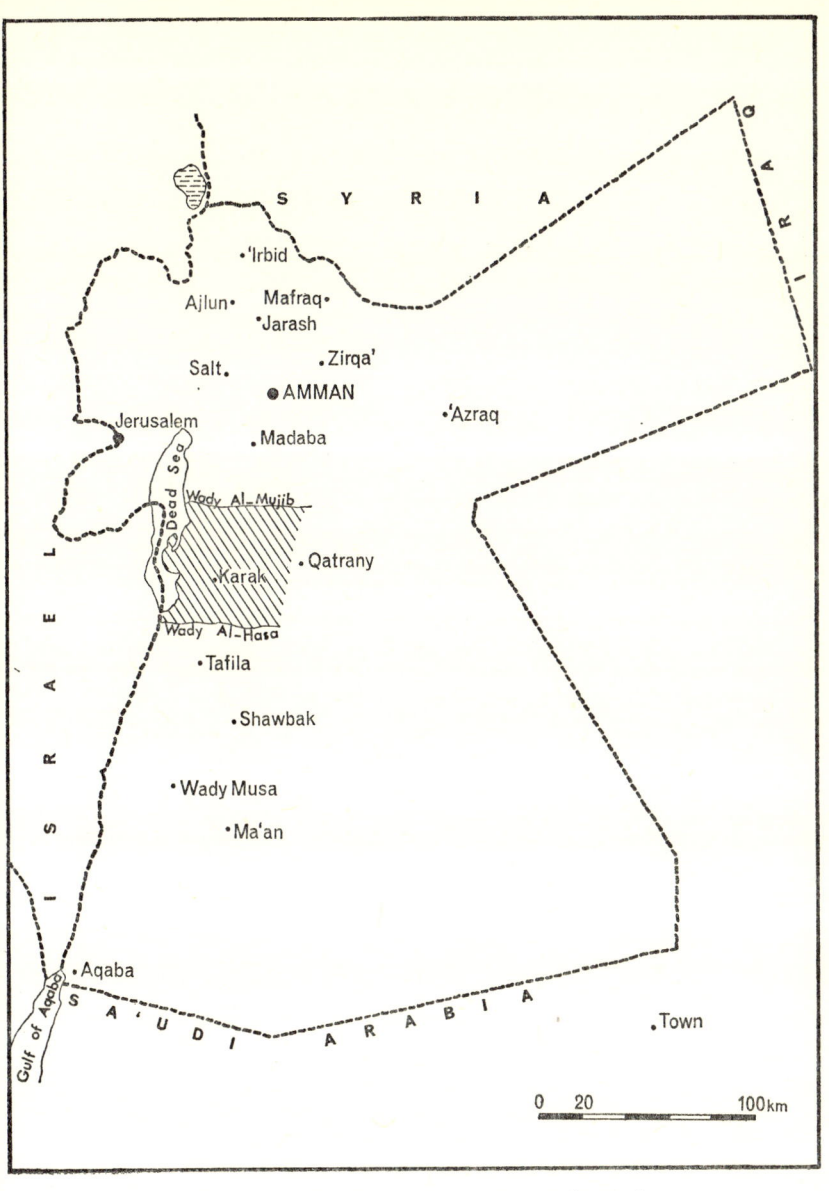

MAP 1. Jordan—East Bank—Al-Karak (shaded)

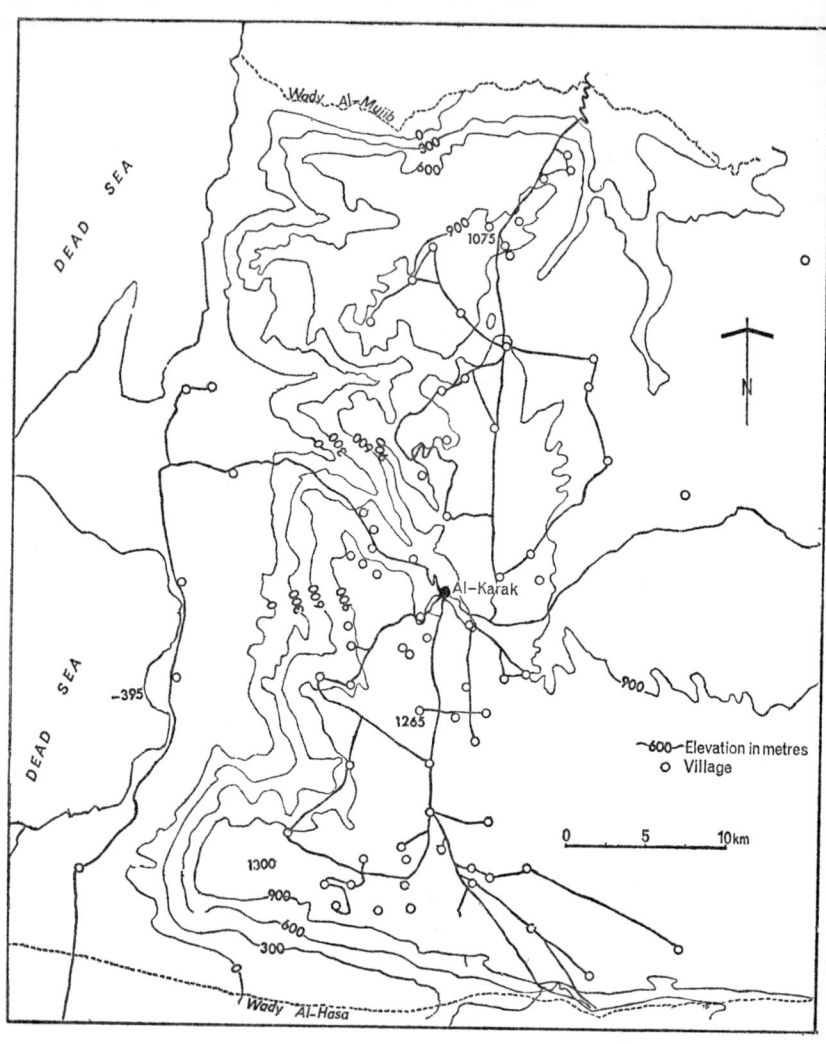

Within the map:
DEAD SEA

Wady Al-Mujib

600
900
1075
900

Al-Karak

-395

1265

900

600—Elevation in metres
o Village

0   5   10 km

1300
900
600
300

Wady Al-Hasa

N

MAP 2. Al-Karak: to show contours

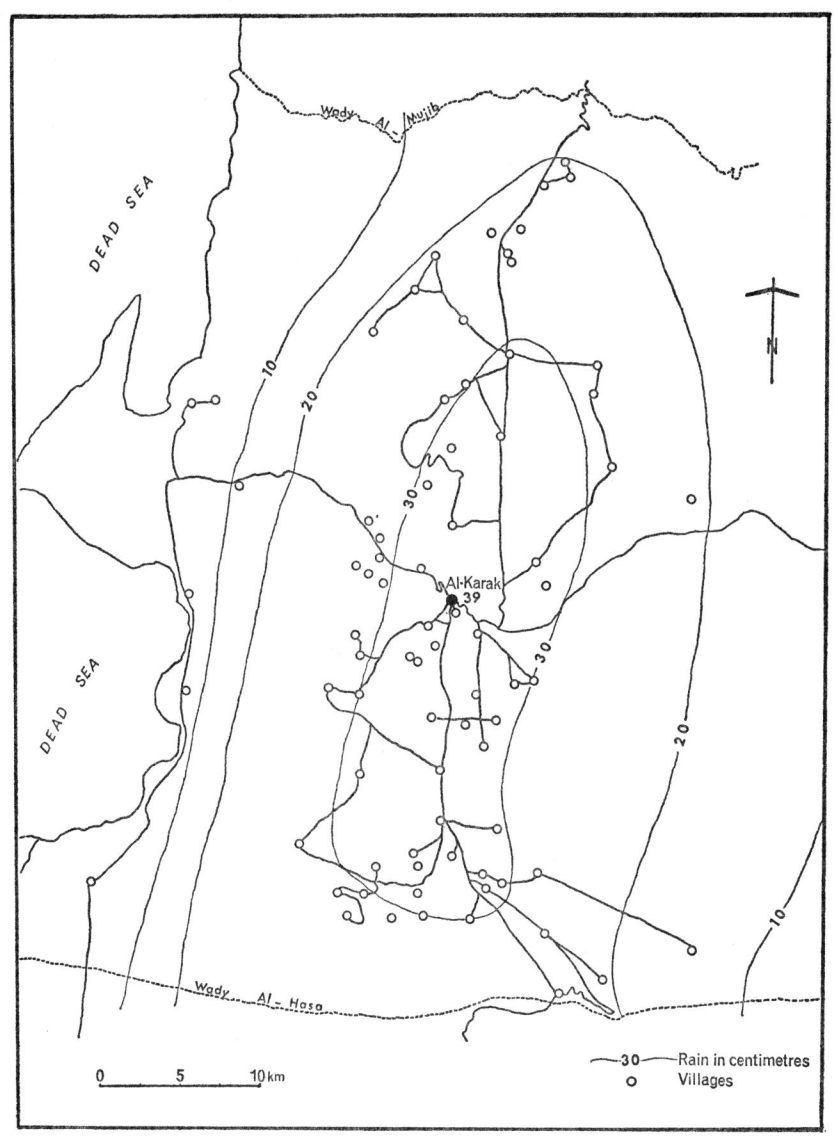

MAP 3. Al-Karak: mean Annual Rainfall

The land on the edge of the Dead Sea has proved fertile with irrigation. On the plateau the soils are in some places light and shallow, suitable only for grains, and in others deep and suitable for fruit-growing. The semi-desert area is used for marginal cereal cultivation when the rains are sufficient. Both here and in the precipitous northern, southern, and western areas of the district, sheep and goats forage on the sparse grass. Large forests once existed in the region, but both the Ottomans and the indigenous population have ravaged them. Reafforestation is now promoted and financed by the central government.

Rain follows the contours of the land. The village population also lies mostly within the 30 cm rain-belt. It will be seen later on in this study that those living outside this belt are also on the margins of the district's political life and hold little political power.

History

Al-Karak was involved in most of the major historical movements in the Middle East owing to its central position, bordering on, or lying close to, Egypt, Palestine, Syria, and Arabia. It was strategically important because of its naturally fortified position on one of the major communications routes of the Middle East. Only in this century have new modes of transport and warfare by-passed it completely. The town has been variously known as Kir of Moab, Kir Haraseth, Petra Deserti, Charac-Moba, Castle of Crac, Pierre du Désert, and Al-Karak. The area first appeared in history in 2400 B.C., during the Bronze Age, with an advanced sedentary agricultural civilization, but this suddenly and inexplicably disappeared in 1800 B.C. About 600 years later, a new civilization, the Moabite Kingdom, developed. It was then that the site of the present-day town of Al-Karak was first settled and fortified. Since then it has probably been continuously inhabited, with possible short periods of interruption. In the tenth century B.C. the Moabites were defeated by, and afterwards paid tribute to, David of the Israelite Kingdom, but under the great Moabite king Mesha the area regained its freedom in 840 B.C. During the late ninth, eighth, and seventh centuries it fell under Assyrian influence and during the next two centuries under the Persians. Alexander the Great conquered it with the rest of Asia Minor, and after his death Ptolemy of Egypt controlled it, along with Palestine and southern Syria.

In the second century B.C. the Moabite civilization gave way to that of the Nabataean Arabs which was centred in Petra, south of Al-Karak. This was a trading kingdom and at times a buffer state between the Ptolemies of Egypt and the Seleucids of Syria. In the middle of the first century B.C. Pompey established Roman control

over Transjordan, soundly defeating the Nabataeans in 32 B.C., but
the kingdom was able to retain a large measure of internal independence as a vassal state of Rome. Internal rule changed hands
in A.D. 106, when various Arab tribes conquered the region and
dissolved the Nabataean Kingdom. In the fourth century A.D., when
the Emperor Constantine (324–37) was converted to Christianity,
most of Transjordan was also converted and Al-Karak became
part of the bishopric of Petra. It came under the Ghassanides in
the sixth century as part of the Byzantine Empire. In the early
seventh century it fell briefly to the Persians, but soon reverted to
Byzantine control, only to fall to the Muslim conquerors.

The first battle between the Muslims and the Byzantines was
fought in the Al-Karak area at Mu'ta in A.D. 629, but the Muslim
forces were heavily outnumbered and defeated. The soldiers of
Islam are said to have fought heroically. Their tombs in what is
now the village of Al-Mazar, close to the field of battle, are considered to be holy and are a place of pilgrimage; and much of the
land aroun dAl-Mazar is owned by the *'Awqaf* institution, which
rents it to local peasants who also have the right of inheritance over
it. After the Muslim conquest Al-Karak was ruled as part of the
various Islamic dynasties, but in the twelfth century the Crusaders
conquered the region. Baldwin I started a fortress-building programme of which Al-Karak was a part, and its imposing citadel,
known as 'Pierre du Désert', was finished during the reign of
Baldwin II. Later, Al-Karak became the centre of Renaud de
Châtillon's rule in Transjordan. This Crusader was continually
opposed by Saladin and more than once earned his wrath by
breaking treaties. When Al-Karak came under attack by Saladin's
forces in 1183 Renaud decided to defend only the fortress, so the
town was quickly taken, but Saladin suddenly withdrew because
of better opportunities elsewhere. Peace was established, but
Renaud broke it in 1187 by raiding rich caravans. After Saladin
had defeated the Crusaders at the Horns of Hattin on the Sea of
Galilee in July 1187, and had put the untrustworthy Renaud to
death, Al-Karak was besieged and starved out in October of that
year. The Ayyubids ruled the area in the late twelfth and thirteenth
centuries and this was the last stronghold to fall to the Mamlukes
under Baibars. Except for brief occupation by Arab forces, it
continued under Mamluke rule until the Ottomans defeated them
in 1517.

The Ottomans[1] set up a government in Al-Karak and garrisoned

---

[1] The source material for this period is sketchy to say the least. This account
is based on J. L. Burckhardt, *Travels in Syria and the Holy Land* (1822); J.
Dissard, 'Les Migrations et les vicissitudes de la tribu des 'Amer', *Revue biblique*

Shawbak, south of the area. Also, significantly, the pilgrimage route
to Mecca, which for centuries passed directly by Al-Karak town,
was moved to what later became the Hijaz railway route on the
eastern edge of the district. This dramatically diminished the
importance of the area, and perhaps partly explains the willingness
of the Ottoman government to let Al-Karak retain virtual independence (with some exceptions) from the mid-sixteenth century
until 1893.

Towards the latter part of the reign of Sulayman the Magnifi-
cent (1520–66), a powerful tribe of Al-Karak, the Tamimiyya,
rebelled against Ottoman rule.

As it would have cost much money to send a regular force to Kerak the
Wali of Damascus asked Yusef al-Nimr of Nablus to deal with the
situation. Yusef at once collected a force and marched to Kerak where
he soon restored order, and those of the Temimiya who were not killed
fled to Hebron. A new governor was then sent to Kerak and one of the
brothers of Yusef, either Othman Agha or Hasan Agha, was appointed
to the command of the troops.

Very shortly after this, the new governor became disloyal and with
the support of the Arabs in his district declared his complete independence of Ottoman rule (Peake, *History*, pp. 84–5).

The Ottomans then tried to regain control through negotiations,
but failed. 'After this the Turks made no further attempt to re-
establish their rule in Kerak and Shobek and so the brother of
Yusef al-Nimr became chief of the district' (Peake, ibid., p. 85).
His descendants and the local Ottoman soldiers in Al-Karak became known as the 'Aghwat tribe. In 1678/9 and again in 1710/11
the Ottomans sent punitive expeditions against the Karakis, but
did not establish permanent rule in the area (Laoust, pp. 219, 231).

From this point to the reoccupation of the region by the Ottomans in 1893, the history of Al-Karak, with a couple of exceptions,
is the history of local tribal politics, relations with the neighbours
of Al-Karak, new tribes entering the area, and the rise of the
Majaly tribe to power. Initially the 'Aghwat, which, together with
its allied tribes, was known as the 'Imamiyya, ruled the area. The
alliance's chief rival was the 'Amr, a semi-nomadic[1] tribe, which

(Jerusalem, 18 Jan. 1905); H. Laoust, *Les Gouverneurs de Damas sous les
Mamlouks et les premiers Ottomans (658–1156/1260–1744)* (1952); Ihsan al-
Nimr, *Tarikh Jabal Nablus wa al-Balqa'*, ii (1961); Col. F. Peake, *History and
tribes of Jordan* (1958); 'Uda al-Qasus, 'Memoirs'. (Unpubl. MS written in the
mid-1920s; abbr. to al-Q. in later footnotes); and oral tradition.

[1] The terms nomadic, semi-nomadic, semi-sedentary, and sedentary are used
throughout this study. The classifications may be considered as four segments
of a continuum. The nomads are the 'true' bedouin who depend mostly upon
camels rather than sheep and goats for their livelihood, live in black tents, and
do not settle in permanent houses. The semi-nomadic people may or may not

may have significantly increased in size in the late seventeenth century through the addition of distant relatives from the Hijaz.

The Majaly originally came to Al-Karak as merchants from Hebron. In the ensuing years they acquired some land, and increased their numbers by bringing in their Hebroni relatives. Then, from the eighteenth century onwards, a succession of brilliant political leaders were able to raise the tribe from a virtually powerless position to that of the leading power of the region and a mover in the whole of Transjordan. In the early 1700s they allied themselves with the 'Amr and massacred the 'Imamiyya alliance, eliminating it as a force in the area. However, the Majaly were definitely the junior partners in the alliance with the 'Amr. While in power the 'Amr were noted for cruelty and ruthlessness, not only in exacting money from the local tribes but also in their brutal personal treatment of the Karakis.

The opportunity for the next round in the rise of the Majaly power came when the Bany Sakhr, a nomadic bedouin tribe, moved up from the Hijaz in the late eighteenth century. The Majaly allied themselves with them as well as with the Bany Hamida and the Hijaya, both local semi-nomadic tribes. This temporary alliance was able to force the 'Amr out of the area, but not to destroy them. In the early nineteenth century the Majaly asked the 'Amr to return, and when they did so, persuaded the Bany Hamida to destroy the tribe's effective power. The Majaly then relegated them to some relatively poor land in the north-east part of the district along the Wady Al-Mujib. The next step was to eliminate the Bany Hamida. Soon after the defeat of the 'Amr, the Majaly incited the local Karakis to attack the Bany Hamida, which they did, seriously reducing their power. The tribe was then forced to move out of its land immediately north of Al-Karak town to the north-west fringes of the district and the Balqa', further to the north of Al-Karak. The Majaly took this land mostly for their own use, but did give part of it to two of the local Christian tribes. Unlike the 'Amr the Bany Hamida remained powerful enough to continue hostilities against the Majaly in varying degrees until the 1920s. Thus by the early nineteenth century the Majaly had eliminated or weakened all the major local contenders for power,

own camels, but definitely raise sheep and goats. They tend to live in one area and, unlike the nomads, move only short distances. Both groups rely to a small extent on planting grains. The semi-sedentary tribes cultivate more crops than do the nomads and the semi-nomads, although they also practise animal husbandry. However, as a rule, only part of a residential group moves the sheep and goats to new pastures, the remainder staying with the crops. They may or may not live in permanent houses. Finally, the sedentary people live in mud or stone houses, depend on crops for most of their income, and what animals they raise are usually under the care of lone herders.

but still had their new allies, the Bany Sakhr, to cope with. The latter were collecting considerable *khawa*, a payment, from most of the local tribes and the Majaly felt compelled to lavish gifts on them.

In the first half of the nineteenth century two outside forces interrupted the play of local politics and gained temporary influence in Al-Karak: the Wahhabis and Muhammad 'Ali Pasha's son 'Ibrahim Pasha. In the early 1800s the Karakis recognized the supremacy of Ibn Sa'ud of the Wahhabis, but his forces never exercised direct control in the area and did not collect taxes. Egyptian forces, however, did occupy the town and region. In 1834 Qasim al-'Ahmad of Nablus rebelled against 'Ibrahim Pasha in Palestine, and after his defeat he fled to Al-Karak. 'Ibrahim Pasha followed him there and captured the town in the same year. The then shaykh of the Majaly was forced to flee and took refuge south of the district with the nomadic Huwaytat, the paramount tribe in the south of Transjordan. Because of this tribe's traditional enmity towards the people of Al-Karak and especially the Majaly, it turned him over to 'Ibrahim Pasha's government, which hanged him in Jerusalem. In 1841 'Ibrahim Pasha withdrew from Syria, leaving Al-Karak free from external rule until its reoccupation by the Ottomans in 1893.

Soon after these events[1] Muhammad Al-Majaly became the paramount shaykh and remained so until his death in 1886. In order to break the hold of the Bany Sakhr, he turned to the Bany 'Attiya, another nomadic tribe which camped in the Wady al-'Araba south of the Dead Sea. In the 1860s the Majaly, the Karakis, and the Bany 'Attiya attacked the Bany Sakhr, applying enough force to remove them from the area. The tribe moved to the north and eventually forced the 'Adwan out of the Balqa'. The relationship between the Karakis and the Bany Sakhr became one of raiding and occasional temporary alliances which continued until the 1930s. The Majaly were now supreme in Al-Karak.

The two decades following the defeat of the Bany Sakhr proved to be the most violent and unsettling in the recent history of Al-Karak. The Karakis raided and, conversely were raided by, the Bany Hamida within the district, the tribes of the Balqa' and Tafila north and south of the region, and the bedouin tribes, the

---

[1] The period from 1840 to the present is much better documented. Many accounts by travellers, missionaries, and Arab functionaries, and foreign and domestic government documents and publications are available. More importantly, most of the period is in the living memory of the elders or, for the very early period (*c.* 1840–90), heard directly from their fathers. On the local history of Al-Karak many sources are cited in the following pages, but the author also checked to see if these facts correspond to local tradition.

Huwaytat and the Bany Sakhr. A major tribal war was also provoked. The Bany 'Attiya were becoming restless, so the Majaly encouraged them to encroach upon the land of the Huwaytat. War broke out in 1877. On one side were the Karakis, two sections of the Bany Sakhr, a section of the Hijaya, the Salayta, the people of Shawbak, and part of Ma'an. On the other side were the Huwaytat, part of Ma'an, and Wady Musa. The Karakis and their allies first attacked Tafila and destroyed some houses, then met the main force south of Tafila and were defeated,[1] after which a heavy raiding relationship persisted until peace was established fifteen years later. From this some interesting alliance patterns may be derived. First, Al-Karak's allies, like Tafila's, were its traditional trading partners, whether they were semi-sedentary, e.g. Ma'an and Shawbak, or semi-nomadic or nomadic, e.g. the Hijaya or the Bany 'Attiya. Other nomadic allies joined in for the potential loot, sections of the Bany Sakhr, for example. This type of pattern existed at all times, not just during this particular war. Thus on the one hand long-term enemies tended to be neighbours involved in the production of the same trading commodities, or their trading partners; and on the other, traditional allies tended to be trading partners and not settled neighbours. Short-term alliances could often be made with most tribes as long as relations with them had not been excessively strained in the recent past and the proposed enemy was not their long-term ally.

Internally, as well, socio-political conditions were not stable. For one thing, there was a continual challenge to the power and authority of the paramount shaykh, Muhammad, by his brother, Khalil. In the last few years of Muhammad's life, when he was getting quite old, both Khalil and Muhammad's son, Salih, were competing with one another for the succession. After Muhammad's death Salih was chosen as paramount shaykh, but much of his power and authority was constantly being usurped by Khalil, so that the question of who was the true leader remained in doubt.[2]

In the middle and late nineteenth century land disputes were endemic. The district was divided into two major alliances, the Eastern and the Western, between which there were constant challenges on land rights, often culminating in bloodshed. A series of sub-alliances also existed, but disputes between two of these, or two mutually friendly tribes, were usually settled by a tribal court or, at the most, by a show of force (Al-Q.).

[1] Peake, *History*, p. 191; Al-Q.; Le P. A. Jaussen, *Coûtumes des Arabes au pays de Moab* (1948), p. 420.

[2] For indications of this see: A. Forder, *With the Arabs in tent and town* (1902), pp. 7–14, 52, and 7–76 *passim*; G. Hill, *With the Beduins* (1891), pp. 190–210; and C. M. Doughty, *Travels in Arabia Deserta* (1888), i. 24.

A Christian religious dispute also caused a major upheaval in the society. The Christian tribes of Al-Karak, which constitute about 10 per cent of the total population, have a long history of mutual tolerance, co-operation, and association with the local Muslim tribes. Greek Orthodoxy had been the only Christian sect in the area, but in the early nineteenth century a few members of this group adopted the Greek Catholic rite following a dispute among themselves. By 1847 they had built themselves a separate church.[1] In 1876 the Roman Catholics established a mission in Al-Karak. After a couple of years they were able to convert some of the Greek Catholics and Greek Orthodox to their rite, again mostly because of local Christian disputes. The local Christian leaders, who felt that they were losing power to this new religion and its priest, harassed these new converts and were able to persuade the Majaly to harass them. This set up a strained atmosphere in which an affair of honour and shame occurred. A Muslim man abducted a Christian woman of the 'Azizat tribe (the majority of this tribe's members had been converted to Roman Catholicism and they also formed the greater part of Al-Karak's Roman Catholics). All the tribes, Muslim and Christian, immediately rallied to the aid of the offended family. The woman was regained and the affair could have been settled by traditional tribal law and custom. But, apparently, the Roman Catholic priest had so incited some members of the 'Azizat that they killed a number of members of the offending tribe. Still, the affair could have been amicably settled, but the priest, probably influenced by the recent harassing of Roman Catholics, encouraged and exhorted them to leave Al-Karak for fear of mass reprisals. As a result, all of them except one section of the 'Azizat and a couple of Roman Catholic sections of other tribes moved to the north of the Wady Al-Mujib. The brother of the abducted woman made subsequent forays into Al-Karak, wounding and killing people and animals.[2] Peace was not established between the 'Azizat and the offending Muslim tribe until after 1930. The exodus of the 'Azizat was a heavy blow to the Majaly, for the tribe had always been one of their staunchest supporters and a provider of fighting men.

During the last few years before the arrival of the Ottomans in 1893, political conditions in the area prepared it readily to accept an outside government. Tribal feuds persisted, and the continuing leadership crisis aggravated the situation. Heavy raiding and

---

[1] W. F. Lynch, *Narrative of the United States' expedition to the River Jordan and the Dead Sea* (1849), p. 357.

[2] Pierre Médebielle, *Kérak, histoire de la mission* (1961), pp. 47–53; Dr. Yusif Shwayhat Al-'Azizat, *Al-'Azizat fi Madaba* (1960?) pp. 50–7; Jaussen, pp. 421–9; Al-Q.

counter-raiding meant a high death and casualty rate. A single raid, for example, cost 8 dead and 22 wounded.[1] Moreover, some form of relationship with the Ottoman government had existed for a considerable time. Various shaykhs of the local and bedouin tribes were paid small amounts, usually in goods, for the protection of the pilgrim route; and for about fifteen years the Ottomans had symbolically collected taxes in the town. From time to time they sent down a small detachment of soldiers; and on their behalf the paramount chief, Muhammad or later Salih, collected some nominal taxes, most of the sum raised being left in the town to pay for soldiers in the event of war.

A series of incidents finally brought about the entry of the Ottoman army into Al-Karak. In 1892 enmity between the Bany Sakhr and the Majaly increased significantly with the capture and brutal killing of one of Khalil Al-Majaly's sons. The Majaly tried to rally all the forces in Al-Karak to fight the Bany Sakhr, but the Bany Hamida backed out at the last moment, and so no attack took place. However, a major tribe of the Syrian Desert, the Ruwala, was raiding in the area and inflicted heavy casualties on the Bany Sakhr. The Majaly, seeing a new opportunity, immediately made overtures for an alliance. The Bany Sakhr felt trapped and called upon the Ottomans to re-establish control.[2] On the side of Al-Karak, the Majaly and most of the other tribes had no objection to this. As for the Ottomans, they had a general policy for the consolidation of control over the whole empire. This opportunity fitted in well with their plans.

In the autumn of 1893 the Ottomans moved a column of troops down to Al-Qatrana on the eastern edge of Al-Karak district and were met by a delegation led by 'Ibrahim Al-Majaly, with the approval of his father, Khalil, and his paternal uncle, Salih. A peaceful entry with a show of force was negotiated. However, the lack of complete Majaly authority among the Karakis is exemplified by the description of the Ottoman arrival by an English missionary resident in Al-Karak at the time. 'A few weeks after the rumour [of the Ottomans coming] several thousand troops camped on the plains opposite our mountain home. Field cannon were mounted on the highest hill overlooking the city, and every plan arranged to take the place.' Every day for a week troops tried to scale the walls, but were repulsed by stones rolled down upon them.[3] The Ottomans, by means of extensive bribery, explanations of the intentions of the government and its favourable economic

---

[1] Forder, *With the Arabs*, pp. 35–6.
[2] Peake, *History*, p. 191; Médebielle, p. 79.
[3] Forder, *Ventures among the Arabs in desert, tent, and town* (1905), pp. 107–8.

results, and the promise of stipends and of amnesty for all past crimes, secured agreement for their entry.

They set up an administration in Al-Karak and established a measure of security. They built a government building, a post office, a telegraph station, a school, and a military hospital. A garrison of about 2,000 men was kept in the old citadel with 200 horsemen. A stipend of 1,000 silver dollars monthly was divided amongst various shaykhs, 200 dollars going to one man, Salih.[1] Although the Ottomans introduced the new Majalla law code, traditional forms of justice prevailed as they do in the contemporary period. Externally, raiding continued, but in a diminished form. Internally, the Majaly still held the upper hand in tribal politics, but a rival tribal leader, Husayn At-Tarawna, was able to gain a measure of power through the formal government structure, which neither he nor his tribe had been able to do before the Ottomans arrived. Local politics appear to have continued in only a slightly altered form, though with less violence.

This relative calm was broken by the revolt of 1910, of which only a brief outline will be given here as it will be described in detail on pp. 106–10. Recent uprisings in the Jabal Druze and Jabal Hawran had given the Karakis the idea of taking up arms. Their main grievances were increasing taxation, restrictions on their use of firearms, and the general Ottoman policy of conscription. The Majaly also believed that the government meant to deprive them of their dominant position in the district. Husayn At-Tarawna, on the other hand, tried to dissuade Karakis from taking part in the revolt and even warned the governor about it. After a successful surprise attack on the local garrison the revolt was quickly put down by Ottoman reinforcements. Reprisals and a heavy fine followed, but none of the chief leaders lost his life. Late in 1911 (the Ottoman Empire being then at war with Italy) an amnesty was declared. The fine was halved, and cancelled in the following year. Moreover, though the Karakis had failed to achieve independence and had suffered heavy casualties, they had at least staved off conscription.

In the first world war Al-Karak, like most of the towns in Transjordan, did not play a significant role. Only a handful of Karakis actively backed the Arab Revolt, although contact was maintained with its leadership throughout. Some joined the regular Ottoman army, but, more importantly, large groups were organized and financed to go out on raids against the bedouin tribes which were supporting the Arab Revolt, especially against the Huwaytat.[2]

---

[1] W. Libbey and F. Hoskins, *The Jordan Valley and Petra* (1905), i. 345–6.
[2] Al-Qasus describes how he and two others led a group of 500 horsemen in an extended raid against the Huwaytat.

Many of the leading Christians of the town were arrested because the Ottomans suspected that they were in touch with the English and French through their Churches.

After the first world war, Al-Karak was rapidly involved in a quick succession of governments: Faysal's Syria, the Arab Government of Moab, and Amir Abdullah's Transjordan. In the first, Al-Karak was a province and a number of non-Karaki officials served in the area along with native Karakis. Security was almost non-existent, both internally and externally, in a manner reminiscent of the years before 1894. When the French drove Faysal out of Damascus in 1920, the status of Al-Karak was left undefined. With the aid of a British officer, Alec S. Kirkbride, the shaykhs set up the Arab Government of Moab.[1] While Amir Abdullah was on his way to Amman from Ma'an, a delegation of shaykhs, accompanied by Alec Kirkbride, went to greet him. During the meeting, the Amir asked Kirkbride: 'By the way, has the National Government of Moab ever been recognized internationally?' Kirkbride replied, 'As regards the local Government, I am not quite sure of its international status. I feel, however, that the question is largely of an academic nature now that Your Highness is here' (Kirkbride, p. 27). Thereupon the short-lived government ended and Al-Karak became part of the Amirate of Transjordan.

Initially, no central control was exercised in the district. Security deteriorated and three major disputes escalated until by late 1921 the town of Al-Karak was under virtual siege. These disputes are discussed at length below (pp. 93 ff., 98–101), but it is enough to state here that eventually a British officer, Captain F. Peake, took the entire Reserve Force to Al-Karak and aided in the establishment of internal order. It was the first use of the Reserve Force by the new government and its success helped to establish the power and authority of the Amir in the whole of Transjordan as in Al-Karak.

Although the Karakis continued to raid outside their territory during the first years of the Amirate, the central government was able to eliminate the practice by the mid-1920s. As the Karaki tribes were semi-sedentary and sedentary at that time, they were easier to control than the semi-nomadic and nomadic tribes of Transjordan. Thus, through the effective use of the Reserve Force and the close relations between the Majalys and the Amir Abdullah, raids ceased by the end of the 1920s, well before Captain Glubb was able to stop them among the desert tribes. Moreover, raiding

[1] Sir A. S. Kirkbride, *A crackle of thorns* (1956), pp. 21–7; M. Al-Mady & S. Musa, *Tarikh al-'Urdun* (1959), pp. 117–23.

between the Karakis, especially between the Majaly and the Bany Sakhr, had become fairly serious with the former suffering heavy losses. The tribes, then, readily accepted an agreement to end the raids.

During the Amirate, Al-Karak was on the periphery of Transjordan and only marginally involved in the concerns of the state. For example, when anti-Zionist demonstrations took place in Salt, Jarash, and 'Irbid, none occurred in Al-Karak.[1] The first demonstration took place a few years before the second world war, when Sulayman An-Nabulsi, later to become a leading Jordanian politician, was a teacher in Al-Karak. On the anniversary of the Balfour Declaration, he led his class into the streets, with the cry: '*Falyasqut wa'd Balfour!*', which, figuratively translated, means: 'Down with the Balfour Declaration!'. The crowd in the streets was ignorant of its meaning, so started yelling: '*Falyasqut Karkur!*' ('Down with Karkour!'). Karkour was a local Armenian shoemaker and he ran out into the crowd, crying, 'Balfour, oh people, Balfour'. Others yelled '*Falyasqut wahid balkun!*' ('Down with a balcony!') and '*Falyasqut wahid min fawq!*' ('Down with one from the top!').[2] It was not until after the second world war that a majority of Karakis became aware of the wider meaning of Transjordan and the Middle East.

The political élite, however, entered into varying relationships with Amir Abdullah and the central government, depending mostly on local political concerns and conflicts. The Majaly retained the position of paramount tribe of Al-Karak and the leadership of the Western Alliance. This tribe, mostly through their head shaykh who was also the most important in the area, Rafifan Pasha Al-Majaly, quickly formed close ties with Amir Abdullah. The Tarawna tribe constituted the major opposition to the Majaly and led the Eastern Alliance. Their head shaykh, Husayn Pasha At-Tarawna, continually opposed Amir Abdullah. For example, he was president of the National Congress in 1929 and later a member of the 'Istiqlal Party, both of which were in opposition to the Amir. On the other hand, the People's Congress, a pro-government and pro-Amir organization, had Majaly among its members. The internal split was also reflected in these tribes' attitudes to the Palestine problem. While the Majaly took no active interest in the Arab cause in Palestine, Husayn Pasha At-Tarawna maintained close political contact with the Mufti of Jerusalem, one of the leading opponents of Zionism.[3]

[1] C.O. 831/5, 5 Nov. 1929. The files for the 1930s mention other demonstrations in the Amirate, but none in Al-Karak.
[2] Haza' Al-Majaly, *Muthakkiraty* (1960), p. 19.
[3] C.O. 831/37, Mar. 1936.

Locally, politics remained little changed from the Ottoman period. Although security continued to be a distinct problem until the second world war, conflicts were not allowed to reach the level of 1921–2. Local tribes still vied for power in the time-honoured manner. The chief regional conflicts (other than cases of personal injury, death, and honour and shame) arose over land because the interwar period saw the sedentarization of most of the tribes and a great increase in land values.

In the contemporary period, the political history and major socio-economic trends of the Kingdom of Jordan are sufficiently recorded,[1] so that there is no need for detail here. Only a few major events and trends are cited to place Al-Karak in a larger setting.

As with all of the states involved in the Arab-Israeli war of 1948, the conflict had important internal results for Jordan, adding the West Bank to its territory and along with it indigenous and refugee Palestinians who were more advanced than the Transjordanians in education and modernity. Then, on 20 July 1951, King Abdullah was assassinated and succeeded by his son Talal, who was soon declared mentally unfit to reign. As a result, Abdullah's grandson, Husayn, not yet having reached the age to rule, was declared king.

The years 1948–50 are a turning-point in the history of Jordan. Many trends were coming to an end. Between the wars, Transjordan had been pacified and consolidated. At last one regime had ruled uninterruptedly for a number of years, and the people were beginning to accept it as their government. Land was registered; values increased; and agriculture began to take on a much more important meaning. But the paternal, almost shaykh-like, rule of Amir Abdullah had come to an end. For example, the old and young shaykhs of the Amirate used to sit around his diwan, kiss his hand, and cultivate a certain amount of respect for and rapport with him, but this type of relationship did not exist, and probably could not have existed, between the shaykhs and the young King Husayn.

After 1950 many new basic services were introduced. A communications network of hard-surfaced roads and telephones was completed. The administration was expanded and became much more efficient. Whereas most departments hardly functioned at all before 1950, today they have branch offices in all sections of the country. Early attempts at education bore fruit; administrative

[1] Mady and Musa; Patai; Harris and others; IBRD; Vatikiotis, *Politics and the military in Jordan* (1967); A. M. Goichon, *Jordanie réelle*, i. (1967); B. Shwadran, *Jordan* (1959); A. Abidi, *Jordan, 1948–1957* (1965).

positions were finally being filled by Transjordanians in significant numbers. The various districts could at last feel that they were a part of the country.

In the 1950s and 1960s a new political balance emerged within the kingdom. Ultimate power was still based on the army, but within the context of a majority of Palestinians rather than Transjordanians. The politics of the big towns and cities which had not even existed in the Amirate before 1948 became a constant and often challenging element. As in the whole of the Middle East, the growth in the popularity of Gamal 'Abd Al-Nasir, the development of Nasserism, and the concomitant Arab Nationalist movement on a mass scale were all felt in Jordan. And parties such as the Ba'th, the Muslim Brotherhood, and the communists began to play leading roles on the political stage.

Political events in the Middle East in and after 1948 buffeted Jordan continuously. After the addition of the West Bank to the country and the assassination of King Abdullah, the pressures on Jordan to join the Baghdad Pact in 1955 and 1956 resulted in extended rioting in the streets, government crises, and martial law. In order to regain popularity and rid himself of the stigma of being called a British lackey, King Husayn dismissed Lt.-Gen. John Bagot Glubb from the command of the Jordanian army on 2 March 1956. Soon afterwards, however, he faced an attempted coup. In 1958, with the union of Egypt and Syria, the troubles in Lebanon, and the overthrow of the Hashimites in Iraq, Husayn's government felt compelled to call in British troops temporarily to help stabilize the country. The 1960s found Husayn's Jordan still under pressure from Nasir, Syria, and Iraq because of his relatively pro-Western policies. Internally, however, the political situation, although by no means entirely peaceful, had somewhat come under his control. The parties considered dangerous to his regime were effectively banned and lost their ability to challenge his power as they had done in the previous decade. Similarly, popular anti-Western feeling declined from its peak in the 1950s, but it rose to new heights as a result of Jordan's defeat in the June 1967 Arab-Israeli war.

During this period, the Karakis were among the king's staunchest supporters. The Majaly and the other tribes supplied many of the officers and men of the Arab Legion and, for the most part, they were noted for their loyalty. Habis Pasha Al-Majaly was commander-in-chief of the army at the time of the 1967 war and was later made minister of defence. Haza' Al-Majaly was many times prime minister until he was assassinated in 1960. Others held many of the most important positions in the country.

Political developments in Jordan and the Middle East in and after 1948 have deeply influenced Al-Karak. The central government has penetrated many aspects of local life and has usurped some local political functions. Schools are now open to a high percentage of the youth. Communications are available and used. The political parties have helped to educate the young and have brought a new form of conflict to the district. All these elements have contributed to the changes which Al-Karak's political system has experienced.

Demography and Economics

Agriculture has always been and still is the economic base and principal economic activity in Al-Karak. In the contemporary period, however, other forms of economic occupation have increased, especially in the town, further differentiating it from the remainder of the district and its villages. Besides the demographic data, the major patterns noted in this section are: (1) the broad ownership of land; (2) the improving economic position of the peasant and his escape from the usurers; (3) the inefficient use of land; (4) the 'foreign' control of the *suq* (bazaar) and manufacturing, and the predominance of one-family shops; (5) the changed nature of commercial transactions and marketing; and (6) the importance of the central government in employment and development.

(1) *Traditional Period.* The population of the district in former times is difficult to establish. Most nineteenth-century travellers gave estimates of about 8,000 people. In 1812 Burckhardt wrote (p. 381) that there were 400 Turkish (Arab Muslim) families with 800 armed men and 150 Christian families with 250 armed men. Based on these figures the population would have been 6,000. In 1870 H. B. Tristram estimated it at 8,000 of whom 1,600 were Christians,[1] and Gray Hill (p. 202) in 1890 at 7,000–8,000. In 1922 the Government of Transjordan put the population of the governorate of Al-Karak, which included Tafila, at 13,500, basing its figures on a house count. The population of the town of Al-Karak was 3,000. This indicates about 10,500 for the district, but in 1948 the first systematic census recorded 39,609 individuals for the district and 3,998 for the town. (Mady and Musa, pp. 311, 448.) This is far more accurate than any of the earlier figures, but it would mean a growth rate of almost 400 per cent in twenty-six years. The reason for the high discrepancy is probably that the people of the Ghawr, the region adjacent to the Dead Sea, and the other tribes of the periphery, the precipitous regions, were either not counted or were greatly underestimated. The population

[1] *The land of Moab* (1873), p. 106.

of the central area was also underestimated, possibly because in those days the tribes were semi-sedentary. Assuming a 2 per cent growth rate, the population would actually have been about 23,000 in 1922, and 15,000–20,000 in the nineteenth century. In 1961 the number of inhabitants was 44,901 and in the town, 7,422.[1]

In the nineteenth century there were only four sites with permanent houses: the town of Al-Karak, and the villages of Kathraba, 'Iraq, and Khanzira (now called At-Tayyaba).[2] The three villages are on the periphery of the area and are populated by tribes with deep historical roots in Al-Karak. However, these were and are of secondary political importance and in recent centuries have been dominated by other local tribes. The remainder of the people lived in the black tents, mostly within one day's riding distance of the town. After the establishment of an outside government, first that of the Ottomans, and then, especially, the Amirate of Transjordan, permanent villages were rapidly built in all the fertile areas. In the early 1920s there were 35 villages[3] with stone and mud houses and today there are 82.

The base of the economy of the district and town has always been agriculture. Grains, animals, and their produce were the mainstay in the nineteenth century. All travellers observed olive groves and the cultivation of wheat and vegetables on the plateau. In the Ghawr millet, tobacco, indigo, and madder were grown for local use and partly for trading. Depending on the rainfall, Al-Karak usually had a surplus of grain which was sold to the neighbouring bedouin tribes, to the Hijaz, and to the people of the pilgrimage. Sheep, goats, mules, and their products were sold to Hebron and Jerusalem. In return, coffee, rice, tobacco, articles of clothing, guns, powder, and grains in periods of drought were bought from Palestine.[4]

In the Ghawr irrigation was used, but on the plateau cultivation was extensive rather than intensive. Each tribe had a recognized area of land and each extended family planted a given portion of it. There was no *musha'* system, i.e. a periodic redistribution of the land, such as was common in Syria. During the spring and early summer segments of many of the tribes moved to the edge of the desert to take advantage of the new grass for their animals (goats and sheep). Families of different tribes, including the Christians.

[1] Dept. of Stat.; *First census of population and housing* (1964), i. 11, 13.
[2] Burckhardt, p. 388; Al-Q.
[3] Al-Q.; B. Salman, *Khamsa 'a'wam fi sharqy al-'Urdun* (1929), pp. 267–74. Although this author does not cite an actual figure his material indicates the same growth.
[4] Burckhardt, pp. 379, 388; Al-Q.; C. Irby, *Travels in Egypt and Nubia and Asia Minor* (1823), pp. 361, 449; Lynch, pp. 342, 356; and Doughty, i. 22.

often camped together in these yearly movements. It should be noted that the tribes of Al-Karak never owned camels.

The *suq* (bazaar) was very small. In the nineteenth century there were about 10 shops; the number increased to 20 by the 1920s and 50 in 1948. Before the turn of the century, commerce was mostly in the hands of merchants who originated from Hebron, but after the Ottoman reoccupation in 1893, merchants from Damascus came to the district and eventually superseded the Hebronis. A few Christian Karakis, however, engaged in trade throughout the period. The merchants who came from Hebron and Damascus usually rented or built houses in the town. By the time the second or third generation came of age, they considered themselves Karakis, only of recent foreign origin. The local inhabitants also considered them Karakis, but with a difference, for they were not of the local tribes and they were merchants. These 'foreigners' tended to marry among themselves and with relatives from Hebron or Damascus; but some marriage with local tribes, however, occurred. There was a limited cash economy, but most transactions were in the form of barter. By greatly over-pricing their goods, a few of the merchants became quite wealthy by Al-Karak standards, and some either bought land from the peasants or took it in exchange for debts which the latter were unable to repay. This was a common occurrence on a limited scale, but it did not deprive a significant proportion of the peasantry of their land.

Land was always the major concern of the Karakis because of their dependence on agriculture. In the 1920s and 1930s internal security within the district greatly increased with the decline of raiding. Permanent villages were built in the traditional camping places. At the same time there was a greater demand for agricultural goods and the value of land was further enhanced.

With the changing power of the various tribes, land disputes have been a common phenomenon in the past hundred years and continue today. Between the wars these increased with the rising value of land. Partly to alleviate this, but chiefly to create a solid and equitable taxing base, the Transjordan Government, with the insistence and aid of the British mandatory power, decided in the 1930s to survey and register the land. Ownership was established by gathering together the leading men of a given area and on their advice registering the land in the name of individuals, families, and, occasionally, whole tribal sections. Land-ownership was based on what was farmed by the particular individual or group at the time, and, as a result, there was no equal division of land during the period of registration. Further, a very small tax was based on the estimated productive value of the land.

Many people, either not understanding the principle of registration or not wanting to pay the tax, allowed others to pay it and register the land in their name. This occurred mostly within the tribe, but at times between tribes, especially on the peripheries of the area, where the people were mostly engaged in animal husbandry and did not see the value of landownership.

Between the wars and in the contemporary period, land has changed hands for a variety of reasons. (1) Some holders sell their land so that they can use the capital for other ventures, such as investment in buildings in Al-Karak, Amman, or other towns. (2) Land is sold in order to obtain enough money to pay a bride price. (3) It often changes hands as part of the settlement of a killing. (4) During periods of drought, large tracts are often sacrificed at very low prices, merely in order that the cultivator may have enough operating capital for the next year. (5) A poor peasant occasionally has to borrow money in order to finance his planting or to buy basic necessities. In the past and to some extent today, he would often pay up to and over 100 per cent interest annually. Not being able to repay the loan quickly enough, he would have to relinquish his land in its repayment. Both Karakis by origin and the 'foreign' merchants have gained land in this fashion. (6) A slightly different pattern is the ruse. This was and is practised mostly in the Ghawr. A merchant or a Karaki by origin will set up a shop, charge highly inflated prices, and get the local people hopelessly in debt. Often, as well, he will lend them money for seeds and tools in order to speed up the process. Within a year or two, by juggling with the figures into the bargain, he places the local peasants so deeply in debt that they will be forced to work for him during the next year to pay it off. But, naturally, he sells them their staples, tools, tea, and sugar, so that the debt continues. In this way the people of the Ghawr have lost almost all their land and are indentured to the new owners through debt. (7) Finally, inheritance follows Muslim law so that each son inherits equally and each daughter receives half of what a son does.

The actual cultivation of land also takes many economic forms. (1) Most land is tilled by its owner. (2) The *murabi'* was an arrangement, common until the 1950s, whereby a man would work full time during the agricultural year and theoretically receive one-fourth of the returns of the land for which he was responsible. Actually, he was paid considerably less, usually just subsistence. This type of work is considered *'ayb*, shameful, for the worker is very poor, which in turn is shameful, and there is an unequal relationship between two men. The people who took this kind of work were most often from the Ghawr or the peripheries of the area and from Palestine. (3) The share-cropping contract varies considerably, according to the quality of the land and what the landowner contributes to the work, e.g. seeds, tools, tractor power. The agreement splits the produce from one-third to two-thirds for the landowner, depending on the above. This form of agreement is not *'ayb*, for the two parties are considered partners. Further, there is no particular preference for the two sides to be from the same tribe or allied tribes. (4) Wage labour is occasionally used, especially at harvest time when many bedouin from outside Al-Karak are so employed. (5) There is the virtually indentured labour in the Ghawr described above.

(2) *Contemporary Period.* Turning to the contemporary period, we find that the population of the area] has grown significantly:

TABLE I

Population of Al-Karak (District and Town)

Year	District	Town
1922	23,000	3,000
1948	39,609	3,998
1952	*c.* 40,500	5,539
1961	44,901	7,422
1966	54,006	..

SOURCES: See above, p. 25; Mady and Musa, pp. 311, 448; *Stat. Yb. 1952*, p. 1; *1966*, p. 2; Dept. of Stat., *Population and housing*, i. 11, 13.

As none of these figures are very accurate, it is futile to establish a definite growth rate. However, Dr. Victor Lorenz, a Czechoslovak urban specialist who has spent a few years in Jordan, basing his figures on the 1952 and 1961 censuses, gives the growth rate for the governorate as 1·2 per cent. Al-Karak district would be about 1·3 per cent, compared with 3·1 per cent for Jordan as a whole.[1] The large difference is explained by a significant emigration of about 0·7 per cent per year,[2] and a lower standard of health.

Tables 2, 3, and 4 (pp. 30, 31, 32) record the employment status and occupation of the active population of the governorate and town of Al-Karak. Many of these figures are referred to in the following pages, but some of those which are not have socio-economic significance. The most important economic activity in

[1] Min. of Interior. *Regional planning in Jordan*, ii/3, by V. Lorenz and A. Dakhgan (1967), 'Rate of Growth in Jordan', Annex, n.p. (Lorenz and Dakhgan in later references).

[2] Dept of Stat., *Population and internal migration* (1967), p. 10.

TABLE 2

Active Population by Status and Industry, 1961 (Al-Karak Governorate)

	Unclassified		Seeking work		Family workers		Employees		Own account workers		Employers		Total	
	%	Persons	%	Persons	%	Persons	%	Persons	%	Persons	%	Persons	%	Persons
Agriculture	..	..	11·7	101	95·6	1,775	44·5	2,497	83·6	6,196	90·8	553	68·0	11,122
Quarrying	..	..	..	..	..	..	2·6	147	0·1	9	0·1	1	0·9	157
Manufacturing	..	..	..	..	1·3	24	1·9	105	5·8	432	2·9	18	3·5	579
Construction	60·0	3	9·5	82	0·1	2	15·2	850	0·3	20	0·5	3	5·9	960
Utilities	..	..	..	..	..	..	0·3	14	..	..	..	..	0·1	14
Commerce	..	..	..	..	2·7	50	0·7	41	9·3	686	3·8	23	4·9	800
Communications & storage	..	..	0·2	2	0·1	2	3·5	196	0·4	28	0·2	1	1·4	229
Services	..	..	1·7	15	0·2	4	21·5	1,206	0·5	36	1·6	10	7·8	1,271
Miscellaneous	40·0	2	76·9	666	..	..	9·8	552	..	1	..	..	7·5	1,221
Total	100	5	100	866	100	1,857	100	5,608	100	7,408	100	609	100	16,353

SOURCE: Simplified from Dept. of Stat., *Population and housing* (1964), ii. 14.

TABLE 3

Active Population by Status and Industry, 1961 (Al-Karak Town)

	Unclassified		Seeking work		Family workers		Employees		Own account workers		Employers		Total	
	%	Persons	%	Persons	%	Persons	%	Persons	%	Persons	%	Persons	%	Persons
Agriculture	..	..	..	..	21·6	11	4·0	37	23·2	118	51·8	29	12·1	195
Quarrying	..	..	..	..	..	..	0·3	3	0·4	2	..	..	0·3	5
Manufacturing	..	..	..	..	21·6	11	5·9	55	30·9	157	21·4	12	14·6	235
Construction	100·0	1	..	..	1·9	1	21·2	197	0·2	1	1·8	1	12·4	201
Utilities	..	..	..	..	..	..	0·7	7	..	..	..	..	0·4	7
Commerce	..	..	..	..	51·0	26	2·4	22	36·9	188	8·9	5	14·9	241
Communications & storage	..	..	..	..	..	..	7·9	74	3·5	18	1·8	1	5·8	93
Services	..	..	..	..	3·9	2	53·4	497	4·9	25	14·3	8	33·0	532
Miscellaneous	..	..	100	66	..	..	4·2	39	..	..	..	..	6·5	105
Total	100	1	100	66	100	51	100	931	100	509	100	56	100	1,614

SOURCE: Dept. of Stat., *Population and housing*, ii. 22.

TABLE 4

Status Percentages of Active Population by Industry, 1961 (Governorate and Town)

		Unclassified	Seeking work	Family workers	Employees	Own account workers	Employers	Total
Agriculture	Gov.	··	0·9	16·0	22·5	55·7	5·0	100·0
	Town	··	··	5·6	19·0	60·5	14·9	100·0
Quarrying	Gov.	··	··	··	93·6	5·8	0·6	100·0
	Town	··	··	··	60·0	40·0	··	100·0
Manufacturing	Gov.	··	··	4·1	18·2	74·6	3·1	100·0
	Town	··	8·5	4·7	23·4	66·8	5·1	100·0
Construction	Gov.	0·3	··	0·2	88·6	2·9	0·3	100·0
	Town	0·5	··	0·5	98·0	0·5	0·5	100·0
Utilities	Gov.	··	··	··	100·0	··	··	100·0
	Town	··	··	··	100·0	··	··	100·0
Commerce	Gov.	··	··	6·2	5·1	85·8	2·9	100·0
	Town	··	··	10·8	9·1	78·0	2·1	100·0
Transport, storage, communication	Gov.	··	0·9	0·9	85·6	12·2	0·4	100·0
	Town	··	1·1	··	79·6	19·3	1·1	100·0
Services	Gov.	··	··	0·3	94·9	2·8	0·9	100·0
	Town	··	··	0·4	93·4	4·7	1·5	100·0
Miscellaneous	Gov.	0·2	54·5	··	45·2	0·1	··	100·0
	Town	··	63·9	··	37·1	··	··	100·0
Total	Gov.	··	5·4	11·4	34·0	45·4	3·8	100·0
	Town	0·1	4·1	43·1	57·7	31·5	3·5	100·0

SOURCE: compiled from Tables 2 and 3.

the governorate continues to be agriculture (68·0 per cent). However, this figure is much lower than it would have been fifty or
twenty years earlier, indicating the economic development and
diversification in the area. The socio-economic differences between
the town and governorate are also clearly demonstrated by the
figures. Agriculturalists form only 12·1 per cent of the active
population in the town as compared with 68·0 per cent for the
governorate. In the whole area, rural and urban, 5·0 per cent are
agricultural employers, in Al-Karak town, 14·9 per cent. This also
indicates that a number of absentee landholders live in the town.
As a final distinction between village and town, the percentage
involved in industry (quarrying, manufacturing, and construction)
is 10·3 in the former and 27·3 in the latter. If construction is
excluded, which is defensible (for over half of these workers rotate
between agricultural and construction work), the difference is 4·4
as compared with 14·9 per cent. Finally, unemployment is high:
5·4 per cent for the governorate and 4·1 for the town. These figures
do not indicate the true position, for the rate of agricultural
*under*employment reaches 20–30 per cent.

For the purely agricultural field, reliable figures over time are
unfortunately not available; no trends can, therefore, be shown.
Some figures for a single year do, however, give indications of
landownership, tenure, and holdings. The 1953 agricultural census
reveals a fairly broad distribution of landholdings, i.e. units which
a man cultivates but does not necessarily own:

TABLE 5

Landholdings in the Governorate of Al-Karak, 1953

No. of holdings	Size (*dunums*)*	Distribution (% of total held area)	
2,744	10–50	7·4 }	20·7
1,997	50–100	13·3 }	
1,864	100–200	24·2	
1,115	200–500	31·9 }	68·5
201	500–1,000	12·4	
42	1,000–2,000	5·7	
7	2,000–5,000	1·6 }	10·8
1	5,000–10,000	0·6	
1	10,000 *or more*	2·9	

* A dunum = 1,000 sq m (0·247 acres). Total area held in lots of 10 or more
dunums = 1,026,366 dunums.

SOURCE: Dept. of Stat. *Census of Agriculture 1953* (1953), pp. 4, 15. Simplified
version in G. Baer, 'Land Tenure in the Hashemite Kingdom of Jordan', *Land
economics*, 33 (Aug. 1957), p. 196.

These figures do not differ greatly from actual property ownership. In 1950 24·5 per cent of privately owned land was in lots of 100 dunums or less, 66·8 per cent in lots of 100–1,000, and 8·7 per cent in lots of more than 1,000 (Baer, p. 196).

It is significant that Table 4 shows only 23·4 per cent of the agriculturally active population as working for, or seeking to work for, an employer. This pattern of broad landholding and a relatively independent peasantry may be explained as follows. The peasants in large numbers have not been ruined by usurious money lenders and as a result deprived of their land. This certainly occurred, but not on a large scale except in the Ghawr. Only since the first world war has land become valuable enough to interest usurers. There has thus been little time for it to fall into their hands. Another reason is that the large tribes of the area tend to aid the peasant more than the smaller and weaker *hamula* which is predominant in Palestine and Syria, where the usurers had a strong hold. This may be attributed to their providing a relatively larger number of creditors who will not necessarily charge high rates of interest, and to the simple physical threat which the group may bring to bear. Also, credit facilities through banks, government departments, and co-operatives were established in Jordan before the second world war and increased dramatically in the 1950s and 1960s. Although they started quite slowly, they eventually gained a firm foothold, and were and are able to provide credit at low interest rates for the peasant, keeping him out of the usurers' hands.

TABLE 6

Agricultural Loans in Al-Karak District

(000 JD)*

Year	Agricultural co-operatives		Other sources		Total	
	Borrowers	Loans	Borrowers	Loans	Borrowers	Loans
1952	..	..	..	37·8	..	37·8
1954	..	..	237	13·6	237	13·6
1956	375	18·8	292	10·3	667	29·1
1958	c. 770	c. 30·8	616	28·7	c. 1,386	c. 59·5
1960	913	38·0	936	28·9	1,849	66·9
1962	1,171	58·8	172	57·9	1,343	116·7
1964	974	32·8	147	48·9	1,121	81·7
1966	57	1·3	227	106·9	284	108·2

* 1 Jordanian Dinar = $2.80

SOURCE: *Stat. Yb. 1952–66.*

The more highly competitive *suq* and better marketing facilities (see pp. 36–8) have also helped to eliminate one source of indebtedness. And looking at broad landholding from another standpoint, a relatively independent peasantry with land and some security is happier with the status quo than it would be otherwise.

In contrast to this relatively rosy picture, the actual land use is not nearly so satisfactory. Except for the vegetables and citrus of the Ghawr, there is virtually no irrigation. Farming is extensive, with little capital investment or labour. In some limited areas, especially in the more precipitous regions, olive groves and vineyards have been planted on a considerable scale. Cereals (wheat and barley), however, are still the principal crop. Tractors are mostly used by the wealthy owners of large estates, but, occasionally, a small owner or operator will hire a tractor and driver for ploughing, planting, and harvest. The use of inorganic fertilizers is minimal, both absolutely and compared with the rest of Jordan:

TABLE 7

Use of Inorganic Fertilizers in the South of Jordan

(metric tons)

Year	South of Jordan	Kingdom
1958	0.2	2,707·1
1960	..	2,347·9
1962	0·6	3,075·8
1964	0·7	7,361·9
1966	19·0	10,231·9

SOURCE: derived from *Stat. Yb. 1958–66*. The 1958 and 1960 figures for the south of Jordan are for the governorate of Al-Karak; the 1962, 1964, and 1966 figures for the governorates of Al-Karak and Ma'an.

The use of improved, selected seeds is also very limited. Because of Muslim inheritance laws, the land tends rapidly to be divided into small parcels. Thus a man with 200 dunums usually farms five, seven, or more scattered plots, which makes the use of tractors and other mechanized equipment less economical and practical. In order to ensure equal inheritance in quality of land, a man will inherit a strip from the top to the bottom of a slope. This further encourages the tendency to plough against the contour of the land, which increases erosion and the run-off of moisture. Goats are another major problem. The government has an extensive programme to increase the number of sheep and eventually eliminate most of the goats; but they have not yet been controlled and the effects of their appetite for small trees and bush are all too plainly to be seen. Nor is nature always kind to the land; the rainfall is highly irregular. In average and good years Al-Karak produces a surplus of grain, and exports vegetables, grapes, and citrus fruits. In poor years, which come with odious regularity every four or five seasons, the mere return of what one plants is considered fortunate. Thus although the peasant is relatively favoured in respect to landholding, ownership, and debt, he has not yet been educated to use his land anywhere near its optimum.

As regards trade and the marketing of produce, far-reaching changes have taken place over the past twenty years in the *suq* or market in the town of Al-Karak. Table 8 compares the ownership of shops in 1948 and 1968.

TABLE 8

Commercial Shop Ownership, 1948 and 1968

1948			1968		
Ownership	No. of shops	%	Ownership	No. of shops	%
Damascenes	25	50	Damascenes	20	10
Hebronis	15	30	Hebronis	10	5
Armenians	5	10	Armenians	1	..
Karakis	5	10	Karakis		
			Muslim	20	10
			Christian	10	5
			Ghazawis	140	70
Total	50	100		201	100

SOURCE: The author's own research.

Most of the 1948 absolute figures have remained relatively constant, while the major alteration is the appearance of a large number of Ghazawis, people from Ghaza in Palestine. The Karakis by origin have increased their share, primarily because of slowly changing attitudes towards commercial enterprise.

As the *suq* changed hands, it changed its character fundamentally. Merchandise used to be sold at 100–200 per cent above cost price, but today the mark-ups are 5–25 per cent. Previously, up to 10 per cent interest per month was charged for credit, today none is charged for up to six months. Ten and at the most twenty items could be found in a shop twenty years ago; today there are hundreds. This new competitiveness is best ascribed to the great expansion of the *suq*, new and better forms of communication with other markets in Amman and elsewhere, and the presence of the Ghazawis, who have a different attitude to commerce from the older Karaki and 'foreign' merchants. One characteristic which has remained constant is the predominance of one-family shops, 92·0 per cent for the governorate and 88·8 for the town (cf. Table 4, p. 32).

There is no over-all organization for the *suq* except an inactive Chamber of Commerce and Industry to which all merchants are required to belong, paying very small fees. The Chamber does concern itself, to a small extent, with the welfare of the merchants through its unofficial member on the local Municipal Council. Also, when a person proposes to set up a new shop, he is required by law to obtain a guarantee from the Chamber that he is capable of doing so. The central government also plays a small part in the *suq*. It haphazardly inspects the hygienic quality of meat and checks the accuracy of, and collects taxes on, balances and measuring sticks. Legally it has the power to control food prices, but very rarely exercises this right.

Most of the villages have shops of their own, the largest ones up to twenty, but prices tend to be 10–20 per cent higher than in the town, and the variety of goods is more limited. As a result, peasants come to Al-Karak to do their major and even minor shopping, if they live near enough.

Throughout history and today the *suq* has been almost entirely in the hands of non-Karakis. Not only were 'foreigners' able to exploit their connections with the Hebron, Jerusalem, or Damascus markets, but the Karakis had and still have attitudes which somewhat preclude them from entering into commerce. They consider the occupation '*ayb* (shameful or disgraceful), because being a merchant would involve dishonesty, selling inferior products as good ones, and over-pricing. Equally, one would have to practice *fannan* (craftiness, slyness, artistry) to make ends meet. They say that being a brigand is more honourable, because one is exercising personal power rather than craftiness. Moreover, if a particular individual does not feel this, social pressure keeps him from entering commerce, for he would be shamed and disgraced. These attitudes are beginning to change as a result of the growing honesty and competitiveness of the *suq* and of increasing education. The Karakis do admit today that the Ghazawis are smart and efficient traders, not invariably dishonest, and more industrious than local people. This is reflected in the proportionately stronger position in the *suq* gained by Karakis in recent years.

'Middlemen' are often a key factor in any economy. In Al-Karak, although a few of these men are 'foreigners', most are of the

original Karaki tribes. In the last twenty years their role has profoundly changed. Previously, it was solely through them that
agricultural produce reached the market, besides which they were
often the providers of credit for the peasant, the usurers. By agreement among themselves they were able to pay the peasants artificially low prices for produce which they then sold at much higher
prices in Al-Karak, Amman, or Jerusalem. Today, however, with
the development of an adequate communications structure and
better education, the peasant has learned that he can hire a truck
and sell his produce at decent prices in Amman. This has also had
the effect of making the local middleman more honest and competitive so that the peasant can deal with him without losing money.
With regard to wheat, the government has stepped in to aid the
peasant and improve the quality of the grain. Previously at harvest
time there was a glut on the market. This, added to artificially low
prices, doubly deprived the peasant of a just return on his labour.
Today when a glut occurs the government buys wheat at the time
at 10–15 per cent above the market prices. It takes only clean,
machine-harvested wheat, thus encouraging the peasant to raise
his standards. Then in the winter and spring months it sells the
wheat at the same price or up to 5 per cent above it. The changing
role of the middleman corresponds generally to the development
of the economy as a whole, the greater degree of competitiveness,
and the more equitable treatment of the peasant.

In local industry the pattern of employment and ownership is
the same as in commerce (see Table 9, below; cf. Table 4, p. 32).

TABLE 9

*Industry by Type and Number of Employees in the
Governorate of Al-Karak in 1965*

	No. of establishments	Workers per establishment		
		1–5	*5–10*	*10+*
Rock crushing	3	..	..	3
Food processing	45	45	..	..
Flour mill	(30)	(30)	..	..
Bakery	(10)	(10)	..	..
Olive press	(5)	(5)	..	..
Clothing	6	6	..	..
Shoes	13	13	..	..
Furniture	2	2	..	..
Traditional industry	10	10	..	..

SOURCE: Dept. of Stat., *Al-dirasa al-sina'iyya li'am 1965* (1967), p. 164.

It is predominantly owned and operated by non-Karakis, for most of the Karaki prejudices and traditions against commerce also apply here. Again, most of those engaged in industry work in their own or their families' workshops (78·7 per cent in the governorate and 71·5 in the town). As for large-scale industry, local people with money are not interested in that sort of investment, communications have only recently been developed, water and electricity supplies are inadequate and unreliable, indigenous skilled labour is scarce, and local leaders are reluctant to increase the number of manual workers in the area.

The construction industry is an important branch of the local economy, employing 5·9 per cent of the active population in the governorate and 12·4 in the town (cf. Tables 2 and 3, pp. 30, 31). Table 10 gives an idea of the recent extent of construction and the various types of housing and structures in Al-Karak.

TABLE 10

Number of Houses and Structures by Type of Construction (*Al-Karak Town and District*)

	houses in town		structures in town	houses in district	
	1952	*1961*	*1961*	*1952*	*1961*
Finished stone	124	296	448	184	518
Rough stone	732	864	864	5,754	7,299
Cement block	1	12	12	1	46
Mud brick	..	1	1	155	728
Reinforced concrete	..	130	135	..	296
Cave	2	4	4	61	240
Tent	2	3	3	3,474	3,367
Total	861	1,310	1,467	9,629	12,772

SOURCES: Dept. of Stat., '*Ihsa'at al-masakin li'am 1952* (1952), pp. 36–40; *Population and housing*, iii. 68–9; Lorenz and Dakhgan, p. 374.

This table shows an average (for 1952–61) of 50 new houses per year in the town and 347 in the district. Although comparative figures for commercial and government construction are not available, over two-thirds of it has occurred in the last twenty years, giving a total for Al-Karak town of about 65 buildings a year. The skilled and semi-skilled workers in this industry come mostly from outside the district and are Palestinians. The unskilled are mostly Karaki peasants who spend part or all of their time in non-agricultural work.

Ownership of land within Al-Karak town is quite broad. In recent years it has also become very valuable, because of its highly limited nature. Most of the major tribes of the central plateau have members in the town who own property within it. The phenomenon of fifty individuals owning one house also occurs, owing to traditional inheritance laws. However, a few individuals, shaykhs of tribes and merchants, with great foresight purchased large plots of land a number of years ago; in the intervening years these have immensely increased in value. The '*Awqaf* institution also holds some large sites, including shops and houses, from which it derives rent.

Finally, the central government plays a significant role in the economy. In the construction field it has built offices for many of its departmental branches in Al-Karak town, and schools, roads, and a few police stations throughout the district. Governmental non-manual employment (largely in teaching posts) accounts for about 30 per cent of the labour force for the town and 6 per cent for the district.[1] Al-Karak provides many officers and enlisted men for the Jordanian armed forces, which in turn brings more money into the area. The government also exercises a measure of control over the local economy. It has the power (occasionally used) to control prices and ensures a minimum degree of honesty in transactions. It haphazardly regulates safety conditions in factories and helps to secure fair treatment of employees. It has undoubtedly been the driving force behind what little economic development has taken place. By creating the communications network it has opened up the area to easy contact with the rest of the country; and its agricultural projects, especially the provision of credit on easy terms, have promoted the relative independence of the peasantry as well as their economic advancement.

[1] These figures are derived from Tables 2 and 3 (pp. 30, 31). Most of the employees in the 'services' section are government employees and teachers.

2

FABRIC OF THE TRADITIONAL
POLITICAL SOCIETY

THIS chapter and the next describe and analyse the traditional
political system. The reason for this is that many elements persist-
ing in the contemporary system have evolved with only slight
alterations from the traditional one. A thorough understanding of
this is therefore necessary if the process of change is to be adequately
presented. Unless an aspect, institution, or practice is specifically
stated to be defunct, it should be presumed still to be operative.
Chapters 4, 5, and 6 will, however, draw attention to the surviving
features of the traditional system, placed in their current setting.
Chapters 2 and 3 are already concerned with change—the movement from independence and isolation to the presence of a central
government, however weak in comparison with that which is in
power today.

The present chapter deals solely with the various groups which
constitute the stuff of political society, all political action within
the system being based on them. These groups are (1) the tribe;
(2) semi-permanent alliances; (3) groups outside the district and
their relation to it; (4) the village; (5) religious groups; (6) minorities; (7) patron–client groups; (8) socio-economic strata; and
(9) the formal government. In a concluding section, the relations
between the various groups will be described in an attempt to show
their interconnections and interdependence and the structure of the
whole society.

The Tribe

The tribe is the single most important political group in Al-Karak
district. Structurally, it may be described as a corporate territorial
group with pyramidal and segmentary qualities. The tribes of the
area, however, differ considerably in relative size, geographical
location, mode of livelihood, and degree of political power. This
section will describe, first, their common characteristics and then
the differences between them.

An understanding of kinship and marriage patterns is necessary
to any explanation of tribal organization as well as being valuable
in itself, for the larger kin groups also have political functions.

Although the tribe is definitely not a kin group but a territorial one, kin groups are basic parts of it, blending into its structure in such a way that it is difficult to distinguish where the kin group ends and the tribal structure begins. Moreover, the local tradition of each tribe often holds that all its members, or all the members of one section, are descended from one man. Many admit that this is not always true, but the myth is kept up. Actually, the sub-lineage or, at times, the lineage of four or five generations is the only true, coherent kin group. The Karakis, like most of the Arabs, reckon kinship through the male line. Politically this patrilineal pattern is significant, for it tends to create neat segregated units and sub-units within the tribe. A man's identity is more strongly attached to this group than to any other; for the behaviour of an individual is considered to be the extension of that of his kin, and, conversely, the actions of a man's blood relatives heavily reflect upon him. The kin unit is further reinforced by the marriage preference for one's parallel cousin (father's brother's daughter).[1] In traditional law, even, an unmarried man has the legal right to marry his closest parallel (paternal) cousin; and not until he has given his permission may she marry another. If no first cousin on the paternal side is available, then two other preferences become operative. Paternal cousins of a lesser degree are frequently chosen, and a cross-cousin (mother's brother's daughter or father's sister's daughter) is also sought. Quite often, because of the general marriage pattern, a cross-cousin is a paternal cousin as well, only of a more distant relationship. This marriage pattern, then, creates a web of both kin and conjugal ties within a relatively small unit, binding its members together. Thus all the children in the male line of a man who lived four or five generations ago may be considered as a corporate group with a common identity and some political functions.

The structure of a tribe may have infinite variations, but all within a basic pyramidal pattern. Schematically, the tribe may be represented as in Diagram 1. For any given tribe and at any given level, however, there may be one to fifteen units. Occasionally one of the steps may be left out because the descending members are few or some have been forgotten. Diagram 2 (p. 44), which follows one line of an actual tribe, may explain the pattern in somewhat less schematic terms.

The significance of this pyramidal pattern is that there is an over-all *vertical* organization of the tribe, not just a series of *horizontal*

---

[1] This point is brought out by R. F. Murphey and L. Kasden in 'The Structure of Parallel Cousin Marriage', *Amer. Anthropologist*, 61 (Feb. 1959), pp. 17–29.

DIAGRAM I

*Tribal Structure**

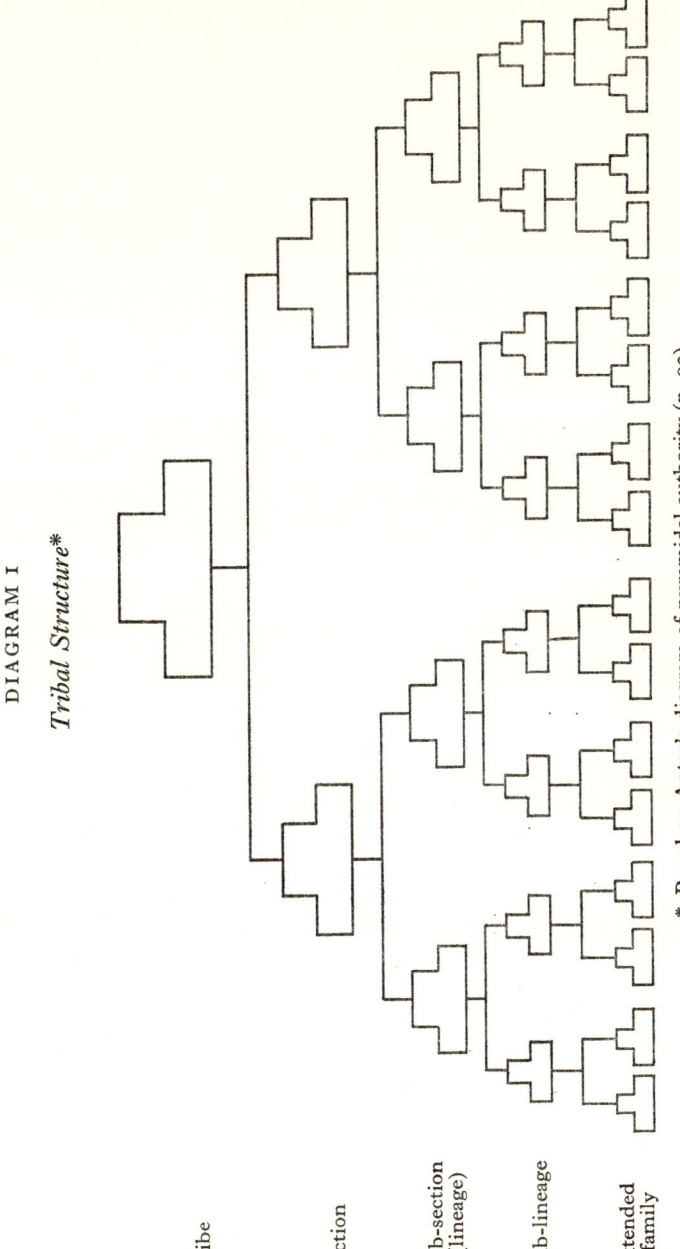

Tribe

Section

Sub-section
(lineage)

Sub-lineage

Extended
family

* Based on Apter's diagram of pyramidal authority (p. 92).

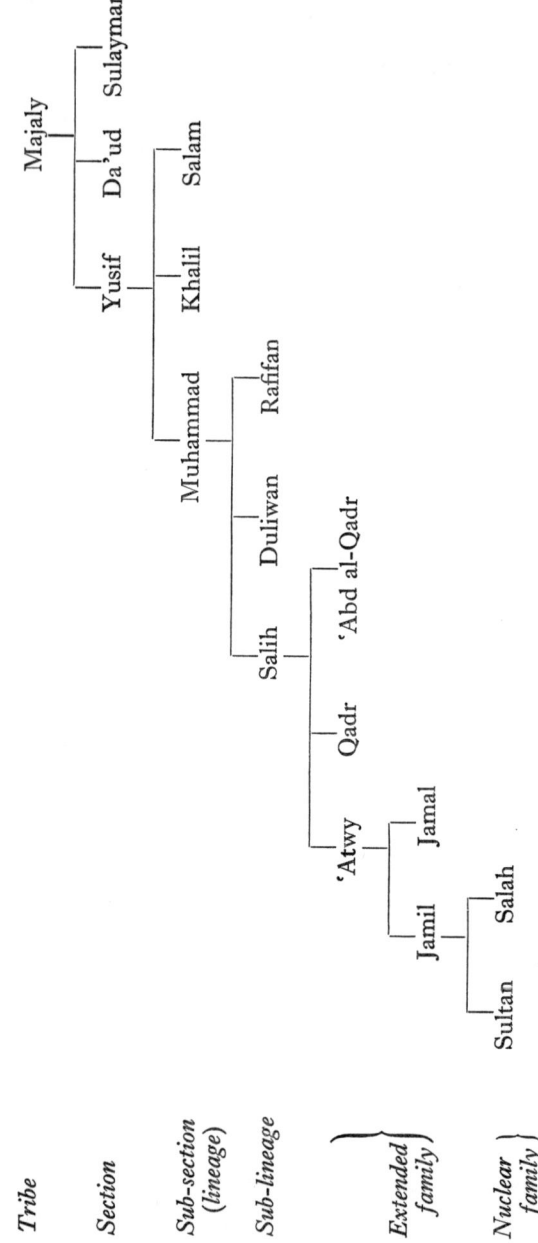

DIAGRAM 2

One Line of the Majaly

units with the same general identity. But the Karaki tribe is also inherently segmentary, each segment at each level has a separate identity and a degree of power and authority of its own. Coupling the two concepts, pyramidal and segmentary, together indicates that the tribe is organized in an ascending series of segments, each being a political group at some times and in some events. Thus each unit at a structurally higher level automatically contains all those groups below it. Nor does any real leadership hierarchy connect the groups; instead, for example, the shaykh of one of the subsections is in turn the shaykh of the section of which it is a part; similarly, the shaykh of one of the sections is shaykh of the tribe.

To demonstrate the meaning of the pyramidal-segmentary system, it is instructive to cite E. E. Evans-Pritchard's classical diagram and explanation for the tribes of the Nuer of the Southern Sudan.

DIAGRAM 3

Evans-Pritchard's Tribal Diagram

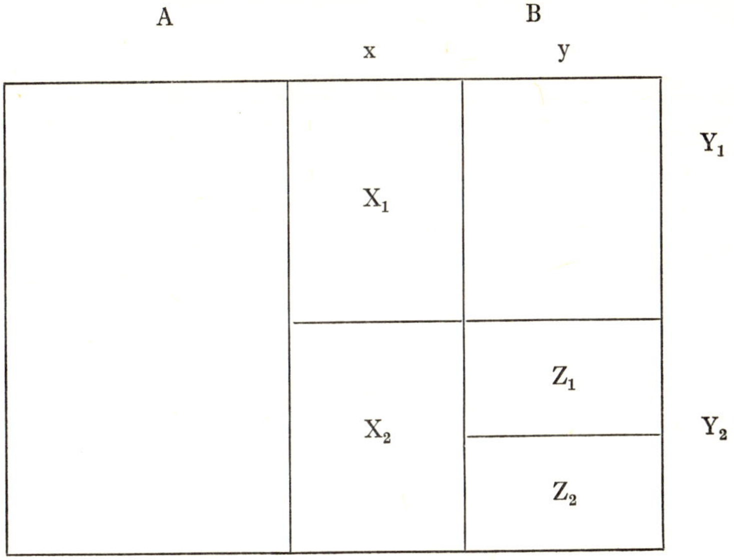

A tribe is divided into territorial segments which regard themselves as separate communities. We refer to the divisions of a tribe as primary, secondary, and tertiary sections. Primary sections are segments of a tribe, secondary sections are segments of a primary section, and tertiary sections are segments of a secondary section. A tertiary section is divided into villages and villages into domestic groups. A member of Z_2

tertiary division of tribe B sees himself as a member of Z_2 community in relation to Z_1, but he regards himself as a member of Y_2 and not Z_2 in relation to Y_1. Likewise, he regards himself as a member of Y, and not Y_2, in relation to X. He regards himself as a member of tribe B, and not of its primary section Y, in relation to tribe A. Thus, on a structural plane, there is always contradiction in the definition of a political group, for a man is a member of it in virtue of his non-membership of other groups of the same type which he stands outside of, and he is likewise not a member of the same community in virtue of his membership of a segment of it which stands in opposition to its other segments. Hence a man counts as a member of a political group in one situation and not as a member of it in a different situation, e.g. he is a member of a tribe in relation to other tribes and is not a member of it in so far as his segment of the tribe is opposed to other segments. . . . A tribal segment is a political group in relation to other segments of the same kind, and they jointly form a tribe only in relation to other Nuer tribes and to adjacent foreign tribes which form part of their political system, and without these relations very little meaning can be attached to the concepts of 'tribe' and 'tribal segment'. That the distinction and individuality of a political group is in relation to groups of the same kind is a generalization that embraces all Nuer local communities, from the largest to the smallest.[1]

This is a theoretical pattern which exists in most disputes or events necessitating group identity, except in cases of loss of life. At times, however, at the lower levels of the tribes, other variations, have been known to occur, although not consistently. It should be noted that added forces come into play at these levels, namely active known kin and pseudo-kin relationships, marriage ties, and personality. In Diagram 4, if Y and Z are involved in a dispute,

DIAGRAM 4

A Lineage

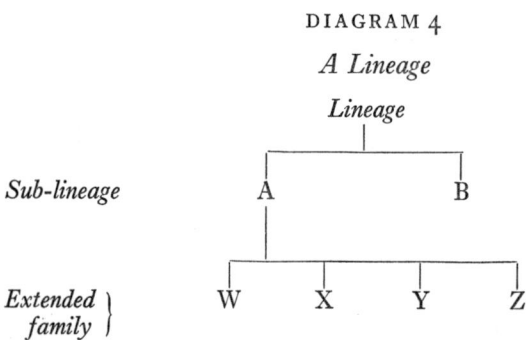

<dl>
<dt>Sub-lineage</dt>
</dl>

[1] 'The Nuer of the Southern Sudan', in M. Fortes and E. E. Evans-Pritchard, eds., *African political systems* (London, 1963), pp. 281–2. Evans-Pritchard's diagram and description are intended only for the tribal structure, but in the case of Al-Karak, kin and pseudo-kin relationships are integrally and inextricably tied in with the tribal structure and should be considered within this general pattern.

ideally W and X should stay neutral, and at times they do. But W may side with Y and X with Z, or W and X may both side with Y or Z. Rarely, W and/or X may divide internally, part siding with Y and part with Z.

In matters involving the loss of life, another distinctive group, the *khamsa*, becomes operative. This unit is composed of a total of five generations, both ascending and descending, of the relatives of either the killed or the killer. It may best be represented by Diagrams 5 and 6.

DIAGRAM 5

The Khamsa

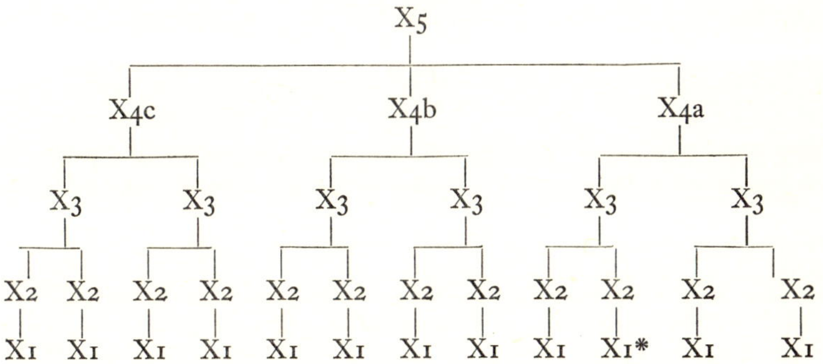

If each X represents an individual and the X_1^* represents the killer or the killed, and if he has no children, as in Diagram 5, then all the Xs are the operative group. If, however, as in Diagram 6, the key person has children, then these count as one generation. Similarly, if he has grandchildren these are counted as two generations. Thus, in the second example, only those Xs with numbers beside them are in the operative group. Moreover, in the dynamics of a killing, which are explained in the next chapter, the *khamsa* of the killer must leave the territory or risk retaliation. However, all those related to the killer only through the fifth generation may pay the *ba'ir an-nawm* (camel of sleep) which allows them to remain without fear of being harmed. Thus, in both diagrams, 4b and 4c and their descendants may stay in their homes.[1]

---

[1] E. Marx (*Bedouin of the Negev* (1967), pp. 64–5), terms the *khamsa* a 'co-liable' group. Then he states that, 'The only term almost exclusively designating a co-liable group, *khams* (five), does not, strictly speaking, apply to the whole group, but only to the men who can trace common descent to an ancestor five generations removed. In Bedouin ideology these men are the men

The tribe is also an actively segmenting group. This process, which takes a period of time, perhaps a generation or more, means a division within a given group, but with the group remaining as a social entity. In this way a new extended family is created if a man has male offspring and they in turn have male children. A new

DIAGRAM 6

The Khamsa with One Descending Generation

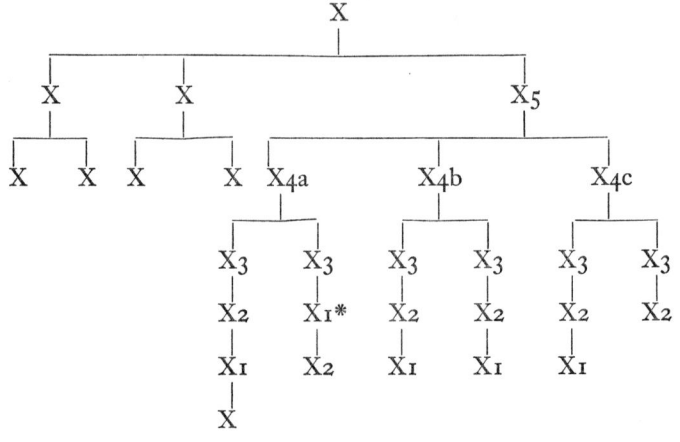

sub-lineage or lineage may be formed by the addition of a genera-tion or two within this pattern. Finally, a lineage (subsection) of a tribe may become a new section, but its former brother sub-sections may remain as part of the original section. This latter phase of segmenting is perhaps the most significant, for usually as the generations pass, new subsections are merely formed under the umbrella of the larger section. The occasion for the formation of

who normally make up a "co-liable group", because men who are further removed can legally exempt themselves from responsibility in certain situations. But the term is definitely also used for a group whose members' common ancestor is more than five generations removed. As long as no part of the group takes active steps towards separation, its members all share full responsibility, as if they were related within the five generations.' In a footnote he adds, 'the differ-ence between the formal and the actual structure of the *khams* can probably account for the many and diverse definitions of the *khams* in the literature on the Bedouin'. For the Karakis, his argument does not hold. In many actual cases described to the author, the strict five-generational group was used. This may be explained by the semi-sedentary and later sedentary nature of the people, for part of a group needs to remain in the area to look after crops and animals. However, in the final settlement of a blood debt, a group larger than the *khamsa* often participates financially.

a new section may stem from the recognition of separate identity due to the activity of this group, or through the setting up of a separate living area, e.g. in the earlier period, a new encampment or, in the later, a new village.

Equally important in this process is the way the Karakis acknowledge their kin relationships. They generally trace these back four or five generations quite accurately with little or no disagreement among themselves. But, by the fifth or sixth generation the reckoning becomes blurred, showing a definite lack of agreement as to what the true kin relationships are.[1] This blurring usually exists among those who claim a direct relationship with the man who is supposedly the father of all those of a lineage (sub-section). Structurally, then, it is easy to break off, segment off, a new group at this level and, conversely, to 'forget' a generation or more, bringing all into a closer, though fictitious, relationship. Occasionally, an outsider and his family may wish to join a tribe, and it is at this subsection level that he is most easily grafted on to the structure because of its only quasi-kinship nature. If a much larger group is to join a tribe, which has been a common phenomenon, it usually does so as a new section. Marriage customs are favourable to all these processes, for, as stated above, they tend to reinforce a small, inward-looking group, commonly not above the sub-lineage level. Intermarriage between the major sections or even subsections of a tribe is not common. Thus if a new group is grafted on to a tribe, its position in terms of kin and marriage relationships is not unlike the already existing relations between the various original sections. This is especially true if the newly added section has been resident in the tribal area, as is almost invariably the case, for a few mutual marriages will have been contracted during that period.

Apart from segmenting, the phenomenon of fission may occur, that is, a section of a tribe may split off to form a separate one distinct in identity and organization. After an internal dispute one section may leave the district and not return. Or a section may segment off, settle in a different region in the district, and eventually become known as a separate tribe.

As to residence, with a few individual exceptions a tribal section tends to reside wholly in one village and most often in one quarter of that village. The larger tribes have sections in two to five villages or more, the smaller ones are often resident only in one or two. Common residence also has political consequences in that it allows

[1] Similar areas of ambiguity were found by Peters in his study of the bedouin of the Negev (*J. of R. Anthropological Inst.* 90 (Jan.–June 1960), pp. 40–2), and by E. Marx (pp. 188–92).

for continual contact and development of common interests. It should be noted that villages usually contain sections of more than one tribe.

The distribution of wealth and material goods within a tribe varies considerably. If the tribe is small and poor, there is very little material difference among its members, if it is large some of its members, sections, and lineages will be much richer than others. Although common economic activity above the extended family level is unknown, the more wealthy members of a tribe performed in the past some welfare functions for the poorest tribesmen. To some extent they still do so.

As regards the nomenclature of the various segments, *'Ashira* is the accepted term for a tribe, but if this is particularly small, it may be called a *hamula*. The section may variously be termed *hamula*, *farq*, *fakhith*, and *fara'*. The subsection (lineage) is most often called *'awlad fulan* or *'ayal fulan*, both meaning 'children of so and so', but *fakhith* and *fara'* are also employed. As with lineages, the phrases *'awlad fulan* or *'ayal fulan* are used for sub-lineages as well. It is the name of the person which is operative here; the local residents know the relationship when they hear it. *'A'ila* means extended family, but not necessarily living in one house. For a residential family, i.e. mother and father and all children, married or not, who live and cook in one house and contribute to its up-keep, the terms *'usra*, *'ahl*, and *'a'ila* are applied. *Bayt* and *dar* mean, most often, a man and all his sons, as well as the physical house. These terms are evidently somewhat loosely used and may be applied to groups which are structurally different. This results from the very nature of the pyramidal-segmentary and segmenting system, for each segment at the various levels performs similar functions and a given group may change its relationship to the whole.

All the tribes in Al-Karak conform to the basic patterns described above, but with some variations. No systematic classification has been adopted here, for the different kinds of tribe are not distinguished by the same criteria. To class them by way of life would give two basic types, by size three or more, by relationship to other tribes five or six. Instead, each type will be listed and described in terms which distinguish it from the rest. It may also be helpful to refer to Maps 2, 4, and 5 on topography, tribal territories, and villages (pp. 10, 55, 58).

(1) *Tribes of the Plateau.* The tribes of the central plateau are the most powerful, completely dominating some of the others and exercising considerable influence over the rest. Today almost all these tribes are sedentary, but before the turn of the century they

were mostly semi-sedentary. In the contemporary period the size of individual tribes[1] ranges from 3,000 members to a few hundred, with a few of less than 100; and their combined membership constitutes over 55 per cent of the total population. Those tribes with about 1,000 members or more have significant power vis-à-vis the remainder; but a large number of smaller tribes, while maintaining their separate identity and integrity, do have special, yet relatively equal, relationships with individual large tribes. The plateau tribes are also characterized by their membership in the two major alliances of Al-Karak.

(2) *The Semi-nomads.* In the extreme north and south of the district live five tribes, the Bany Hamida and 'Amr in the north, and the Nu'aymat, Kharasha, and Batush in the south. These today are generally semi-sedentary, but before the contemporary period they were semi-nomadic. Although they call themselves Karakis and are considered to be so by the plateau tribes, they do not belong to the major alliances, and they neither have significant political power today nor in the recent past, even though their average membership is over 1,000. Their social customs are closer to those of the true bedouin of the desert than to those of the plateau tribes, and in nomenclature they follow the bedouin terminology in calling the tribe a *qabila* or *qaba'il* and the tribal section, depending on its size, *'ashira* or *hamula*. It will be recalled that the Bany Hamida and the 'Amr formerly played an important part in Al-Karak's history, but that they were driven out to the remote northern regions. Here, as in the extreme south, the land is markedly inferior to that on the plateau, so that their economic base is of poor quality. They also have fewer schools, and thus are less well educated than the people of the plateau. Significantly, each of these tribes has no more than one family resident in the town of Al-Karak.

(3) *Tribes of 'Iraq Village and the Bararsha.* The Bararsha and 'Iraq tribes live south and west of Al-Karak town on the edges of the plateau and in the precipitous region dropping to the Ghawr. They are a series of small tribes joined in two separate alliances, but not members of the two major alliances. The Bararsha has about 3,400 members in 15 tribes, and 'Iraq village about 900 in 4 tribes. Like the tribes of the plateau, they were semi-sedentary and are now sedentary. Local tradition holds that before the Crusades most of these tribes lived in and around Al-Karak town and some were Christian, but because of their co-operation with the Crusaders, they were banished by Saladin to the area where they now live. Then, at some unknown time, the Christians went over

[1] See App. 1, pp. 178-9, for a complete list of tribes and their villages.

to Islam. Like the semi-nomads, these tribes are less well educated than the plateau tribes and their land, on the whole, poorer. Over the generations they have suffered from unequal relationships with the plateau tribes, paying *khawa* mostly to the Majaly, but also to other large tribes. Probably because of their relative poverty, they often turned to brigandage, especially during the inter-war period. A significant percentage of them have lost their land to members of the plateau tribes, but not nearly to the same extent as the Ghawarna.

(4) *Ghawarna*. The Ghawarna are the dark-complexioned people of the Ghawr. Although they are Arabs long resident in the region, they are most appropriately dealt with in the minorities section below (pp. 65–6) because their relationship with the other tribes of the district is characterized by racial discrimination.

The Semi-permanent Alliances

The next step is to show how the tribal units are linked together in a formal political sense. Three basic forms of semi-permanent alliance exist in Al-Karak: small tribes attached to larger ones; the alliance of relatively equal tribes; and the major Eastern and Western Alliances of the district.

(1) *Attached Tribes*. As may be deduced from the diagram of the tribal alliances of Al-Karak (p. 53), there are numerous tribes which may be designated as attached. These tribes, which vary in size from 50 to 500 individuals, are joined in alliances which essentially stipulate protection by the larger and support by the smaller. For example, if the smaller tribe enters into a dispute with a larger one, the former's ally is obliged to come to its support. However, if the superior member of the alliance is in conflict with another tribe, the smaller tribe is not required to aid the larger, though in practice it usually does so. In the earlier periods of little or no state security, the smaller tribes camped with or near their allies in order to secure protection. With the sedentarization of the plateau Karakis, some of the attached tribes formed their own villages and others settled in the villages of their superiors. Although it is extremely difficult for a member of an attached tribe to become shaykh of a major one, it is not unknown. Usually, when this happens, the smaller tribe loses its separate identity and becomes a section of the major one. On balance the attached tribes have many of the rights of the major tribe without all its obligations. However, in terms of political power, they remain decidedly inferior to the major tribes. The advantage of this relationship to the larger tribe is that it gains prestige by others seeking its protection and that it potentially has much larger numbers to call

DIAGRAM 1. *Tribal Alliances of Al-Karak* (et al denotes that the following tribes are 'attached')

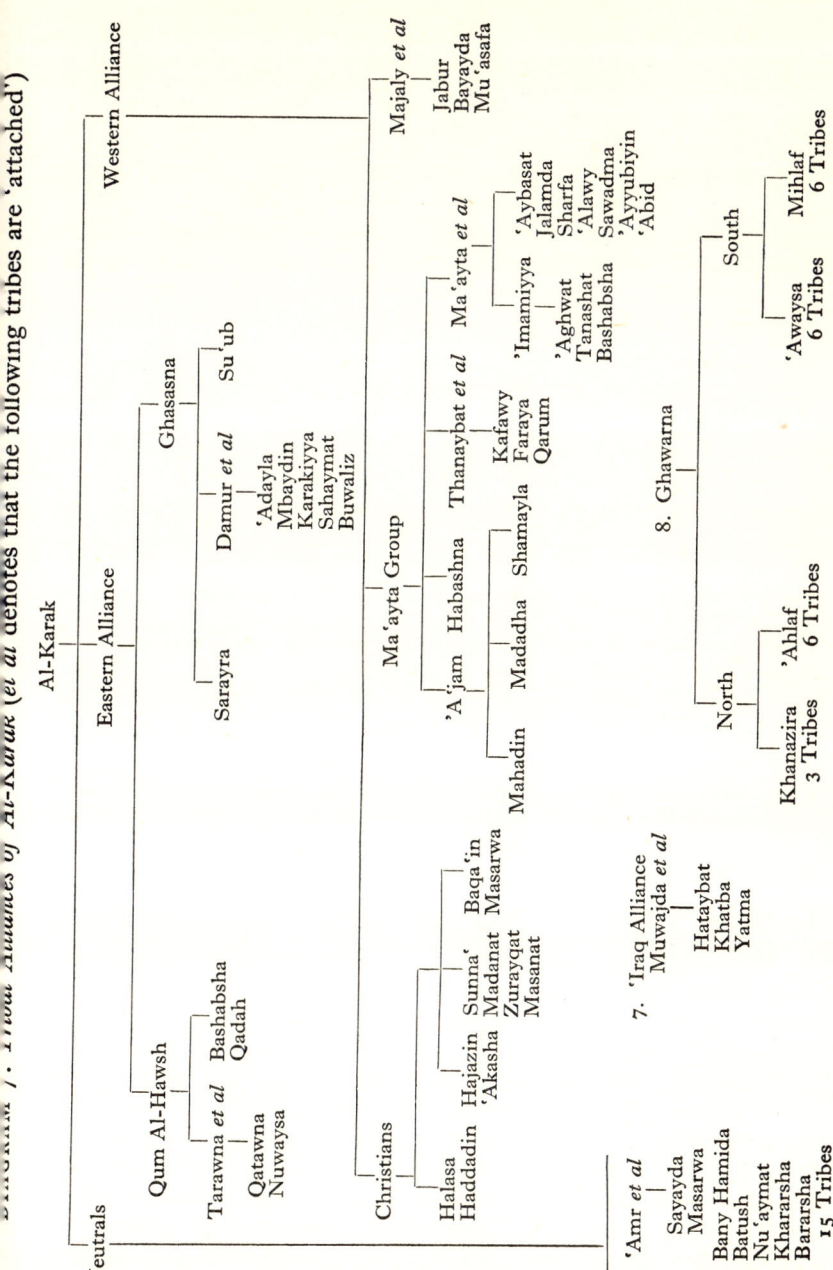

Al-Karak

Neutrals

Eastern Alliance

Western Alliance

Qum Al-Hawsh

Tarawna *et al*
Qatawna
Nuwaysa

Bashabsha
Qadah

Christians

Halasa
Haddadin

Hajazin
ʿAkasha

Sunnaʿ
Madanat
Zurayqat
Masanat

Baqaʿin
Masarwa

7. ʿIraq Alliance
Muwajda *et al*

Hataybat
Khatba
Yatma

Ghasasna

Sarayra

Damur *et al*

ʿAdayla
Mbaydin
Karakiyya
Sahaymat
Buwaliz

Suʿub

Maʿayta Group

Mahadin

ʾAʿjam

Madadha

Habashna

Shamayla

Thanaybat *et al*

Kafawy
Faraya
Qarum

Maʿayta *et al*

ʾImamiyya

ʾAghwat
Tanashat
Bashabsha

ʿAybasat
Jalamda
Sharfa
ʿAlawy
Sawadma
ʾAyyubiyin
ʿAbid

Majaly *et al*

Jabur
Bayayda
Muʿasafa

8. Ghawarna

North

Khanazira
3 Tribes

ʾAhlaf
6 Tribes

South

ʿAwaysa
6 Tribes

Mihlaf
6 Tribes

1. ʿAmr *et al*

Sayayda
Masarwa

2. Bany Hamida
3. Batush
4. Nuʿaymat
5. Khararsha
6. Bararsha
   15 Tribes

upon for certain actions it may contemplate. In sum, the arrangement may be perceived either as a patron-client relationship between two groups or just an extension of the tribal segmentary system with the attached tribe as a more loosely tied tribal section.

(2) *Minor Alliances—Tribal Groupings between Relative Equals.* The two sets of alliances examined in this section and the next may be considered, in a political sense, as extensions of the tribal structure. Evans-Pritchard's identity and opposition pattern is equally valid for these two structural levels. The diagram then would be:

DIAGRAM 8

Tribal and Alliance Patterns

Al-Karak

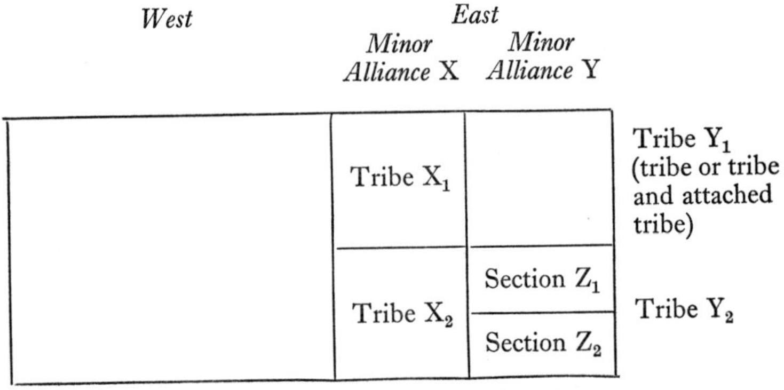

West	*East*		
	Minor Alliance X	*Minor Alliance* Y	
	Tribe X_1		Tribe Y_1 (tribe or tribe and attached tribe)
	Tribe X_2	Section Z_1	Tribe Y_2
		Section Z_2	

These alliances are long-standing political agreements and relationships between equals, or relative equals, and are operative against their opposing structural equal. But this is not to say that when two tribes of separate minor alliances are involved in a dispute the alliance automatically comes into force. On the contrary, only if one side or the other feels that it can no longer adequately cope with the situation does it call in its allies. Until this time they render it passive, moral support. As with the whole segmentary tribal system, there is a degree of flexibility, and upon sufficient and major cause, a tribe may break off and join another group or remain independent. As to territory, it is evident from the tribal map (p. 55) that most of these allied tribes live contiguously. Further, more marriages are contracted between them than between non-allied ones. In sum, these alliances may be considered as an extension of the corporate pyramidal-segmentary structure of the tribal system.

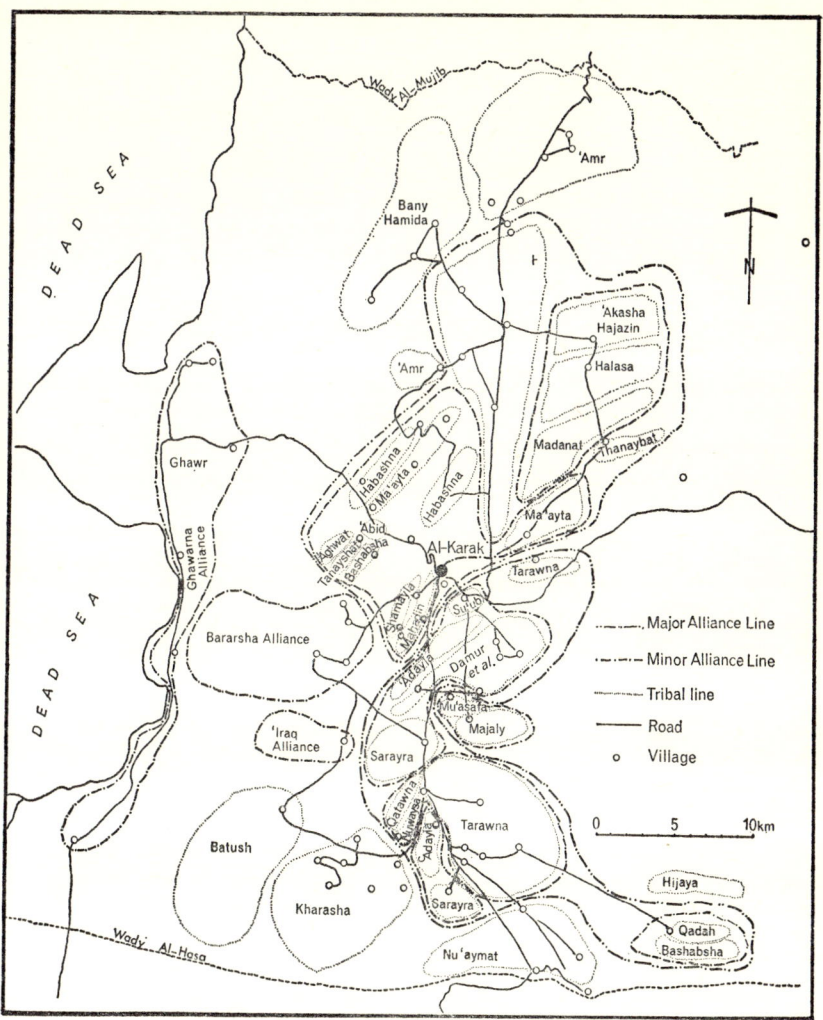

MAP 4. Tribes and Alliances in the District of Al-Karak

Although this is not indicated in Diagram 7, the Majaly and Ma'ayta have long, traditional close relations approaching this form of alliance. Local tradition holds that the two tribes are descendants of the same man, but by different mothers. In most political activities the Ma'ayta side with the Majaly and vice versa. However, this does not hold good for the Ma'ayta's attached tribes, for there is a long-standing tradition of enmity between them and the Majaly.[1] These tribes do join with the Majaly in terms of the major alliances.

(3) *Major Tribal Alliances—East-West Split.* The tribes of the plateau are divided into two major groups, the Eastern Alliance and Western Alliance, which are referred to locally as *sharaqa* and *gharaba* respectively. These alliances are the final phase in the pyramidal-segmentary system, and the details of the relationships are the same as for the minor alliances, only on a larger scale. Karakis think that the origin of the split is based on boundaries drawn by the Ottomans in the sixteenth century for purposes of taxation, dividing the tribes into three groups: Western, Christian, and Eastern. After the reoccupation in 1893 the same boundaries were used. The Ottomans were probably merely recognizing an already established reality, for the division is a natural one, given the nature of the terrain. The tribal and alliance map (p. 55)[2] shows that the tribes of each minor and major alliance live in contiguous territories with one notable exception: a section of the Majaly and a couple of its attached tribes, which are by local tradition related by blood, live in the area of the Eastern Alliance. This land was acquired from the 'Amr after the Majaly helped it to defeat the 'Imamiyya and to gain the leadership of Al-Karak district in the eighteenth century.

The Majaly has a special position in another sense as well, for it is the paramount tribe and provides the leadership for the whole of Al-Karak. Some of its leaders like to claim that the tribe is a member of no alliance, arguing that its leadership position dictates neutrality in these affairs. In practice, however, the Majaly maintains a dual position as leader both of Al-Karak and of the Western Alliance. As may be easily recognized, the very nature of the pyramidal-segmentary structure dictates this posture. On the one hand the Majaly gains its essential support through the Western Alliance which enables it to maintain its supremacy in

[1] The 'Imamiyya have not forgotten that the Majaly helped the 'Amr to put an end to their rule at the beginning of the eighteenth century. The other attached tribes of the Ma'ayta have long had close relations with the 'Imamiyya, and are therefore not over-friendly with the Majaly. When the 'A'jam alliance, formerly a part of the Eastern Alliance, changed sides, it joined the Ma'ayta because of the help that tribe extended to it. Subsequently, however, the three tribes of the 'A'jam have been involved in numerous minor disputes with the Majaly, perpetuating the historical enmity.

[2] Because of limitations of space and the large number of tribes, only the major ones can be shown on this map. And although nearly all the members of any one tribe live in the designated area, a few may live in a totally different one, even in that of a different major alliance.

Al-Karak. On the other, when non-plateau tribal questions or external relations come into play, the Karaki tribes, as a rule, fall into position behind Majaly leadership.

A certain amount of flexibility exists within the system, but it takes time for change to resolve itself. For instance, in the middle of the last century the Mahadin and its 'A'jam allies, the Shamayla and Madadha, were members of the Eastern Alliance. During this period a dispute involving the loss of life developed between the Tarawna, the paramount tribe of the Eastern Alliance, and the Mahadin. The Mahadin, being (even with their 'A'jam allies) a relatively small tribe in relation to the Tarawna, appealed to the Damur for aid, but met with a refusal. The Mahadin then turned to the Ma'ayta which gave them support, after which the Mahadin left the Eastern Alliance, joining the Western one and, within that, the Ma'ayta Group. For lack of an opportunity or reason, it was not until fifty years later that the other members of the 'A'jam followed suit, and that, reportedly, because of an accident. During a major fight between the Eastern and Western Alliances, members of the Shamayla were just looking on until a stray bullet from the Eastern Alliance killed one of their men. The tribes then joined in the fight on the side of the Western Alliance and have remained members of it ever since. That these tribes were able to change sides was largely because their territory lies on the edge of the Eastern Alliance area, and, by switching, they just moved to the edge of the Western Alliance. Actually, the structure of the wadis around the town of Al-Karak places the 'A'jam more naturally in the Eastern group, which probably accounts for their original membership, but their relative position allowed them to shift more easily than a tribe located further south and east.

(4) *Alliance Reflections in the Town.* The map of Al-Karak town[1] shows living patterns of the 1960s; the picture was considerably different fifty or even twenty years ago. Before the establishment of a central government and thereafter of internal order, there were three distinct living areas. The *suq* divided the Eastern Alliance from the Western Alliance and the Christians lived in the north-eastern section. In normal times and especially in periods of tension, no one from the Eastern section ventured into the Western and vice versa. However, because the Christians were part of the Western Alliance, there was free intercourse between their

[1] Cf. p. 58. As it is impossible to show all the 1,300 or so houses in the town on this map, only the major pattern is shown, that is where most of one tribe or group lives, plus the mixture that is current today. Normal orientation is reversed because this is the way one thinks of the town. The southern end stands considerably higher than the northern and contains the greater part of the *suq*, the chief government offices, and the citadel.

respective sections at most times. The minor alliances and individual tribes also tended to live in their own subsections of their alliance areas. In contrast, the *suq* was considered to be neutral territory

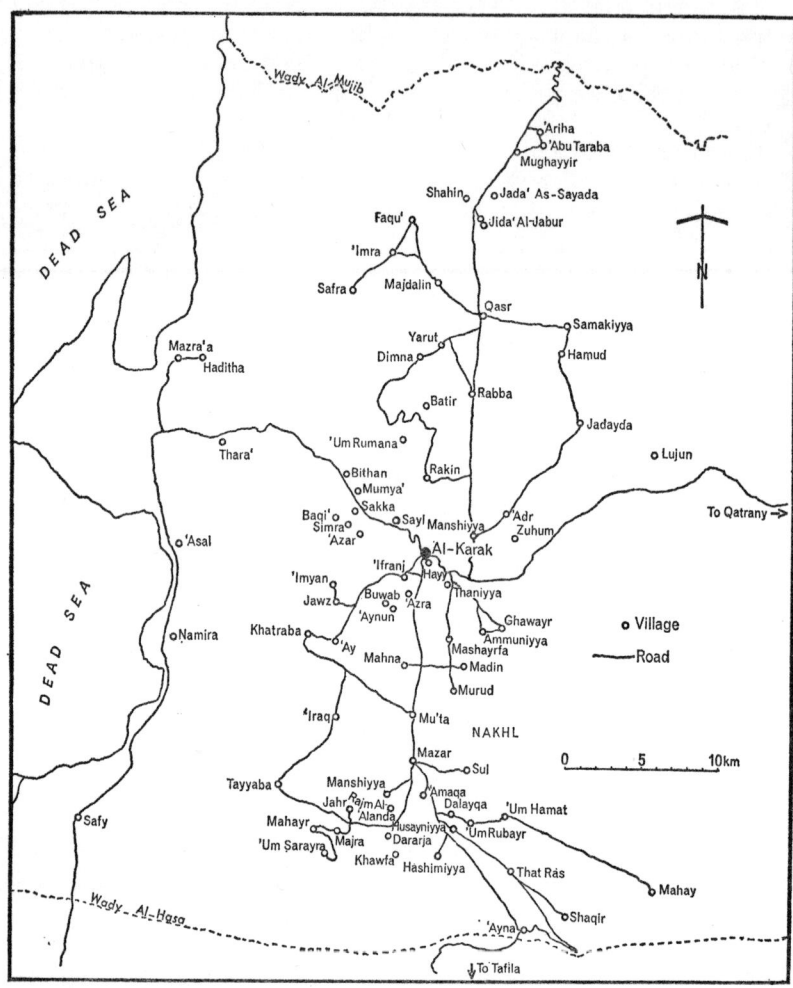

MAP 5. Villages in the District of Al-Karak

where no violence should occur. This concept was extended to the whole of the town in the interwar period.

Living patterns have changed considerably: one finds Christians living among Muslims, members of the Eastern Alliance living in the Western section, and, conversely, Western in Eastern. However, as may be seen from the map, the old patterns still predominate, which may be explained by the preference for living close to relatives and, equally important, by landownership.

(5) *Al-Karak District.* The top of the segmentary-pyramidal structure is Al-Karak district. All the tribes identify themselves as Karakis vis-à-vis the surrounding districts and, when necessary, they operate as a unit against them. In the days of raiding, for example, all who wished to join a band and were not prevented by a current dispute did so. Further, there was no raiding between Karaki tribes, although brigandage and theft did exist.

Groups outside the District

The importance of the outside groups is not their internal organization, but their relationship to the Karakis. The major groups will, therefore, be mentioned and then the various possible relationships will be described.

The groups to the north and south closely resemble the Karakis in their history and structure. They are sedentary (formerly semi-sedentary) tribes, arranged in a segmentary-pyramidal pattern. The other major groups are the bedouin tribes which live in the desert to the east of Al-Karak and to the south in the Wady al-'Araba. They have a structure similar to that of the Karaki tribes, but are usually much larger. Moreover the tribe is not a coherent whole, the section being the most important operative unit. Before the first world war these tribes were either nomadic or semi-nomadic; today their members fall into all categories, but are predominately semi-nomadic and semi-sedentary. The agricultural cycle of the Karakis and the animal-husbandry cycle of the bedouin are complementary. From late winter to early summer while the crops are growing, rain in the desert provides grazing for the animals of the bedouin. By the time the crops have been harvested, the desert grass has dried up and the bedouin bring their animals to the Karaki fields to pasture them on the stubble, providing natural fertilizer much appreciated by the Karaki agriculturists. When the rains begin again in the late autumn, the bedouin move to the desert for the new grass and the Karakis prepare their fields for new crops, completing the cycle.

Political relationships between the Karakis and outsiders took four basic forms, with many variations which tended to give the terms and their corresponding meaning a certain ambiguity but also a flexibility. These formal relationships with the tribes and adjoining areas began to lose their importance in the inter-war period owing to increasing security, the decline of raiding, and the elimination of tribal wars. Their only significance today is that the relations between Karakis and the corresponding outside groups are closer where strong ties once existed and strained where the relationship was one of heavy raiding or war. Thus continual enmity remains between Karakis and the Huwaytat and close relations with the Bany 'Attiya.

(1) *War.* A tribal war was a declared state of hostility between two tribes or alliances in which the side initiating the action sent a messenger to the other, formally stating its intentions. The state of war was usually preceded by a long period of strained relations involving a heavy raiding relationship. A tribe might declare war out of fear for its territorial integrity or livelihood, or it might do so (or provoke a declaration of war by the other side) in an attempt to increase its power. After the end of hostilities which could last for weeks or drag out over decades, peace was established through formal negotiations.

(2) *Raiding.* A raiding relationship existed between Al-Karak and any outside group with which this was not specifically forbidden. The raid was a highly formalized action in which the intention was to take animals and movable goods, but not to inflict physical injuries or loss of life. Unless extremely hostile relations existed between the two groups, any wounding or death was referred to tribal courts.

(3) *Suhba.* The *suhba* was a negotiated agreement, most properly termed a treaty of friendship, between two groups, e.g. between Al-Karak (or a Karaki tribe) and an outside group. It implied, first, that neither party had the intention of going to war against the other and, secondly, that the two parties desired better relations in the future after past disputes had had time to be forgotten. For example, it will be recalled that the Bany Hamida were instrumental in destroying the effective power of the 'Amr and later were themselves defeated by the Karaki tribes. After this, both tribes lived side by side in the northern part of the district. With the passage of time, they established a *suhba* relationship and eventually a *bin'amma* treaty. The *suhba* agreement did not preclude mutual raiding, but it did prescribe that the raid was to be carried out in a friendly manner and that the raided goods and animals should be returned for a price much below their actual value. Further, if there was a killing between the two parties, it was not to be a cause for general hostility, but merely an affair between the *khamsas* of each individual.

(4) *Bin'amma.* The *bin'amma* was a negotiated agreement implying a close relationship with many potential variations. Its basic terms stipulated that there was to be no raiding between the two

parties; if a raid did take place, then all goods and animals were to be restored with apologies. In order to maintain this agreement, each side appointed an *'alim* ('one who knows') to look after the interests of the other side in his territory. A variation on this pattern was the relationship between the Karakis and the Bany 'Attiya. The latter were allowed to pasture their animals at will within the district; and the Karakis collected no *khawa* from them, as they did from some sections of the Bany Sakhr at the time. But the Karakis wanted ghee, dried yoghurt, sheep's wool, and goat hair from the Bany 'Attiya. So a bargain was struck whereby if a lone man could successfully fill his cloak with the desired goods and get away unobserved, he could keep them. If he were caught, he would lose his cloak with no further recriminations. The relationship also involved, depending on mutual negotiations, defensive and/or offensive arrangements which could be directed against a given tribe or tribes or could form a blanket agreement.

Villages

In the traditional period villages were for the most part non-corporate territorial groups; only in the last ten years have village councils been formed, creating a degree of corporateness, and even then not in a majority of the villages. The average village contains sections of two or three tribes, which are usually linked by one of the forms of alliance: attached; minor alliance; or at least the same major alliance. Traditionally, there were no common activities in the village, rather, it was merely a place of common residence where people farmed adjoining fields. In the villages with mixed tribes, numerous marriages are contracted between the groups (except Muslims and Christians), showing a preference for village as well as tribal and kin endogamy. As regards religion, although half of the rural Christians live in two solely Christian villages, Samakiyya and Hamud, a significant proportion live side by side with Muslims in Ar-Rabba and 'Adr which were settled around the turn of the century. Two villages founded in the contemporary period, Lajun and Majdalin, are also mixed. New villages are formed for two basic reasons. As new land is tilled, villages are built in the area so that the farmers will be close to their fields. Or a village may be formed by a new section of a tribe segmenting off and establishing a new place of residence. These processes may take a few years before the permanence of the village is established. In sum, from a political standpoint, the village has only an indirect role by bringing two or more groups together in extended common residence and permitting common marriage in the case of Muslims.

Religion

Although religious differences are minimal in Al-Karak in comparison with the whole of the Middle East, they do have some
political effect and, as regards the Christians, they constitute a
limitation. Islam claims approximately 90 per cent of the Karakis,
the remainder being Christian, but this small figure does not
adequately reflect their position. The Christian tribes live only on
the plateau; and of the residents of this more important area, they
constitute close to 20 per cent.

A number of Islamic institutions exist in the district, but none
which ties the Muslims together in any coherent fashion. The town
and most of the villages have mosques with their religious shaykhs.
These used to keep a few informal schools, teaching boys to read
and recite from the Quran and some simple mathematics, but this
instruction ceased after the Ottoman and the Amirate governments
established their own schools. Islamic law, the *shari'a*, has only
recently come into force, mostly in the last seventy years, and then
only for personal status, marriage, divorce, treatment of women
and children, and inheritance. The customary tribal law was used
before this and continues to predominate today. The overwhelming majority of the Muslims belong to the Hanafi school of law,
but no socio-political significance is attached to those who do not.
The *'Awqaf* Institution owns property and sometimes takes part
in welfare and civic programmes for the town, but it is controlled
from Amman, with only a local committee of advisers. It should
be noted that the Sufis neither established branches of their orders
in the district nor gathered adherents. To sum up, although Islam
definitely has a strong religious and social role in Al-Karak, no
real direct or indirect political importance should be attached
to it. Admittedly it did have a role in the Muslim Brotherhood in the contemporary period, but this is discussed in later
chapters.

The Christians have a stronger organization, resulting from
a number of interwoven, reinforcing factors. Their very status as a
minority with a strong common identity tends to pull them
together. Although in general the tribal system decidedly holds
a stronger political position than religion, Christianity adds one
more uniting element to the tribal alliance, even though it is also
the *raison d'être* of that alliance. Again the more structured and
organized nature of the church in comparison to the mosque gives
the Christians a greater cohesiveness than the Muslims. Moreover,
the Christian missionaries, Roman Catholic and Protestant, set up
schools in the 1870s and 1880s which continued during the tradi-

tional period with only a couple of short breaks, and the Roman Catholic school still functions today. Although the Muslims were and are welcome to attend the schools, the Christians have definitely benefited more from them, gaining a much higher educational standard than their Muslim counterparts and another reason for greater identity. As regards corporateness, the Christians are only corporate through their tribal alliance. Their leaders are usually dependent on this group rather than on other organizations. Priests have provided political leadership upon occasion, but not consistently.

The Christians are internally divided. The Greek Orthodox membership is the largest, containing the following tribes: Sunna', Madanat, Zurayqat, and all but one section each of the Halasa and Haddadin. The Greek Catholic (Uniate) membership is the next largest, composed of the Baqa'in, Masarwa, and half of the Hajazin and 'Akasha, Masanat (a section of the 'Azizat of Madaba), and one small section each of the Halasa and Haddadin. Until early in the nineteenth century, all Karaki Christians were Greek Orthodox, but a couple of tribes were converted to the Greek Catholic rite and later in the 1870s and 1880s some tribal sections of both rites were converted to Roman Catholicism. After this, only individuals or families have been known to change their affiliation. There were three basic motives for conversion. First, the newly introduced churches proselytized energetically, persuading some in this manner, especially because the degree of local religious knowledge was minimal. Secondly, the Roman Catholic Church usually required conversion to its rite if a person wished to marry someone of its faith. Thirdly, as a result of disputes between tribes or internally within a tribe, some groups changed church membership in order further to emphasize the split. Originally, the non-converted tribes and their leaders felt that the new rites and their priests, often non-Arabs, were a challenge to their authority, and they opposed them on these grounds. In the contemporary period this difference does not seem to have very much political importance on the district level, although it does occasionally affect relations within a village.

The relations between Christians and Muslims have always been extremely cordial and close. Members of each side participate in some of the other's ceremonies and, in the past, even adopted some of their customs. For example, in the visiting that takes place during the Muslim and Christian holy days, the opposite members invariably take part. Also, Muslims quite often join with the Christians in the Easter procession through the streets. In respect to mutual customs, before the turn of the century, many Muslims had their children baptized and a few Christians took more than one wife. Even today, a Christian with a barren wife may take a second without divorcing the first. Finally, the people continually express their mutual tolerance for one another and are quite proud of their mutually good relations as compared with the rest of Jordan and the Middle East.

This tolerance and mutual respect are reflected in political relations. The Majaly have always been particularly close to the Christians with significant benefit to both. On a number of occasions, outsiders have challenged a person or group for being Christian and the Majaly were quick to defend them. For example, in the early 1920s upon hearing that a Damascene Muslim was swearing at the Christians and saying that they would go to Hell, Rafifan Pashal Al-Majaly immediately banished the man for ten years. The Christians co-operated closely with the Majaly in the days of wars and raids, providing some of the best men-at-arms, and, on the whole, they have consistently done so in non-violent political relations. In other spheres as well, Christians have held many high positions. Because of their higher standard of education as well as their acceptance, they have continually held proportionately more local-government positions than the Muslims, or just the Muslims of the plateau. Further, Al-Karak sent Christians as its representatives to Faysal's government in Damascus and to the Salt conference in 1920.

Differences and minor strains do, however, exist. Although the Christians are considered to be wholly Karakis and Jordanians, the leader of Al-Karak district could never conceivably be a Christian. In that they are a minority in the area, but favourably treated, they do not seem troubled by this, but they do criticize the central government for not allowing Christians to attain the top official and political posts at the national level. Also, the Christians generally feel that they are superior to the Muslims on several counts. They cite their higher level of education and claim that their morals are superior, asserting that no thieves or brigands come from their community. Finally, in private they strongly criticize the Muslim custom of paying a bride price, saying that this means that the woman is being treated no better than an animal. In contrast, the plateau Muslims hardly criticize the Christians at all; they have nothing but praise for their level of education and the excellent state of mutual relations within the community. The semi-nomads and tribes of the periphery occasionally express lack of tolerance and distrust, but this is not manifested in action.

Minorities

The term minority is used here to describe the various groups of people which, because of individual and particular characteristics, do not (or are not allowed to) integrate themselves into the pyramidal-segmentary political structure. They are considered to be different both by the Karakis and by themselves. For purposes of description, they are divided into six categories: Ghawarna; former slaves; Hebronis and Damascenes; Armenians; iron-smiths; and gipsies.

(1) *Ghawarna.* The Ghawarna are the dark-complexioned people of the Ghawr, slightly over 6,000 in number, who are subject to economic and political domination with heavy racial overtones. They are divided into two major alliance groups, the northern based in the villages of Mazra'a and Haditha, and the southern based in Safy and Fifa, the latter village being south of Al-Karak in the Tafila district, but in the Karaki sphere of influence. Each major alliance is in turn divided into two minor alliance groups, three of which are composed of six tribes and one of three. The origin of these tribes is obscure, but they are known to have been long resident in the district and are considered to be Arabs. However they have always been grossly exploited (see p. 28). Before the extensive development of agriculture in the area, all the major tribes, especially the Majaly, by threat of force collected *khawa* from them. After their land started becoming valuable, the major tribes and the Hebronis and Damascenes began taking it by ruse and threat. Generally, the central government has condoned and even abetted this ill treatment. Because some of the people who own part of the Ghawr lands also have considerable influence with the government, nothing is done to aid the Ghawarna. On the contrary, whenever a government administrator is found to be aiding them against the wishes of the landowners, he is transferred to another post away from the region.

The Karakis' social attitude towards the Ghawarna has all the typical elements of racial discrimination. For example, it is held that no honourable person should marry one because of their dark skins, and the attitude is carried out in practice, for intermarriage is virtually unknown. Moreover, it is generally thought that they should hold only menial manual-labour jobs, and never rise to a position of authority or power over a light-complexioned Karaki. Some of the educated Karakis criticize these attitudes, but this is strictly the view of only a few individuals.

To indicate the extent of the power of the Karaki tribes over the Ghawarna, a famous example which is often cited in Al-Karak is helpful. One man, Za'al Al-Majaly, was particularly infamous for his ruthless control and physical maltreatment of the Ghawarna. Between the wars he acquired considerable holdings in the region and treated the people as virtual slaves. When, in his opinion, a man was not working hard enough, or did something of which he did not approve, Za'al put him in prison. Having no actual gaol of his own, he ordered the man to sit among thorn bushes until he was released which might be from a day or up to a week later. And such was his power and the consequent fear on the part of the Ghawarna that the man invariably obeyed.

In the interwar period, there were two significant exceptions to this pattern.[1] First, the head shaykh of the Habashna, Muhammad, offended by this maltreatment, decided to live with a couple of Ghawarna tribes for a time in order to explain their rights to them. Through these efforts he was able to prevent them from losing part of their land. Secondly, a potash plant was built close to Safy in the 1930s. Fresh water was required for the washing process and it was decided to buy it from the tribes of Safy. The British agent in charge made sure that the local tribes got this money and he did his job so well that the people of the village did not work at all from 1935 to 1948 when the Arab-Israeli war ended the arrangement.

In the contemporary period the Ghawarna are treated rather better. Economic domination continues, but harsh physical treatment is a thing of the past. Za'al Al-Majaly's prison no longer exists. A few primary schools have also been built, but no secondary ones.

(2) *Former Slaves.* Before the turn of the century, some of the major Majaly shaykhs possessed personal slaves. They were usually well treated and respected, and were provided with a horse, a pistol, and a rifle, all symbols of prestige. After the slaves were given their independence, some intermarried with the Ghawarna, losing their former slave status and identity and taking membership in one of the tribes. But a number of individuals remained in the plateau with the Majaly and have attained a curious mixed position. On the one hand, because of their dark colour and their former slave status, they are subject to discrimination. Like the Ghawarna, they are not accepted as potential marriage partners, nor are they allowed to rise to positions of authority. Officially, they have taken the tribal name of Majaly, but the local Karakis refer to them as '*abid al-Majaly* (slaves of the Majaly), implying recognition of their former status and consequently disrespect. On the other hand, some have been treated quite favourably. For example, the paramount shaykh from 1842 to 1886, Muhammad

---

[1] Both these examples are from an interview with Sir Alec Kirkbride.

Al-Majaly, had a favourite slave named Salama, and when Muhammad died, Salama inherited land equally with Muhammad's three sons. As a result, his descendants and others live and own land in Ar-Rabba, one of the principal Majaly villages. A more recent example occurred a few years ago when a second-generation former slave killed another man in a car accident. The custom is for the *khamsa* of the man responsible to make a substantial payment to the *khamsa* of the deceased person. The son of the former slave, being of only a second generation in Al-Karak, had a very small group from which to gather money for the payment. Rather than see all these people financially ruined, the Majaly section which lived in the same village, Ar-Rabba, took up a collection for the payment. It is not rare for a larger group than the *khamsa* to make the blood payment, but what is significant here is that the son of a former slave was in a sense accepted as a member of the Majaly tribe by this action. In sum, the former slaves are discriminated against on account of their colour and former status, but are also treated much better than the Ghawarna, partly at least because of the prestige of their fathers.

(3) *Hebronis and Damascenes.* Politically, the Hebronis and Damascenes fall into the same class as regards internal structure and external influence and activity. Each group is a series of independent extended families, but has no organization as a formal coherent unit. The groups do, however, maintain considerable common contact in business and social affairs and each has an informally recognized leader. One seat on the Municipal Council is always reserved for a Hebroni, representing the interests of both groups, particularly on the commercial side. As a general rule, Hebronis tend to marry local members of their group, or members of their *hamulas* in Hebron and the same applies to the Damascenes. Occasionally, a man may marry a woman from one of the Karaki tribes and when this occurs the children of the marriage often feel a certain loyalty to and identity with their mother's tribe. The Hebronis and Damascenes are not members of the tribal alliances and consider themselves to be neutral in this respect. Nor did they participate in the external politics of the area: wars, raids, and temporary alliances. Although some members have attained great wealth by Karaki standards, they have never gained much political power. These people are considered to be Karakis (see p. 27), but with a difference, for they are not of the local tribes and are merchants. For the most part, they think of themselves as Karakis, but because of their economic and social status they know that they may never obtain significant political strength, despite their economic wealth.

In recent years some of the Hebronis and many of the Damascenes have left Al-Karak because the newly arrived and commercially interested Ghazawis have outcompeted them in the *suq*. Also, another incident caused a large and wealthy family to leave. When Haza' Al-Majaly was assassinated in 1960, a Damascene family, the Shammut, was implicated. The individuals involved were from Salt, the Karaki Shammut being very distant relatives, well outside their *khamsa*. Nevertheless, because of the great prestige and importance of Haza', they feared local retaliation, left the district, and sold their considerable assets.

(4) *Armenians.* By the end of the 1920s, there were 40–50 Armenian families in the district, but today only four or five remain. They came as a result of Ottoman persecution, to escape conscription, and for better economic opportunities. Although accepted and protected within the society, they were not considered part of it. They had different social customs, retained their language, only learned Arabic poorly, and tended to marry among themselves or with Armenians from other towns. Their economic activities usually revolved around commerce, industry, and construction. They built most of the flour mills and olive presses and made most of the shoes. Some of them rented and bought land very early in the Ghawr and were the first people to farm it intensively and efficiently, demonstrating its high economic potential. They were and are important municipal employees in the utilities department because of their technical knowledge and skill. Most of these families have left because of better economic opportunities elsewhere and because much of their handicraft is now replaced by imported manufactured goods. The few who remain are municipal employees, landowners, and the local commercial pharmacist.

(5) *Iron-smiths.* The Khaza'y are a small tribe of traditional iron-smiths, typical of similar groups found in Transjordan and the Syrian Desert[1] which move from camp to camp and village to village, seeking work. The Karakis do not consider them as equals, probably because of their particular mode of livelihood, but they are not ill treated, for their trade is needed. In recognition of their neutral status in the days of the raids, if they lost animals or goods, these were restored automatically by the raiders. The Khaza'y may be considered to be a technical, functional group whose trade is valued and therefore protected by all concerned.

(6) *Gipsies.* The gipsies are similar to the Khaza'y in that they have no political power, but they are a despised people and are often ill treated. Their camps may be found on the edges of all the

---

[1] Cf. Alois Musil, *The manners and customs of the Rwala bedouins* (1928), pp. 181–2.

fertile areas of Jordan and it is from these that they practise their trades. They are petty thieves and do some work in gold, but their most important function is entertainment. At weddings and other occasions, they are hired to play music and their women sing and dance. Also, Karaki men visit their camps for pleasure, singing, dancing, gambling, and prostitution.

Patron–Client Groups

A patron–client relationship may exist between two individuals, between an individual and a group, or between two groups. The position of the two parties may depend, among other factors, on wealth, power, status, or a combination of these. This vertical group implies a superior and an inferior, but it does not necessarily mean that the relationship is one-sided in favour of the superior party. Rather, the aim of the connection may be for the mutual benefit of both sides. For some of the following, political meaning may only be secondary to economic, but in each case the two overlap.

(1) *Murabi'*. This is an individual-to-individual, temporary, contractual relationship whereby a poor man, the client, attaches himself out of economic necessity to a richer man, the patron, giving his labour during the agricultural season in return for subsistence and, if needed, a measure of protection. Although the poor man cannot contribute much support to his superior in the context of the whole political system, the fact that his superior has another person or persons attached to him adds to his prestige. The association is not an equal one, because of the extreme poverty of the client which brings dishonour on him and forces him into clientage, but it is freely entered into by both parties; there is no physical or moral compulsion and it may be terminated by either side.

(2) *Sharecropping*. A sharecropping agreement is also a temporary contractual relationship, but a much more equal one. Unlike *murabi'*, it is honourable for both patron and client, and is entered into for the economic benefit of both. As regards politics, it is indirectly and at times directly beneficial to both as well. For the patron, the existence of a client adds to his prestige and, in that the client is most probably an ordinary member of his tribe or an allied one, the man's political support has some weight. From the standpoint of the client, as long as the contract lasts, he is assured of a measure of political protection and aid.

(3) *Attached Tribes*. As has been mentioned above (pp. 52, 54), many small tribes have semi-permanent attachments to larger ones which result in considerable political and social benefit to both

parties. The superior tribe gains prestige, potential numbers, and support, while the attached tribe enjoys aid and protection and the prestige of being associated with a powerful group.

(4) *Bararsha and 'Iraq Tribes.* Traditionally, most of the Bararsha tribes and those of 'Iraq village were subordinate to the Majaly and the remainder to other major plateau tribes. This relationship was neither equal nor freely contracted, for the superior tribes by threat of force required them to pay *khawa*. The patron did, however, afford the client tribe a measure of protection against other tribes both in the district and outside. In turn, the clients provided fighters in the event of raids or war. The collection of *khawa* was eliminated in the interwar period, but the tribes retained a position of inferiority to the plateau tribes in all political affairs. Until very recently the Majaly could demand and obtain their support virtually at will. They have also lost proportionately much more of their land to the usurers than the plateau tribesmen.

(5) *Ghawarna.* The Ghawarna's unequal relationship with the Karaki plateau tribes is sufficiently described above (pp. 65–6).

Socio-economic Strata

In the traditional political system, socio-economic strata certainly existed, but were of minor importance, for they had no coherence and very little identity attached to them. From both a social and an economic viewpoint, entrance into one of these strata was mostly ascriptive, one was born into it. However, traditional achieving ability also had a role, for a man was able to push himself into a higher stratum by creating wealth and using it in the proper way; or, conversely, an individual might squander his wealth and either he or his children would slip into a lower stratum. As to identity, there was no direct relationship between one's degree of wealth and one's social standing. A man saw himself, and was seen by others, as being distinguished from his equal in material goods according to how he gained and used his wealth. Thus no one considered a rich merchant the equal of a rich or even a moderately well-off Karaki landowner, and a poor Ghawarna or Bararsha was a very different person socially from a poor plateau tribesman. It was membership in the other social groups which defined a person's position; and it was within these groups that wealth and social strata were of greater importance. For example, within the upper stratum of the plateau tribes, a certain amount of common identity, but no real coherence or loyalty, could be discerned.

In the contemporary period, socio-economic strata take on greater significance, and, at least for a small segment (the educated middle stratum), a strong feeling of common identity. This is discussed at length in Chapter 4 (pp. 131–3).

Formal Government

Although the local and central governments are interconnected by law and in practice, they have distinct institutions and offices and for descriptive purposes are most easily dealt with separately. In the contemporary period, formal government has increased greatly in importance and in scope, and, as such, is described at length in its new form in later chapters.

(1) *Local Government.* Before the contemporary period, organized local government only existed in the town of Al-Karak, where the first municipal council was formed in 1895. The legal duties of the council were and are to provide basic utilities, new roads, town planning, and some welfare. For these purposes it taxes houses and shops, charges for water and electricity, and collects sundry fees. The central government also provides some regular financial aid and grants long-term credits for civic projects. The council's authority is greatly limited by law, for major projects, tax rates, resolutions, and business other than daily housekeeping must be approved by the central government.

Under the Ottomans and the Amirate, the actual selection of the council members reflected two major factors: the population make-up of the town and the power position of the tribes in the district. Thus, although the Majaly have never had more than six or seven extended families resident in the town, except for a short time after the 1910 revolt, a Majaly has always been head of the council; and from 1918 until today, Duliwan Pasha Al-Majaly, brother of Rafifan Pasha, has held this position. On the other hand, the Habashna, a relatively weak tribe, has a larger proportion of the population of the town than any other tribe and it consistently has a member on the council. The Christians, who have a significant proportion of the town's population and are strong in the district, claim 2 or 3 of the 9 seats. As regards the major alliances, the Western Alliance usually has 2 or 3 more seats, bringing its total to 6 or 7. The Eastern Alliance, with one-quarter of the population, rarely has more than one member. The Hebronis and Damascenes are allotted one and occasionally two places, reflecting their numbers and economic importance. The semi-nomads and tribes of the periphery of whom there are very few in the town and who lack power in the district, never have a council seat.

Before the late 1950s, although the council did provide certain minimal municipal functions, it was noted for its desultory and mediocre performance. Its members used the council as a means of gaining prestige, political in-fighting, and obtaining funds through petty corruption. Also, very few of the important decisions were made in connection with this formal body, but rather through one of the following three methods. First, a few of the local leaders, always including Rafifan Pasha and Duliwan Pasha, formulated proposals and presented them to the council for formal approval. Second, the central government, as part of its general development programme, submitted measures for which it expected and obtained passage. Third, the more usual method was for the district leaders and central government personnel to work in concert, for relations with Amir Abdullah's government were usually excellent.

(2) *Central Government*. The nature of the relationships of both the Ottoman and Amirate governments with the people of Al-Karak was very much the same, best described as a progressing continuum. The main features of change were that the central government gradually imposed greater security, the collection of taxes steadily became more efficient, and the central government increasingly contributed more to the economy and welfare of the area.

The principal formal institutions consisted of the governor, the police and the army, the law courts (see pp. 86–7), and the mukhtars. Except for a short time at the beginning of the Amirate, in order to ensure neutrality the governor was always a man from outside the district. His office symbolized the whole of the government, for while purely administrative decisions, such as acquiring more medicine for the local health centre, were dealt with directly by the department concerned, any decision with the slightest political importance, such as hiring a new employee, had to go through his office. Although the police came under a separate chief, they should be considered as an instrument of the governor for the implementation of the government's policies as well as the maintenance of order and security. In the background lay the army as the ultimate force which could be called in when needed. The government maintained a consistent policy of manning the police and army in the area primarily with non-Karakis so as to avoid conflicts of interest. In the traditional period, few government departments had offices outside Amman, and few policy decisions were made for, or carried out in, the provinces. Rather, it was a period for building up the basic structure of government: police, army, taxation, land registration, and the state legal apparatus. Only gradually were other functions affected: commercial and industrial regulations, health institutions, credit facilities, and welfare.

Other than through local employees, two of the formal institutions created permanent connections between the central government and the population; and many less formal methods were also employed. An Administrative Council of local notables and senior officials occasionally functioned. The purpose of this council, from the point of view of the Karakis, was to advise the governor and central government on the needs of the district and to communicate complaints about the execution of policies; from that of the government, to facilitate the implementation of official decisions. The second institution, which still functions today, is the office of mukhtar. The mukhtar is at the same time the local representative of the government vis-à-vis the tribe and that of the tribe vis-à-vis the government. Until after the second world war he represented one large tribe or three or four small ones, and was paid a small salary. He is now unpaid and represents fewer people, each large tribe having 6 to 8, usually one per tribal section, and a small tribe having one of its own. The mukhtar records vital statistics, and helps in the collection of taxes and in finding and identifying any person under his jurisdiction upon demand from the government. He protects the rights of the individual in the event of his house being searched, and helps to solve minor disputes. He plays a very important part in determining inheritance, as he is expected to know all the precise kinship relations of the deceased.

The central government also paid stipends to the chief shaykhs, on the one hand to keep them from opposing the government, on the other to induce them to help it to function. Because the central government was at first so weak, the Ottomans and the Amirate not only worked through the local leaders but actually, though informally, delegated much of their authority to them. This was a pragmatic policy recognizing the inability of the government even minimally to fulfil its functions without the aid of the shaykhs; it was also a means of using their already existing traditional authority with the people.

As may be observed from the above description, the central government was and is an integral part of the political system. Admittedly, it has a special position, for it commands the ultimate power of the army, but its structure and functions are intertwined with that of the society.

Political Structure of the Whole Society

In the foregoing pages the political society has been broken down into its structural parts, and it is now necessary to recreate the structure of the whole traditional society. The pyramidal-segmentary system ties the majority of the population together, starting with the true kin groups, the sub-lineages or lineages, and working stage by stage through the tribal sections, tribes, minor and major alliance groups, and finally Al-Karak as a whole. Of these groups, loyalty, identity, organization, and discipline are strongest with the kin group, for a man's actions are considered to be those of his kin and vice versa. To a lesser degree this is true on an ever diminishing scale up the pyramidal organization. The kin groups, tribes, and alliances are the bases of the traditional political structure; all other groups either reinforce these or are forms relating to them. The villages and the town provide common residence, a milieu for daily contact, and opportunity for creating intergroup marriage ties, strengthening the bonds amongst the tribal groups. Conversely, the separate villages are united through common tribal and alliance identity. Islam has a certain force which unites its adherents in a common culture, but, politically, it has little direct or even indirect influence. Because of the greater organization of the Christian church and its minority status within the area, this religion has a stronger binding force than Islam in Al-Karak. Although the existence of two religions is a natural social divisive force, this effect is minimized by common residence, the inclusion of both in the alliance structure, and, perhaps most importantly, a long tradition of living and co-operating together in mutual respectful tolerance. The patron–client relationships unite individuals and groups within tribes, the small and large tribes of the plateau, and the dominant plateau and subjected periphery tribes. And, in turn, patron–client groups are tied together through the patrons being of the same tribe or alliance. In contrast to these vertical groups, the weak horizontal strata contribute their minimal identity across tribal and patron–client divisions, and the various levels are united by all the pyramidal and vertical groups. Finally, the central government is connected to all of these groups through the Administrative Council, the mukhtar, the staffing of some posts by local Karakis, informal relationships with Karakis, and political activities in which all participate.

The minority groups, although minimally dealt with above, should be mentioned separately because of their special status. The Ghawarna are tied to various tribes by unequal economic bonds and patron–client relationships, as are the Bararsha and the people of 'Iraq village in a weaker sense. Some former slaves are integrated to some extent in the Majaly tribe and also share a common residence and religion with them and other tribes. The Armenians are somewhat identified with the Christian Karakis as a result of a common faith, and with the whole society by a common residence and their necessary and beneficial economic role. The Hebronis and Damascenes can claim a common religion and residence with the Karakis, some marriage ties, and economic and commercial bonds. Finally, the iron-smiths and gipsies have no real ties with the society except the services which they provide.

The town of Al-Karak has a special position in this structure, for representatives of the vast majority of the tribes and groups reside within it. It is here that they work, live, and practise politics together and that most of the decisions affecting the whole and even minor sections of the area are made. The establishment of the district's central-government offices within the town further reconfirms its central role.

In sum the society is divided into a series of groups each with its own degree of identity, loyalty, and corporateness; but, in turn, each of these units has numerous links with the others, binding the large majority of the people of Al-Karak into a structural whole.

3

DYNAMICS OF THE TRADITIONAL POLITICAL SOCIETY

THE intention in this chapter is to describe and analyse in three stages the dynamics within the traditional political system. (1) Some considerations on the concepts of legitimacy, authority, and power applicable to Al-Karak are put forward. These are essential for what they reveal of the limits and possibilities of action on the part of the society's leaders. (2) The acquisition and maintenance of the various political leadership roles are surveyed with reference to the whole of the society as well as its parts, relating each role to the group structure presented in the previous chapter. An attempt is also made to describe and explain the special position of the Majaly, the paramount Karaki tribe. (3) We enter upon the true dynamics of the political society by citing examples of different types of political action. The categorization and ordering of the various examples are not pure, for in practice each kind of political action overlaps another. Although this overlapping is kept to a minimum by the choice of examples, it is included where it occurs and is explained as such. Only thus can one be true to the data as well as to the system and its dynamics. Moreover, the cases are chosen in order to point out the many kinds of problems which arise and are solved within the society. Subject to this explanation, the various categories are: disputes solved by the traditional legal mechanism; land disputes; intertribal affairs; major alliance relations; and external relations.

As in the previous chapter, many elements of this traditional system are substantially the same in the contemporary period. If a particular pattern or slightly altered form of it is still valid, this is noted, but if considerable change has taken place, then other examples will be given in Chapter 5. In this way, both continuity and change in the system are indicated.

Some Notes on Legitimacy, Authority, and Power

It is argued here that in Al-Karak there was no legitimacy in the past, and only recently has the Jordanian regime been able to establish a minimal claim to it in the minds of the Karakis. Taking three basic types of legitimacy, first, there is no ideological base for belief in the system (e.g. socialism, fascism, Islam, traditionalism).

Secondly, the traditional desire that the non-formal governmental structure should continue to exist is not accompanied by any sense of moral obligation to obey the leaders. Thirdly, personal legitimacy based on charisma has never been a lasting force in Al-Karak, though Qadr Al-Majaly did perhaps command this kind of loyalty and legitimacy for a short time before and during the revolt of 1910.

The political system itself was unfavourable to legitimacy. First, the paramount power within the area repeatedly changed hands ('Amr, Bany Sakhr with the Majaly, Majaly with its allies, the Ottomans, the Amirate of Transjordan, and the Kingdom of Jordan), each one exercising power and authority in a different manner, none staying long enough or penetrating deeply enough into the society to establish itself as legitimate, and quite often having to rely on the use of force. Again, in the absence of the central government's army, unless the leader of a group, other than a kin group, exercised some form of sanction over his followers (e.g. force over the Ghawarna), he could not give an order and expect to have it obeyed. Rather, all decisions were made in con-sultation with other leaders of the various levels, the top person's opinion carrying slightly more weight than those of the others, but it was still the decision of the individual and his kin group whether to obey or not. The authority commanded by an individual in a particular office was very weak; it was other factors that persuaded a man and his group to go along with the leader: expediency, traditional inertia, material gain, sense of common identity, social pressures, and the leader's own political ability. The phenomenon of self-help ran throughout the political system. Whatever the issue, a stolen sheep, personal injury, a land claim, or raiding, at all levels a man or group established a position of power before demanding a decision from one of the leaders over the affair. In this sense, the leader functioned as a mediator or, more often, an arbitrator upon the agreement of both parties.

Traditional politics in Al-Karak may be viewed as a continuing balance between self-help, the use or potential use of power, on the one hand, and, on the other, the exercise of authoritative decisions, followed out of expediency, not legitimacy. The intro-duction of an outside government with its ultimate power in the form of an army blended into both.

Leadership

The traditional leadership roles of the society are based on different combinations of groups and varying balances of ascriptive and achievement criteria. In this section, position by status is presented at the outset, followed by a description of the various leadership positions. These include: the shaykhs at the various tribal levels, shaykhs of the alliances, *shaykh al-masha'ikh* (shaykh of the shaykhs, paramount shaykh of Al-Karak), *'aqid* (raid leader, defunct role after the mid-1920s), village leader, traditional *qadi* (judge), religious shaykhs and priests, minority group leaders, patrons, and central-government positions.

(1) *Status*. As stratification tends to unite people of the same stratum, status, through the mutual competition for it, tends to divide them, especially those of the same stratum. For example, in contrast to strata classification, a man who has considerable wealth may be regarded as a member of the upper stratum and he may be able to buy a certain amount of power; but he may not have very high status, through his failure to use his wealth in the pre-scribed patterns which give one prestige, or because he has gained his wealth in a manner that is not highly approved of in the given group or society. Therefore, status or prestige sets one person off from another; it divides and does not unite. This has political meaning on two scores. First, the very competition for it may be politically related and this competition may also make it more difficult for two persons, otherwise equal, to co-operate in a political venture. Second, the possession of status may put a person in a more powerful political position within the society.

The following list is composed of those characteristics which give an individual his status in society. They are subdivided into three groups: (*a*) ascriptive, those criteria over which man has no choice; (*b*) ascriptive and achievement, those which may be given or which may be gained through a man's ability, or a combination of the two; and (*c*) achievement.

a. *Ascriptive*

(i) *Kinship and tribal membership*: because a man is considered as an extension of his kin and, to a lesser extent, of his tribe, the prestige and power of the group contribute greatly to his own position.

(ii) *Age*: older people are generally held in respect. If a man's status is high, age enhances it, if low it makes only a minor difference.

(iii) *Sex*: males are highly favoured in all political roles; women have little political significance except through the creation of marriage ties.

(iv) *Colour*: in any competition for status or position, the people of the Ghawr and the former slaves are seriously hampered, if not entirely frustrated, by their dark skins.

b. Ascriptive and Achievement

(i) *Landholding*: the more land a man possesses, the greater the prestige.

(ii) *Other material wealth*: wealth honourably gained (e.g. fees for deciding judicial cases or sheep and goats won by raiding) enhances status, whereas wealth gained by trade gives only a minimal political advantage.

(iii) *Occupation*: honourably gained wealth permitting one not to work gives the highest prestige, then, in descending order, come middle- and small-sized landowners, soldiers, very poor farmers, and artisans and merchants. In the contemporary period, this ranking is considerably altered.

(iv) *Honour*: one's honour must be maintained; any loss of it means a considerable decline in status. A person born of a dishonourable family or group lacks honour and it is difficult to recoup it.

c. Achievement

(i) *Spending patterns or generosity*: wealth generously and judiciously spread adds very greatly to a man's position and it may also create political debts.

(ii) *Bravery*: in raiding and in war before the 1920s and at all times in individual relations, a man's courage had to be proved and maintained if he were to enjoy status and honour.

(iii) *Prudence and intelligence*: these two qualities help to maintain and increase a man's rank and are highly respected.

(iv) *Leadership ability* is one of the most important aspects of a man's character as regards political status.

(v) *Piety*: prestige is enhanced by knowledge of, and conformity to, religious doctrine and local customs. Blatantly transgressing many of the moral precepts hurts a man's position, but infringing one or two, e.g. the Islamic prohibition of alcohol, is acceptable and may add to a man's prestige if he is already highly regarded. These exceptions are permitted, for they tend to enhance one's virility.

A man's status, his place in society, depend on how he combines these qualities. If he totally lacks, or is incurably negative in, any one of them, he may not rise to great heights in the eyes of the other Karakis. But for example as regards birth, if a man is born of one of the plateau tribes, or even of the semi-nomadic ones, but of an insignificant, though honourable group, he still may attain considerable status and political power through exceptional ability.

Thus, although each category is strong in meaning, the society is flexible enough to allow a capable man of humble birth to rise within it.

(2) *Tribal Leader.* Moving from the general to the particular, it is now desirable to examine how a man gains a position of tribal leadership. As a result of the pyramidal-segmentary nature of the tribal and alliance system, political leaders are found at all levels: kin group, lineage (subsection), section, tribe, and minor and major alliances. On the ascending organizational scale, moreover, the leader of one of the sub-lineages of a lineage is also the leader of the lineage, and the leader of one of the lineages (subsections) is leader of the section. The same pattern continues all the way up to the *shaykh al-masha'ikh* of Al-Karak. For each of these positions, the qualifications are basically the same. However, for each higher level, progressively higher standards must be attained and maintained.

The eldest son often inherits his father's position of leadership. Only if a brother or a paternal cousin is significantly superior in ability is he able to usurp it. For the upper level of the tribe, someone from outside the immediate kin group of the individual's brothers, paternal cousins and uncles must be decidedly superior in all other qualities in order to gain the role. For the attached tribe alliance, it is almost a prerequisite for attaining leadership to be a member of the major tribe, though a member of one of the attached tribes has been known to do so. In this role, he may be regarded as shaykh of the major tribe, especially if his smaller tribe is thought, however fictitiously, to be related to the major tribe by blood. This may also result in the minor tribe becoming a section of the major one. Finally, the position of *shaykh al-masha'ikh* has been more often determined by inheritance than have other leadership roles (Diagram 9). The hereditary element in this office was emphasized in order to stem the stiff and often bitter competition for it, with the result, however, that its holders have lost some of its inherent power and authority to stronger men who usurped its functions though not its title.

To be generous and thus to fulfil one of the leadership requirements, one must have wealth. Usually, a potential shaykh inherits his initial wealth, but it has been known for individuals without any to become shaykhs thanks to other personal qualities. Afterwards, because of the opportunities arising from his position, a man may gain sufficient wealth. He can then practise his generosity in a more demonstrable and meaningful manner. The various methods for obtaining wealth include: occupying unclaimed land, buying land and making it productive, collecting rents from land, keeping part of the bride price for one's daughters,[1] accepting fees for settling disputes, and receiving semi-obligatory gifts. Other methods which died out between the wars were raiding, and collecting *khawa*, money, goods, and produce from the Ghawarna, Bararsha, and 'Iraq tribes.

DIAGRAM 9

Occupants of the Role of Shaykh al-Masha'ikh[2]

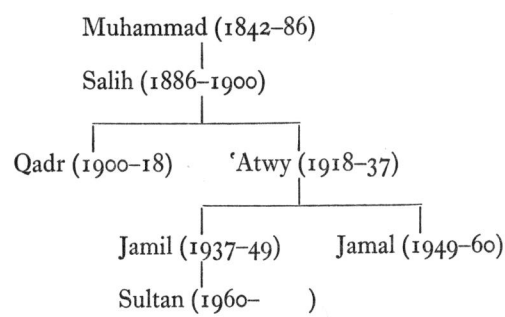

After one has acquired wealth, its distribution is one of the chief ways of obtaining and keeping the support of followers. Direct payment to retainers and overpayment for services rendered is common. The shaykh was (and still is to a lesser extent) a provider of welfare for the poor of his group. Weddings, Muslim and Christian feast days, special occasions, and the arrival of important guests provide opportunities for lavish meals and the demonstration of one's generosity. Often, for example, the shaykh of a tribe, besides inviting the important members of his tribe, welcomes any of the others who may wish to come. At special times of the year it is customary to slaughter a camel or a few sheep and distribute the meat to the poor. Thus, a fine-tuned system of spreading material benefits creates various attachments and obligations which the shaykh may turn to political advantage.

[1] The ideal is for the father of the bride to spend more on the wedding and goods given to the bride than the total sum of the bride price. However, more often than not, this is not the case unless the father is already quite wealthy.

[2] Salih was the eldest son of Muhammad, although Muhammad's brother, Khalil, probably had much more leadership ability than Salih at Muhammad's death. Salih was succeeded by his eldest son, Qadr, who died without male offspring. The position then fell to his brother, 'Atwy, who was followed by his eldest son, Jamil. When Jamil died, Sultan, his eldest son, was a minor, so Jamil's brother, Jamal, succeeded. He was killed in 1960 with Haza' Al-Majaly, and Sultan, although in his mid-twenties, became *shaykh al-masha'ikh.*

The equitable settlement of disputes can be one of the most important methods of gaining support. On the one hand, the shaykh gains very high prestige if he can maintain peace and harmony amongst his people and neighbours. On the other, both parties to a dispute feel indebted to the person who has solved it. If one or both of the groups had no connection with or obligation to him previously, the solving of a dispute creates one, and, if a connection already existed, this reinforces the tie. Further, the action heals rifts within the group, or between groups which support the shaykh, creating a more integrated body linked with him.

Although the political strength of marriage ties is usually ephemeral, they are nevertheless continually sought. A man of lower rank seeking political advancement aspires to the daughter of a political leader. Conversely, a man gives his daughter in marriage expecting in return a measure of future political support. A shaykh may marry women from three or four different tribes to create or reinforce ties, however tenuous. By themselves, these conjugal bonds have little practical political importance, but in conjunction with numerous other forms of mutual interest, they may add a modicum of strength. From another viewpoint, the men who are the most influential in marriage arrangements are almost invariably the political leaders. Those who hold these key positions can create debts as well as forge kin and conjugal group bonds which are favourable to them.

Before the mid-1920s, the personal qualities of bravery, good horsemanship, ability to lead a raid were all necessary for a traditional shaykh. If the tribal leader was not the ʿaqid, the raid leader, and was young enough to hold that position, the actual holder of it presented a constant challenge to him. He could counter this opposition by creating marriage ties and giving proof of other leadership qualities, but if he failed, he often lost his position.

The actual selection of a shaykh is an informal process and usually agreed upon by consensus. When a shaykh dies or becomes too old to perform adequately the duties of his office, the lesser shaykhs, and often any members of the relevant group who wish to attend, meet and discuss who is to succeed him. Most often the new shaykh is already agreed upon and the meeting is purely a ritual; if not, a decision is made only through discussion and a final consensus, not by voting.

Finally, a short example may give some idea of how a shaykh of a large tribe day by day exercises his authority and maintains his position. He may visit a village where a section or two of his tribe live and while there he will solve problems which cannot be dealt with by local leaders. He may render decisions on disputes ranging from stolen sheep to divorce settlements. He may, on the one hand, receive semi-obligatory gifts, and, on the other, distribute welfare to the needy. He may act as a broker for a marriage contract or perhaps influence a recalcitrant father in favour of a suitor. All these actions help to maintain his contacts, show that he is able and willing to exercise his authority (thus helping to maintain it), and, generally, reinforce his position of leadership.

(3) *Village Leader.* In the contemporary period, many of the villages have formal councils, supported and partly controlled by the central government, but, traditionally, the village leader was, and often still is, a tribal leader at a given level. If the village has more than one tribe represented, it also has a series of different leaders. However, the headman of the superior tribe usually has greater power unless he is personally much inferior to another of the leaders.

(4) *Qadi (Judge).* In Al-Karak for the last hundred years there have always been five or six judges (*munahy*) qualified to solve major disputes involving blood or honour, and numerous other judges (*mushahy*) for other disputes. The *munahy* judge, usually a major shaykh in his own right, almost invariably inherits his position after having listened to his father solving blood and honour disputes for years. Again, if he is not capable or highly respected, an uncle or a brother takes the position. The *mushahy* judges are men at all levels of the tribe who are known to be able to solve disputes equitably and who are also customarily minor shaykhs. In choosing a judge for a particular dispute, although the two parties may select anyone they wish, the choice most often devolves on one of the recognized men.

(5) *Patron.* Though the patron–client relationship has already been discussed (pp. 69–70), something must be said here about how this can reinforce a man's other leadership roles. The patron may acquire wealth which will support his position as shaykh. His influence over others and their dependence on him enhance his prestige and power. Finally, the relationship may strengthen other, e.g. tribal, bonds.

(6) *Mukhtar.* The mukhtar is a man in an ambiguous position, for he is at the potentially conflicting service of his tribe and of the central government. He is chosen by a consensus of the heads of the families whom he represents, but with the legally required approval of the government. The family heads look for a man who is honest and respected and who has the time to devote to the job. If the local leader wants the position, it is his for the asking, but often he does not, because of the time it consumes and the conflicts

of interest which are inherent in it. Because the government's wishes are known and taken into consideration when he is chosen, it is extremely rare for a man to be refused official approval. In the performance of his duties, the mukhtar may be subject to two opposing demands. On the one hand, he is of a particular tribe, section, and subsection and necessarily feels the customary loyalties, and, on the other, he is the representative of the government which, at times, may demand that he contravene these feelings.

(7) *Religious Leaders.* These have rarely exercised political leadership except occasionally in the case of Christians. Briefly, the shaykhs of the mosques, who may be either from the area or not, are appointed and paid by the government. The responsible government official consults with the leaders in the town and villages to obtain their confirmation of the appointment, but this is mostly a formality. The local leaders have the right to have a religious shaykh dismissed, but again this rarely occurs. The religious *qadi* is also government appointed, and, because of his role in inheritance and family law, he is invariably chosen from outside the district and rotated frequently to ensure his neutrality. The Christian priests are appointed by their Churches from outside the district and paid by them. At times priests have been chosen from the area under pressure from the local tribes.

(8) *Government Officials.* The senior officials of the central government are leaders in a sense, for they are the local representatives of the power of the state. The government appoints to the most important positions (governor, judges, and heads of the police and local army units) men who have minimal connections with the district, so that they will not use their power unjustly. The value of this is recognized both by the government and by the local population. Not until the contemporary period did the centrally appointed men have considerable power in the area. Formerly, the degree of central control, although increasing, was slight. Moreover, the shaykhs of the Majaly, except for a period around 1910, ingratiated themselves both with the Ottomans and Amir Abdullah and were allowed to exercise much of the power which the governor currently possesses.

Special Position of the Majaly

The Majaly are recognized by all groups as the paramount tribe of Al-Karak, and from it the *shaykh al-masha'ikh* is invariably chosen. This tribe has a few characteristics which distinguish it from the others, lending it the ability to maintain its superior position. In the first place, its members have a greater feeling of tribal cohesion than other tribesmen, and from cohesion, ability and desire to co-operate and perhaps to make sacrifices for the tribe emerge, heavily contributing to its strength. Reinforcing this strong tribal feeling is the very superior reputation enjoyed by the group, a sense of being a Majaly which nurtures and sustains itself. Also, the superior wealth of the tribe and the knowledge that it is at least partly distributed may have contributed, in the days of raid and war, to a man's willingness to risk more, knowing that his family would be well cared for. Further, because this tribe has been a successful leader for a long period, it has a great deal of land. Virtually each tribesman, in turn, has land and, unlike the other tribes, an unconscious if not conscious effort is made on the part of the leadership to see that no man is deprived of his land except by fair purchase. The Majaly are also more inmarried than their fellow Karakis. Rarely is a woman allowed to marry someone of a different tribe, though its men do occasionally take women from outside the Majaly. As has been noted above, marriage ties, although not strong in themselves, contribute to the strength of other bonds.

The Majaly have also been fortunate in producing a number of leaders renowned for their strength and wisdom. Moreover, not only has there been one top man, but many individuals capable of leading the whole tribe. Although there certainly have been times of conflict between them, in general they work out a division of labour. One, for example, would deal primarily with tribal affairs and another with external relations. With the introduction of a central government, these leaders were quick to adapt to the new circumstances, co-operating with the new power and even turning it to their advantage.

As regards the traditional alliance system, the Majaly maintain a position both within it and above it. After the 'Amr were defeated, the tribe assumed the position of the rightful ruler of Al-Karak; from it came the leaders of the district. But it was semi-sedentary, as were the other plateau tribes, and maintained close relations with the Western Alliance, especially the Ma'ayta and the Christians, to the point of being considered the alliance's leader. Without these relations, the Majaly could not have maintained the power it possessed; because of them its claim to the same position as the 'Amr was undermined. As a result, it was constantly challenged by the Eastern Alliance, especially the Tarawna. Over the Bararsha and the tribes of 'Iraq village and the Ghawr, the Majaly held much greater power than all the other plateau tribes combined, which bolstered up its claim of being the paramount tribe and gave it greater wealth. Finally, tribes outside Al-Karak, and after 1893 the central government, recognized the superiority of the Majaly within the district.

Disputes Settled through the Traditional Legal System

Disputes are settled at all levels of the society through highly developed, sophisticated, traditional mechanisms. These institutions and methods have been sufficiently recorded by a number of authors[1] and are common to most of the tribes of Transjordan and many of those of the Syrian Desert. Thus, the principal considerations in this section are limited to, first, the place and nature of traditional law and dispute-settling practices, secondly, the general way in which disputes are solved, and, thirdly, a couple of actual cases with political complications. Though the examples discussed in the following sections are often finally resolved in tribal courts, the problems are primarily political and are dealt with as such.

It is necessary to distinguish between different kinds of law which are employed in Al-Karak and the place of traditional legal customs among them. Before the Ottoman reoccupation only the customary law was present, but since that time other systems have been introduced. Basically, three bodies of law are directly relevant to the district, each with its own court system and judges.[2] First, in Jordan the applicable part of Islamic law (*shari'a*) is concerned with inheritance, marriage and divorce, child support and welfare, and personal status. The Christians have their own court systems for these matters. Secondly, the civil (*madaniyya*) code includes all commercial laws and regulations and the criminal (*jaza'iyya*) statutes cover all crimes as defined by the state. Finally, the customary law (*'urf*) covers many sections of the other two bodies of law. *'Urf* and other relevant legal systems usually function simultaneously, if they are both applicable. If *'urf* and written law conflict, the matter enters the relevant government court and the judge decides which is to be employed.

Further to elucidate this division, it is necessary to draw a distinction between *haq 'am* (public right) and *haq khass* (private or particular right). Public right involves the law of the state whereby a man is a citizen of the state. If he commits an infraction of the law, it is against the state, whether or not it affects another individual. The concept of private right allows a person to take up proceedings of a personal nature with the expectation of direct

[1] Faruq Al-Kilany, *Al-muhakim al-khassa fi al-'Urdun* (1966); 'Arif Al-'Arif, *Al-qada' bayn al-badu* (1933); 'Uda Al-Qasus, *Kitab al-qada' al-badawy* (1936); Salman. *Khamsa 'awam fi sharqy al-'Urdun* (1929).
[2] Al-Kilany (*passim*) lists a number of special courts and bodies of law in Jordan, but these are not directly relevant to this study.

compensation against someone who has harmed him as defined by customary law. Two parallel systems of law may thus both be applicable at the same time for the same offence. In practice, as is shown below, when a person is subject to two systems, the effect is not a doubling of the punishment, but two complementary punishments, each taking into consideration the other.

Self-help runs throughout the traditional dispute-settling mechanism, whether it be for the case of a stolen sheep, claim over land, injury, or death. When a man (or a group) feels that he has been wronged and wishes the wrong to be corrected by the traditional legal institutions, he must establish a claim through a counter-stealing or the threat of violence in order to force a settlement. The existence of self-help within traditional dispute-settling runs concomitant with the tenuous nature of authority in the traditional system. No *qadi* or shaykh consistently has sufficient power or authority to solve disputes unless the complainants provide themselves with strong bargaining positions. As a result of the emphasis on self-help, a member of a minority group feels inhibited from taking any action which may create a dispute because of the lack of a large effective unit to support him.

For choosing a tribal *qadi* for a particular case, there are set formal procedures, but in practice these follow a certain pattern. If the case is between members of the same tribe, a *qadi* of that tribe is most frequently chosen. If it is between two strong tribes and has caused considerable enmity, a *qadi* from a neutral tribe is customary, but if little general enmity exists, one from either tribe is usually chosen. If the two tribes are allied, then the judge is virtually always from one of the two. If the case is between an attached tribe and its superior, the *qadi* of the superior presides; if between a small attached tribe and another major tribe, the attached tribe is considered as a part of its superior and the *qadi* is so chosen.

In the case of an intentional killing, the procedure is as follows. After the act, there is a period of three and one-third days called *fawrat ad-dam* (outburst of blood) when the *khamsa* of the dead person may kill any member of the *khamsa* of the killer. By customary law, any person killed during this period in the area of Al-Karak is not regarded as payment for the original killing and no one is to be held responsible. To eliminate this threat, the *khamsa* of the individual responsible may take out an *'atwa ad-dam* which is a guarantee that no member of the *khamsa* will be killed during this period. It is usually negotiated by important intermediaries such as neutral shaykhs, the *shaykh al-masha'ikh*, the governor of the district, and the head of the local police. The *khamsa* of the killer also leaves the district and seeks protection in the north or the south, but, as mentioned above (p. 47), the kin related only through the fifth generation may pay the *ba'ir an-nawm* in order to remain in the area. After the period of *fawrat ad-dam* has passed, if the *khamsa* of the deceased kills anyone of the other *khamsa* outside the district, then the crime is considered to have been expiated and no other action should be taken. As a guarantee against such attempts an *'atwa lidifa'* is taken out by the same procedure as the *'atwa ad-dam* and renewed until the case is solved.

After a period of time varying from one week to a year, the two parties meet before the chosen *munahy* judge. If guilt is not established or admitted, he establishes it. The settlement is negotiated, but follows standard patterns. By custom the payment is divided into two parts, the *tulba* and the *gharra*. The first is 100–500 dunums of the best land belonging to the *khamsa* of the guilty party. The second is a young unmarried woman who must be given to the closest male relative of the deceased who will accept her. After she has born a child to the man, she may return to her family, but in practice, if she is well treated, she usually stays with the man as his wife. However, the *tulba* and the *gharra* have often been replaced by a payment (*diya*) in cash or kind. The practice of demanding an unmarried woman has virtually lapsed today, but is still valid and must be complied with if demanded. In cases involving Christians, the *diya* always replaces the *gharra*. The payment, which is customarily negotiated, is from 1,000 to 1,500 dinars and is divided amongst the *khamsa*, one-third from the guilty individual, with the remainder paying in proportion to their degree of kinship to him. If the *khamsa* is poor, the tribal section or the whole tribe may provide the payment. Also, it has been known for the payment to be small or even not to be demanded, but the guilty *khamsa* invariably insists on making some payment so as not to create unwanted obligations. Finally, the *qadi* is paid 100–200 dinars out of the *diya*.

In the case of an accidental killing, the procedure has some variations. The two *'atwas* are taken out, but the guilty *khamsa* does not leave the area. However, it is often stipulated that no member of the *khamsa* may come near the village of the deceased person. In the town, the members of the responsible *khamsa* tend to stay in their homes and do not appear in public. The payment, in this case called *diya Muhammadiyya*, is significantly smaller, 300–400 dinars, and is often waived altogether.

In the case of an intentional killing between a Karaki and a non-Karaki, another variation appears. Although the *'atwas* are taken out, no one leaves his home, for they are not of the same district.

However, members of the responsible *khamsa* are not allowed to visit the territory of the deceased. The payment, called *diya 'ajnabiyya*, is 300–400 dinars.

Crimes involving the violation of a woman are usually the most difficult to handle. By custom and permitted by law, the family of the woman may kill her, the man who violated her, and another member of his family. In practice, the settlement can take many forms. If the affair becomes publicly known, the honour of the family demands that the woman be killed and this almost invariably occurs. If the woman was forced, most often the man is killed as well. The killing of a second man may be replaced by a payment negotiated with the aid of a *qadi* of about 1,500 dinars. However, in an unpublicized affair where the woman is willing, the payment is about 400 dinars. In another manner, if the man and woman are not married and the affair is not publicly known, the two may be married.[1] If the woman is married, anything from a number of killings to forgetting the affair is possible. In this case, as in the above, the woman's kin are responsible for her, not her husband and his kin. This is true in all cases involving women, for they are still considered as members of their fathers' lineages.

In less serious cases, there are also set patterns and formalities. For example, if Hamad steals a sheep from Abdullah, Abdullah will in turn steal a sheep from Hamad and place it with a neutral party. He will then go to the shaykh of the tribe, section, or lineage, state what has occurred, and demand his sheep back. The shaykh, a *mushahy* judge in this case, will put pressure on Hamad and Hamad's kin group to return the sheep and to give up sheep stealing. The kin group is extremely important, for it is the only real group which can force one of its members to do what it dictates. The ultimate threat is to expel the man from his kin group, leaving him without any attachment and virtually defenceless. To take another example, Kamal, a poor man of a weak group, feels that he is being harmed or threatened by Samir, a man of considerable stature and power. He will ask another strong man, perhaps his patron, perhaps another member of his tribe or an allied tribe, to intervene for him. Kamal's protector will then inform Samir, either directly or through a *mushahy* judge, that Kamal is under his protection and that their relationship needs to be improved. Usually the affair

---

[1] The distinction between publicly and not publicly known is crucial. In the former case, the honour of the family demands a violent reaction, but in the latter, other solutions are possible and are preferred. Antoun in his study of a Jordanian village reflects this in his statement: 'When a critical societal norm is violated, the community has two ways of treating it. It can attempt to minimize the breach or hide it. But failing that, it must punish it rigorously.' R. T. Antoun 'On the Modesty of Women in Arab Muslim Villages', *Amer. Anthropologist*, 70 (Aug. 1968), p. 687.

can be settled over a meal and be forgotten, but, failing this, the protector has to demonstrate his support for Kamal in tangible ways.

The state's legal mechanism meshes with the traditional legal institutions, encouraging their use. For an intentional killing, the guilty party is sentenced to about five years in prison, but to about fifteen years if he refuses to let the case be put before a tribal *qadi* as well. For an accidental killing, the person is imprisoned for a few months, but for considerably longer, a few years, if he does not accede to traditional law. In the contemporary period the state's proof of guilt is usually accepted by the tribal *qadi*, but if a man protests his innocence traditional methods are used. Also, the government recognizes the customary counter-killings as a legal settlement. Thus, if a man kills his sister for being involved with another man, or if there is a killing during the period of *fawrat ad-dam*, no substantial action is taken.[1] The killer may sit in prison for a month or two, but after consultation with a tribal *qadi*, he is freed. In minor cases of personal injury and theft, the government often leaves matters entirely to the traditional courts.

The following short examples introduce complications and political elements in legal disputes besides showing the importance attached to guarantees and the traditional legal system.

About the turn of the century a man from a tribe of southern Palestine which had a *suhba* relationship with the Mahadin (Western Alliance, Ma'ayta Group) came to Al-Karak. Under the agreement he was to be protected by the Mahadin while in the area. This tribe also had an outstanding blood debt with the Sarayra (Eastern Alliance, Ghasasna) which gave the latter the right to kill him, which it did. To recoup its honour and to avenge the killing, the Mahadin immediately killed two members of the Sarayra. In the case that followed, the *qadi* decided that the Mahadin had to pay the *diya* for the Palestinian and the two members of the Sarayra. Because the Mahadin had not met its obligations of protection, it was responsible for the Palestinian's death, and, although its honour demanded the counter-killings, its original omission was the cause of these two deaths. It was therefore responsible for them as well.

Rafifan Pasha Al-Majaly was a noted judge, but also had a reputation for injecting politics into his decisions. One of his cases unfolds as follows. A member of the Shamayla (Western Alliance,

---

[1] In 1932 a law was passed forbidding all counter-killing. (Al-Kilany, p. 18). But in practice it is not enforced. The government officials and police do intervene as quickly as possible in order to prevent retaliation, but the government does not prosecute individuals for such offences.

Ma'ayta Group, but usually at odds with the Majaly) was killed by a member of the Karakiyya (Eastern Alliance, attached tribe to the Damur). The next day, a brother of the dead Shamayla killed a close relative of the killer, but, because this was in the *fawrat ad-dam* period and there was no '*atwa ad-dam*, it did not count as payment. The shaykhs of the Karakiyya admitted the tribe's guilt, but said that it would not abide by any decision, for it was poor and could not make any payment. The Damur eventually persuaded the shaykhs to let the case be heard by Rafifan Pasha and to abide by his decision. A month after hearing the case, Rafifan Pasha dictated the settlement. Because the dead Shamayla was an important man and because of the initial intransigence of the Karakiyya to accede to tribal justice, he decreed a *diya* of £1,250 (Ottoman gold), an extremely large sum, worth about four times the ordinary paper money. He then, however, declared that the official exchange rate was to be used, making the actual payment about 1,700 dinars.[1] The Damur collected the amount from its own members, because the Karakiyya could not pay it. The Shamayla were incensed, feeling that they had been cheated by Rafifan's trick, but finally accepted the settlement.

The case demonstrates a number of political points. The choice of Rafifan Pasha as *qadi* was acceptable to both parties because of his prestige, but also because the known friction between the Shamayla and the Majaly influenced the Damur and Karakiyya in their acceptance. The Damur's insistence upon a trial and the final decision both strongly reflect the importance attached to the traditional legal system by the society. Finally, room for manipulation and political gain is shown by the decision itself, whereby the Shamayla was both honoured and slighted.

As may be seen from the above, self-help functions throughout the system from an intentional killing to a stolen sheep. In each type of case, the judge is asked to give a decision and his authority is invoked in support of a solution which will be accepted by both sides; but he has no power to execute his decision. The offended party, however, provides itself with a bargaining force, e.g. the threat of a counter-killing by the *khamsa*, a sheep in the hands of a neutral, or a protector, in order to ensure the compliance of the offending party. Further, points of honour require the relevant group or individual to provide the necessary self-help for the offended party. The *khamsa* of a murdered person or a man asked to be a protector does not stop to consider whether the service should or should not be provided, but proceeds to act almost

---

[1] Figures given by informants which may not be the actual exchange rates at the time.

automatically. Not to react in such a way brings shame and loss of status.

The traditional legal system with its associated institutions is the strongest base for authority within the political society. One might argue that within it lies the legitimacy of the political system which, in turn, gives legitimate authority to the holders of its offices. But the ever-present need for self-help seriously weakens this claim, for it is not the authority of the system which influences men to obey decisions, but the potential force, in however formalized a manner, which the offended party brings to bear.

Land Disputes

Because of the pre-eminent role of land within the economy and the resulting significance of disputes concerning landownership, the subject merits separate treatment. The following four cases are chosen to indicate the different kinds of land disputes and how each is resolved. Also, from the viewpoint of time, they show a basic continuity in both the nature of the problem, and the way in which disputes are approached and settled.

(1) *'Adr Dispute 1890–4.*[1] Before the arrival of the Ottomans, the plateau tribes of Al-Karak gained control over land east of the village of 'Adr, taking it from bedouin jurisdiction. The Western Alliance unilaterally decided that one-third of the land was to be allotted to the Muslims of this alliance, one-third to the Christians, and one-third to the Eastern Alliance, basing the allotment on the old Ottoman tax division. The Eastern Alliance objected, saying that each major alliance should get half. To reinforce this position, the Eastern tribes occupied part of the land which was to be given to the Christian tribes and which also lay between the two alliance groups. Rather than create a virtual civil war, the Christian tribes persuaded the Eastern Alliance to put the case before a *qadi*. Part of the original difficulty lay in finding a truly neutral *qadi*, for all those in neighbouring districts and bedouin tribes had an interest in seeing the Karakis fight among themselves, but eventually the two parties agreed upon one in the Jabal Hawran.

Both sides put their arguments before the judge, the Christians contending that this division was historically sound and based on Ottoman laws. The Eastern Alliance claimed that conditions had substantially changed, in that the Christians were now an integral part of the Western Alliance, and, as a result, the land should be divided accordingly. The *qadi* decided in favour of the Christian tribes. But when the parties returned to Al-Karak and the

---

[1] 'Uda Al-Qasus discusses this dispute in some detail.

Christians demanded the implementation of the decision, Khalil Al-Majaly, the uncle of Salih Al-Majaly, *shaykh al-masha'ikh*, forbade them to take possession of the land. Khalil feared that the action would seriously divide Al-Karak when it was facing grave external challenges: the growing threat from the Bany Sakhr and the rumours of an impending Ottoman occupation. This decision greatly angered the Christian leaders, especially those of the Halasa and the Haddadin, who did not have the excellent relations with the Majaly enjoyed by the other Christian tribes and who stood to gain the most by the division. Two shaykhs from these tribes went to the Balqa', seeking another favourable ruling in the hope that it would induce Khalil Al-Majaly to reverse his position. They remained out of the district till after the arrival of the Ottomans, whereupon they returned and put the question to the new Ottoman governor, Husayn Hilmy Pasha. He ruled in favour of the Christians, basing his decision again on the old Ottoman tax division. With the force of the Ottoman government behind the partition, the Eastern Alliance accepted it.

(2) *Bany Hamida–Al-Majaly Dispute (1870s and 1921–2)*. The Bany Hamida and the Majaly had strained, violent relations from the time when the former were roundly defeated by the Karaki tribes. The Bany Hamida had been forced to move and took up residence in the north-west part of the district and the southern part of the Balqa', north of Al-Karak district. Part of the land which the tribe inhabited, south of where the village of Shahin is now situated, was also claimed by the Majaly. In the 1870s the dispute escalated to the point of large raids and pitched battles, resulting in considerable bloodshed. Eventually the Majaly with the help of the 'Akasha and Hajazin (allied Christian tribes) defeated the Bany Hamida, driving them out of the region of Shahin, and the three victorious tribes settled the newly acquired land. Then the 'Amr took advantage of the temporary weakness of the Bany Hamida and seized some land north of Shahin.

In 1921 the Majaly, hoping to take advantage of the power vacuum in the early months of Amir Abdullah's reign, attempted to seize all the remaining Bany Hamida land. The Majaly shaykhs encouraged the Bany 'Attiya, a bedouin tribe allied to Al-Karak in a *bin'amma* relationship, to encroach upon the land of the Bany Hamida in the Wady 'Ibn Hamad, which led to great friction between the two tribes. At last the Bany 'Attiya called upon the Majaly for aid and the two tribes drove the Bany Hamida out of the district entirely. However, the latter appealed to Amir Abdullah for justice, and in the following year he persuaded the Majaly to restore the land to them.

(3) *Al-Majaly–At-Tarawna (1890s and 1920s)*. The Majaly and Tarawna tribes had a long dispute[1] over the Nakhl, a stretch of rich grazing land north of the village of 'Um Hamat. This had been owned by the 'Amr, but after their defeat the Majaly claimed it as heir to all rights of the former rulers. However, after the entrance of the Ottomans, Husayn Pasha At-Tarawna persuaded the government to declare the Nakhl to be *miri* (government) land, making it open to fresh claims. Then Husayn Pasha asked for it because of its proximity to Tarawna territory, and this was granted by the Ottomans. After the Amirate was formed, the Majaly re-opened the question, physically occupying the Nakhl in order to establish a basis for their claim. The case was put to Amir Abdullah, who decided that Husayn Pasha should pay Rafifan Pasha Al-Majaly 1,500 dinars for half of it, the other half remaining with the Majaly. The decision was based on the Majaly's pre-Ottoman claim and, undoubtedly, was influenced by the tribe's good relations with the Amir.

(4) *As-Sarayra–Bany 'Attiya (1968)*. The land on the eastern edge of the district is mostly government-owned and its sparse grass is used for pasture. In one area, the Bany 'Attiya and the As-Sarayra both claimed traditional grazing rights. They came into conflict in 1968 over these claims, started shooting at each other from afar, and the army had to intervene in order to stop the violence. The case was put before a neutral *qadi* and, on the basis of evidence presented by witnesses of the Sarayra, Bany 'Attiya, and other tribes, he decided that the Sarayra had a better claim to continual use of the land than the Bany 'Attiya and awarded the grazing rights to them.

These examples demonstrate the same basic pattern for settling disputes found in the previous section: self-help and the use of a *qadi*'s authority, plus the pivotal role the central government can play. However, each case has its own peculiarities, reflecting the politics of the area. In the first, the major and minor alliances and considerations for the unity of the whole district came into play. Although initially the Western Alliance attempted to obtain the lion's share in a land division, it eventually gave up its claim in the interest of greater unity, temporarily angering one of its minor alliances. But this minor alliance was able to use the arrival of the Ottomans to revive its claim, which indicates how the local tribes can use the central government to their own ends. In the second case, the raiding between the Karakis and Bany Hamida shows that at that time the latter was not considered to be a Karaki tribe, for, as has been mentioned above, Karaki tribes never raided one

---

[1] 'Uda Al-Qasus also mentions this dispute in his memoirs.

another. Again, the establishment of a central government made a great difference. In the 1870s none was present and the Bany Hamida lost the land, but in 1921–2 the Bany Hamida was able to regain land through the intervention of Amir Abdullah. The third case demonstrates the use of the central government by the local tribes. In the first phase, Husayn Pasha stopped the Majaly with his shrewd manœuvring of the Ottomans, and, in the second, Rafifan Pasha regained half the land and a substantial payment through the intervention of Amir Abdullah. Finally, the fourth case was included primarily to show that these disputes continue at the present day in substantially the same traditional patterns.

Intertribal Affairs

(1) *Intertribal Latent and Temporary Hostility*. Between a number of tribes, a state of latent enmity exists, continuing over an extended period of time. The two opposing tribes may be in the same major alliance, but never in the same minor one, and they almost invariably do not live in the same village, but do live close enough for casual contact. The condition is characterized by frequent arguments and bitterness, often resulting in physical injury and occasionally death. A statement, joke, or challenge which would cause only comment or laughter between members of mutually friendly tribes, can, between mutually hostile ones, be the spark for renewed conflict. When violence does flare up, it is not necessarily limited to small groups, but may call into action whole tribal sections or the tribe itself. In contrast, fights between individuals of two friendly tribes can be more easily reconciled and forgotten. If such an affair results in an injury, only the immediate families are involved, and in the case of death, the *khamsa*.

Whenever violence does flare up between two parties, it is the duty of those present to attempt to separate them. Further, the tribal leaders are expected to intervene, using their prestige and authority, as quickly as possible in order to impede the escalation of the affair. When the case comes before the tribal court, not only does the *qadi* decide it according to law, but he is expected to gather together the leaders of the opposing groups and create a lasting reconciliation. He is usually successful in cases of temporary hostility, but rarely in those of latent hostility turned violent.

Since the establishment of a central government, the police or army becomes involved in these affairs whenever significant violence breaks out. If two individuals are involved one or both may spend a few days to a month in gaol before the case is brought before the state and traditional courts. If the dispute involves tens and twenties, all except important personages usually spend a night in gaol. The state distinguishes between individual and group clashes, temporary and latent ones, the latter being much more important, for they can have long-term detrimental effects on peace and security in the area. The state, through the governor or chief of police, works closely with all the local leaders to re-establish a calm atmosphere. Potentially, if an affair cannot be calmed down, eliminating the threat of violence, the king himself may intervene.

As regards physical violence, the individual is subject to conflict-ing social pressures. On the one hand, he may feel that he must defend his personal honour, but, on the other, the ideal of harmony within the society may push him in the other direction. Further, because any individual is the extension or represesentative of his kin, his actions automatically involve the whole. His kin may push him to act when he thinks inaction is the best course, and, con-versely, not to act when he thinks action is called for. Quite often a man enters into a dispute without conscious thought, but, never-theless, these pressures still work on his mind.

(2) *Intertribal Political Manœuvring*. Despite the strict pyramidal-segmentary political structure given in Chapter 2, considerable room for manœuvre remains within it. Two competing Majaly shaykhs may support opposing Christian shaykhs, as in the late 1920s when Rafifan Pasha backed 'Uda Al-Qasus and Shlash Al-Majaly promoted the interests of 'Aysa Al-Madanat. As long as the competition remains on a peaceful plane, it does not violate the structure. Rather, each is seeking more political support in order to lay claim to greater power and a better political position. This type of manœuvring exists at all levels of the system and is merely one of the methods of seeking and attaining leadership positions.

Dynamics of the East-West Split

The theme of this section is the division of the plateau tribes into two sections, but, because of its comprehensive nature, other features of the political society often come into play. The incidents related here are intended to bring out the various manifestations of the division and how leaders tried to manipulate it to the advantage of themselves and of their groups. What is at stake is leadership of the entire area, or each leader's share of it—in other words, political authority and power.

(1) *Land Disputes*. In the section on land disputes (pp. 92–5), two of the examples, 'Adr, and Al-Majaly versus At-Tarawna, were directly concerned with the East–West split.

(2) *Ottoman Period.* Under the Ottomans the Majaly maintained its supremacy in Al-Karak, but the Tarawna was able to gain some significant positions. The Ottomans recognized the paramount position of the Majaly, awarded its shaykhs the largest portion of the stipends, and often worked through them, using their authority. The Ottomans also set up some formal organs of government which included local Karakis, and, in each, the Western Alliance retained the upper hand. Two Majalys and one Christian sat on the original Administrative Council and only later was a representative of the Eastern Alliance added. In 1895 the municipal council for Al-Karak town was established and its membership was always disproportionately in favour of the Western Alliance. In 1902 a judicial court was formed with two Christians, one Majaly, and one Tarawna. Although the Western Alliance, and particularly the Majaly, dominated the formal government organs and continued to enjoy considerably more authority and power than the Eastern Alliance, Husayn Pasha At-Tarawna and his tribe were able to gain more say than they had enjoyed before the coming of the Ottomans. Husayn Pasha was so well satisfied with these gains that when, in 1910, the Karakis of both alliances planned a revolt, he had no part in it. He even informed the Ottoman governor of the impending rising, but his information was disregarded because of his known antipathy for the Majaly.

During this period the Christian leaders enjoyed a favourable relationship with the Ottomans. At the beginning of the Ottoman reoccupation, for lack of other suitable housing, the governor resided in the house of the local Greek Orthodox priest. The priest and the governor also happened to come from the same province in Anatolia and they got on very well together, which was greatly to the Christians' advantage. Moreover, the Christians were the best educated of all the Karakis, owing to the efforts of the Roman Catholic and Protestant missionaries. As in any bureaucracy, reading and writing skills were required, thus the Christians could more readily fill the posts open to Karakis. Finally, because the Christians were part of the Western Alliance and had traditionally good relations with the Majaly, the Majaly shaykhs both aided them in obtaining posts and benefited by their holding them.

The Ottomans, like the Amirate after the first world war, were not legitimate in the eyes of the Karakis. The early central governments held their positions through a balance between the use of power and the distribution of awards in exchange for minimal obedience. As was pointed out in the section on land disputes (pp. 92–5), the local tribes manipulated the central government for their own ends, incorporating the new power and forms into their

political struggles. Finally, below the superficial new layer, traditional politics carried on as usual.

(3) *The Hawshat al-Kafawy.*[1] The year 1921 was a violent one
for the Karakis. Besides the clash between the Majaly and Bany
Hamida, two other violent conflicts broke out: the *Hawshat al-
Kafawy* and the *Hawshat al-Babur*, the latter being discussed in
the next part of this section. The *Hawshat al-Kafawy* was primarily a conflict within a minor alliance, but is presented here
because the East–West split was injected into it, demonstrating
how the politics of the area overlap. It also forms a good, almost
necessary, introduction to the next example.

In the village of Al-Jadayda live the Thanaybat (Western
Alliance, Ma'ayta Group) and its attached tribes which include the
Kafawy. Although the Thanaybat is part of the Ma'ayta Group,
severely strained relations between the Ma'ayta and the Thanaybat existed in 1921. Once after the Thanaybat stole some goods
from the Ma'ayta, some Ma'ayta tribesmen immediately went to
Al-Jadayda and retrieved them, but as they were returning to their
encampment, a member of the Thanaybat killed a Ma'ayta.
Ordinarily, this is cause for retaliation by the *khamsa* of the deceased, but a couple of days previously in Al-Jadayda a dispute
over a woman had occurred between the Thanaybat and the
Kafawy. The Kafawy, a very small tribe, taking note of the strained
relations between the Thanaybat and the Ma'ayta, went as a *dakhil*
(one who seeks protection, literally, 'one who enters') on the
Ma'ayta. With this background, after the death of one of its
tribesmen, the Ma'ayta rode in force on the village of Al-Jadayda,
killed a couple of men, destroyed a few houses, and stole a number
of sheep and goats, many of which they killed indiscriminately. To
counter the overwhelming force of the Ma'ayta, the Thanaybat
sought and received the support of Husayn At-Tarawna and the
Eastern Alliance, and because of this, the majority of the Majaly
and some Christians joined the Ma'ayta.

Rafifan Pasha and Duliwan Pasha Al-Majaly on the Western
side and Husayn Pasha on the Eastern actually attempted to calm
their respective groups, but with no visible effect. The passions
of the individuals were inflamed by past relations and current
events, and by the two primary opposing groups, the Thanaybat
and the Ma'ayta. As each side was making ready for a pitched
battle, the Habashna (Western Alliance, Ma'ayta Group) rode in
force between the two, separating them. This tribe's leaders
considered that the losers would inevitably be the Western Alliance,

---

[1] Sir Alec Kirkbride confirmed and elaborated a number of points concerning
this affair.

particularly their own minor alliance, the Ma'ayta Group; also, as a member of this alliance, the tribe was expected to intervene in its internal affairs. The affair was terminated with many of the Thanaybat leaving the district for five years, for the tribe was guilty of killing a Ma'ayta and was considered to be the culprit in the affair over the woman. A long period was necessary to temper the high passions and intensive enmity between the two tribes and, even though the guilty part of the Thanaybat left, the Ma'ayta continued to harass the remaining members of the tribe for a year.

This affair demonstrates a number of features of the dynamics of Karaki politics. It could have remained the internal concern of a minor or perhaps major alliance had the Thanaybat not asked Husayn Pasha At-Tarawna and the Eastern Alliance for aid. But the making of the request indicates the potential flexibility of the system. Structurally, the dispute should have been solved internally, but the traditional customs also allow a person or a group to demand protection from anyone in the area or from neighbours outside it. Further, according to the same local custom, Husayn Pasha could quite honourably have merely provided protection, a defensive measure. But he chose a more active role, although not intending violence at least courting it. With the entrance of the Eastern Alliance on the scene, the Western one had to involve itself as well. Finally, the role of the Habashna was pivotal. It had the choice of intervening on either side, which might have been expected given the passions aroused, but it also had an obligation to enter as a peacemaker within its own alliance group. The Habashna chose the more honourable course, which also benefited it through preventing the partial destruction of its own minor alliance.

(4) *The Hawshat al-Babur*.[1] Violent though the *Hawshat al-Kafawy* was, the two major alliances were prevented from clashing. However, the passions were there and were soon channelled into a major fight in the *Hawshat al-Babur* late in 1921.

The initial confrontation took place close to Al-Karak in the neighbourhood of the village of Ath-Thaniyya between its occupants, the Su'ub (Eastern Alliance, Ghasasna) and the Mbaydin

---

[1] This affair, which is best described as local civil strife resulting from internal causes, was erroneously termed by Abidi (p. 14) a rebellion against the authority of Amir Abdullah and inaccurately described by Vatikiotis (pp. 47, 62) as a rebellion against Amir Abdullah's 'integrating authority' and an uprising against the 'Amman-appointed governor'. The governor at the time was Rafifan Pasha Al-Majaly, the paramount shaykh of Al-Karak. His appointment was an early temporary expedient on the part of Amir Abdullah's government. Not until after the *Hawshat al-Babur* did the Amirate place a neutral non-Karaki as governor of the district.

(Eastern Alliance, Ghasasna, Damur attached tribe) on the one side, and, on the other, the Habashna which had an encampment close by. As both sides were pasturing sheep and goats in the region, they began arguing over grazing rights, and eventually began exchanging rifle fire. Given the strained atmosphere of the *Hawshat al-Kafawy* and the clash between these particular tribes, another incident took place in Al-Karak town. At a flour mill, an Mbaydin and a Habashna argued over who was to be first to have his grain milled. The argument quickly developed into rock throwing and shooting, and within the day both sides brought in more armed men. The Su'ub, Damur, 'Adayla, Sarayra, Tarawna, and Qadah came to the aid of the Mbaydin and the Christian tribes rallied to the support of the Habashna, as did members of the Majaly when they saw that the shooting was not going to cease quickly. The Ma'ayta delayed a week before joining in on the side of the Habashna, for it bore a grudge against the tribe for impeding the attack on the Thanaybat in the *Hawshat al-Kafawy*. The 'A'jam (Shamayla, Mahadin, and Madadha) did not join at first because of its close association with the Ma'ayta and because of mixed allegiances. The Mahadin about fifty years previously had changed loyalties from the Eastern to the Western Alliance, particularly the Ma'ayta, because of a dispute with the Tarawna (cf. p. 57). The Shamayla and Madadha were not completely reconciled to the change, partly because of long-standing latent hostility between the Shamayla and the Majaly. However, as a few Shamayla were looking on at the fracas, one was killed by a stray bullet coming from the Eastern side. The three tribes then promptly joined the Habashna.

After considerable bloodshed in the first days, both sides settled down to a siege which was not broken until Captain Peake arrived with the Arab Legion. He marched to Qatrany on the eastern edge of the district and then, with a small body of cavalry, force-marched to Al-Karak, arriving before the Karakis expected him. This was considered important in Amman, for it was feared that the Karakis, given their bellicose mood and the only recently established Amirate, might unite and oppose the Legion. Captain Peake was, however, easily able to obtain a guarantee from Rafifan Pasha that the Karakis would not oppose his force. With the arrival of the main body of the Legion, he established order by imposing a curfew, forbidding arms to be carried in the town, and arresting those who broke the rules. He states that he imprisoned 150 men in the first three days for contravening these regulations (*History*, p. 107). Large patrols were also sent continually to the rural area to ensure that no other outbreaks of violence occurred.

Amir Abdullah appointed Ash-Sharif 'Aly bin Al-Husayn Al-Harathy to act as his personal mediator. He, in turn, set up a committee of reconciliation composed of 'Atwy Al-Majaly, the *shaykh al-masha'ikh*, Rafifan Pasha, and Husayn Pasha. These men in conjunction with the other major shaykhs resolved their differences and established peace. But there were a number of deaths to account for, and, because of the nature of the clash, it was virtually impossible to establish responsibility for each through witnesses. The judges therefore used the *bisha'a*, a hot iron which is placed on a person's tongue. It is thought that if the hot iron burns him he is lying, and if it does not he is telling the truth. Further, although *'atwas* were taken out in all cases, it was decided that no *khamsa* should leave Al-Karak, for if all those responsible did so, a large percentage of the plateau tribes would have had to go. Each man and his *khamsa* or tribe did, however, pay the *diya*. Payments were awarded to the Shamayla and Halasa on the western side and to the Su'ub, 'Adayla, Karakiyya, and Qadah on the Eastern. The Habashna, 'Adayla, and others had offsetting blood debts. In terms of killing the greatest number, the West won the fight, but it also had to pay for its victory.

Although clashes between the two sides have broken out since the *Hawshat al-Babur*, this was the last one to involve extensive violence and bloodletting. The Amirate had made effective use of the army, and the Karakis, aware that it is always potentially ready, have refrained from such excesses. Before his death, Amir Abdullah often visited Al-Karak, helping to maintain peace between the two factions. It is, however, possible that a clash—necessarily on a smaller scale, for this one lasted over a month—could occur again. This has happened in other parts of Transjordan and the king has felt it necessary to intervene personally to re-establish peace.

(5) *The Interwar Period—the Amirate.* Although politics in Al-Karak between the wars may be considered as an extension of the pattern under the Ottomans, some features perceptibly changed. Raiding ended in the mid-1920s as did tribal wars. Internally the incidence of violence somewhat lessened, but that of theft remained high. The *khawa* compulsorily collected from the tribes of the Ghawr, 'Iraq village, and the Bararsha ceased, only to be replaced by the seizure of land, especially in the Ghawr. As in the Ottoman period, skills in reading and writing became more important, and fighting ability and good horsemanship less so. Traditional political power struggles continued, but the ability to manoeuvre in Amman's politics began to become significant, particularly for the top leadership.

In the early days of the Amirate, Rafifan Pasha established excellent relations with Amir Abdullah. Their very first meeting set the tone for the future.[1] The Amir is reported to have asked Rafifan Pasha why the Majaly and Al-Karak did not substantially contribute to the Arab Revolt. Rafifan Pasha replied that the Ottomans had ruled justly, that he and Al-Karak had on the whole enjoyed good relations with them despite the 1910 revolt, and that he had pledged his loyalty to their government. But, he added, 'now that they are gone and that we have an Arab Prince, we are quite pleased at the turn of events'. He then emphasized that he, his tribe, and Al-Karak would be as loyal to Amir Abdullah and his government as they had been to the Ottomans. Apparently, Amir Abdullah greatly appreciated the frankness of this reply at a time when all he was hearing from other sedentary and semi-sedentary Transjordanians was that they had supported the Arab Revolt, either overtly or covertly, knowing all along that this was not true. The Amir also knew of the paramount position of the Majaly in Al-Karak and he was quite willing to work through local leaders who were loyal to him.

Both Amir Abdullah and Rafifan Pasha benefited from their initial rapport and their resulting co-operation. Within Al-Karak the Amir informally delegated some of his power and authority to Rafifan Pasha, instructing the local officials to work closely with him. Although the interwar period was full of small disputes and occasional refusals to pay taxes,[2] Rafifan was able to help maintain a modicum of order at minimal expense after the *Hawshat al-Babur*. The Amir also took Rafifan's eldest son, Habis, as his protégé and put him into the Arab Legion, where he advanced quickly through the ranks, eventually to become its commander. Other members of the Majaly and the Western Alliance also benefited greatly, becoming Legion officers and high officials. Nor should the Amir's decision on the Nakhl land dispute in favour of the Majaly be forgotten. In other fields, Rafifan Pasha used his prestige and contacts to influence tribal leaders outside Al-Karak on behalf of the Amir.

In contrast, relations between Husayn Pasha At-Tarawna and Amir Abdullah were strained and often bitter. It is said in Al-Karak that while the Amir was visiting the town in the early years of his reign, the two entered into a violent argument, ending with

---

[1] This account was first heard from Karaki sources, secondly from a Palestinian Roman Catholic priest who had served in Al-Karak for a few years, and thirdly from Sir Alec Kirkbride.

[2] Taxes were never fully paid during this period, because of the unequal way in which they were apportioned. Some families and tribes simply did not have the money.

Husayn Pasha knocking the Amir off his chair and drawing blood. This is an extreme example, but it shows an honest contrast with Rafifan's position. The two Karaki leaders were often at odds and their competition was reflected in opposing positions. Partly because he was very religious and partly in opposition to Amir Abdullah and Rafifan Pasha, Husayn Pasha formed close relations with the Mufti of Jerusalem, Al-Hajj 'Amin Al-Husayny, an adversary of the Amir. Husayn learned anti-Zionism from the Mufti and supported his political position, even buying rifles and dispatching them to him in the 1930s. Also, in the late 1920s and 1930s Husayn Pasha was one of the leaders of the anti-Abdullah National Convention and 'Istiqlal Party, while Majalys joined the pro-Abdullah People's Convention.

In other spheres of Amman politics, the East–West division was present. Mady and Musa, in their book on the history of Jordan (pp. 334–61), list eight interwar parties with Karaki membership, in none of which were individuals from both major factions present. The relative power of the two divisions was reflected in the membership of the consultative council:[1]

Karaki Membership of the Consultative Council

	Western Alliance	*Christian*	*Eastern Alliance*
1929	Rafifan Al-Majaly	'Uda Al-Qasus	'Attallah As-Sahaymat
1931	Rafifan Al-Majaly	Mitry Az-Zurayqat	Husayn At-Tarawna
1934	Rafifan Al-Majaly	Mitry Az-Zurayqat	..
1937	Rafifan Al-Majaly	'Ibrahim Ash-Sharayha	..
1942	Rafifan Al-Majaly[2]	Yusif Al-'Akasha	Husayn At-Tarawna

Rafifan Pasha retained his seat continuously until his death and the Christians were guaranteed a position because of their minority status. The Eastern Alliance was occasionally able to gain a seat, depending on the number of places apportioned to Al-Karak and whether Al-Karak was joined with Ma'an in an election district or not.

The division between East and West continued throughout the interwar period with the same basic forces working against each other, although through Amman politics they did take on some

[1] The law of 1928 setting up the consultative council provided for indirect elections for its membership. H. M. Davis, *Constitutions, electoral laws, treaties of states in the Near and Middle East* (1947), pp. 315–20. The electoral law and the constitution of the parliament were changed in 1947.

[2] Rafifan Al-Majaly died in 1945 and was replaced by his son, Ma'arak Al-Majaly.

new forms. With the passing of Rafifan Pasha in 1945 and Husayn Pasha in 1951 an era ended, leaving the way open to the changes of the contemporary period.

The examples and description in this section demonstrate the dynamics of the East–West division and many features of the political system. The phenomenon of self-help and the tenuous nature of traditional authority are evident, as is the pyramidal and segmentary nature of the political structure. Strict lines of division may, however, be broken out of necessity, as in the *Hawshat al-Kafawy*. Further, the integral nature of the central government within the local system is apparent, for it both manipulates and is manipulated. This is not incompatible with its possessing and using superior force as in the *Hawshat al-Babur*, but merely indicates that it is in a special position.

External Relations

Al-Karak's external relations consisted of various alliances, trading relationships, raiding, and war. Since all have been discussed above at various stages, this section is devoted to only two major features. First, raiding was perhaps the most common form of external relations, with the possible exception of trade. Second, the revolt of 1910 is the most important single event in the district's modern history and for this reason alone it should be described. Further, it does bring out political features not discussed previously.

(1) *Raiding Patterns*. The classical raiding pattern is well demonstrated by a confrontation between the Majaly and the Huwaytat. A party of men from the Huwaytat raided a Majaly encampment on the eastern edge of the district, taking horses and mules. The men of the Majaly encampment then quickly collected reinforcements from the whole of the Majaly, the Christians, and the Ma'ayta, rode to the southern part of Transjordan, and counter-raided a Huwaytat encampment, taking camels. The raiding party left these animals with a neutral, the Sarayra (Eastern Alliance, Ghasasna), and sent a messenger to the relevant Huwaytat section through a Tafila shaykh, asking for a mutual exchange of raided animals. The two parties met, with the Tafila shaykh acting as intermediary, negotiated the return of the animals to their original owners, and the affair was terminated.

Raiding and counter-raiding did not always follow this simple pattern, for example the series of raids and even battles which took place in the few years before the Ottoman reoccupation. In the late 1880s the Karaki shaykhs established a policy of taxing any person who came to the district for the purpose of trade with the exception of those linked with Al-Karak by the *bin'amma* alliance. They implemented the policy efficiently, collecting fees on all camels laden with goods entering or leaving the district. The reaction of Al-Karak's neighbours was not favourable. Markets being limited, they were tied to trading with the area, but they retaliated by raiding any unprotected individual Karaki or caravan they could, which resulted in Karaki counter-raiding. This continued at a moderate level until 1890 when, as a few members of the Eastern Alliance were returning from a trading expedition outside the district, they were set upon by a party from a Bany Sakhr section and in the fracas one of the Karaki women was violated. The Karakis quickly returned to their encampment and sent a messenger to Al-Karak town who immediately returned with a large force of horsemen drawn from all major plateau tribes. This raiding revenge band rode out to where the Bany Sakhr section was camped and took many of their sheep, goats, and camels. Some of the Karakis returned to the district with the animals, but the remaining raiders, mostly Eastern Alliance members, followed the fleeing Bany Sakhr, seeking restoration of honour and revenge for their violated woman. Eventually, the Bany Sakhr turned and made a stand, killing nine Karakis and wounding many of the rest.

The Karakis retreated to the district to heal their wounds, but a few months later they set out again. This time they successfully raided the Bany Sakhr's animals, plundered their goods, and destroyed what they could not carry. This heavy raid caused other sections of the Bany Sakhr to join with the defeated one in a large-scale attack on the Karakis. In the battle that followed, the sons of two important Majaly shaykhs lost their mounts and were forced to seek protection as *dakhils* on a section of the Bany Sakhr which had not taken part in the battle. In doing this, they were invoking the strict letter of tribal law and custom, but they were asking far too much of the Bany Sakhr section to protect them after a major battle with other sections of the same tribe. As it turned out, the brother of the Bany Sakhr *'aqid* (raid leader), hearing that they were in the camp, came and killed them. Following this affair, very heavy raiding continued between the Karakis and the Bany Sakhr. As was mentioned in Chapter 1 (p. 19), the Ruwala, a major bedouin tribe of the Syrian Desert, started raiding the Bany Sakhr and soon afterwards the Ottomans occupied Al-Karak, considerably relieving the tension.[1]

The first example and part of the second reveal striking similarities to the internal political system. The counter-raiding, the

---

[1] On taxing and raiding in the 1880s and early 1890s see Al-Q.

placing of the animals with a neutral, and the use of a neutral
shaykh as an intermediary all have their parallels in the methods of
resolving similar problems within Al-Karak itself. The second
example shows how violence is caused and builds up. First, the
Karakis disturbed the traditional balance with the introduction of
a tax on trade, causing more raiding. Then an affair of honour forced
the degree of violence much higher. Finally, but for the arrival of
the Ottomans, the incursion of the Ruwala and a possible agreement with Al-Karak could have intensified the hostility, perhaps
to the point of causing war or forcing the Bany Sakhr to abandon
the area.

(2) *The 1910 Revolt.*[1] The first time the shaykhs of Al-Karak
seriously considered revolt was about 1900 when their stipends
were diminished, but with the arrival of more Ottoman soldiers,
they dismissed the idea. In the ensuing ten years, taxes were in-
increased, resulting in grumbling discontent, but not to the point
of revolt. In 1910 the Ottoman government in Damascus apparently
decided that it was time to increase considerably its control within
the district. Samy Pasha, who had just finished quelling the revolts
in Jabal Druze and Jabal Hawran, sent a telegram to the local
governor, Tahir Bek, stating that taxes should be increased, that
breech-loading rifles should be confiscated, that the carrying of
arms in the streets of Al-Karak town should be forbidden, that
a census of the male population should be carried out in preparation for conscription, and that landownership should be registered.
He further asked the governor if he required more troops to carry
out this new policy. Tahir Bek put these demands before the
administrative council, the high officials, and important shaykhs,
asking for their comments. They all expressed their disapproval
and asked that the new measures should be rescinded. Tahir Bek
finally had to tell them that he had no actual control over the
policy, admitting his lack of authority, and sent a reply to Samy
Pasha that he would carry out the new measures, but required
additional troops.

The shaykhs of Al-Karak then asked 'Uda Al-Qasus, a well
educated, respected Christian of the Halasa, to go to Damascus
and put their case before the Waly. Their list of complaints included the lower stipends, the higher taxation which they considered oppressive, conscription and the partial disarming of the
population, and the refusal to give Qadr Al-Majaly, *shaykh al-*

---

[1] There are numerous sources on this event: F.O. 195/2343, 2370, 2371
Damascus Consul, Nov.–Dec. 1910, Jan.–June, July 1911; Forder, *In brigands'
hands* (1919), pp. 125–31; Mady and Musa, pp. 18–26; Médebielle, pp. 121–4;
Peake, *History*, pp. 93–4; Al-Q.; Vatikiotis, pp. 35–6.

masha'ikh, a seat on the administrative council. The latter two points require more explanation. Although the Karakis felt an honest grievance about each of these complaints, the prospect of conscription was the major concern and the real cause of the revolt. Rumours were rife that in Jabal Druze and Jabal Hawran the Ottomans had drafted virtually all the young men into the army, sending them to serve in faraway places. Further, they genuinely feared, and not without cause, that if they were deprived of their most effective fighting men, they would be open to attack by their bedouin neighbours, especially their traditional enemy, the Huwaytat. As regards Qadr Al-Majaly and the administrative council, the previous *shaykh al-masha'ikh*, Salih Al-Majaly, had been accorded a seat. Thus Qadr and the other Majaly shaykhs felt that the Ottomans were trying to deprive the tribe of its special role in the district.

Although 'Uda Al-Qasus was received politely in Damascus by the Waly, he was told that these measures applied equally to the whole of the Empire and must be accepted by all its subjects. On his return to Al-Karak, he informed the shaykhs of the Waly's reply and, that night, they decided upon revolt. At about the same time, more Ottoman soldiers arrived and the governor proceeded with the census. Seven separate committees for taking the actual count were formed and despatched to the countryside, each with a military escort.

The revolt started relatively favourably for the Karakis, but ended in failure with great loss of life and property. To begin with, it was quite well organized, but politics and human passions partly destroyed the initial element of surprise. Part of the plan was to disperse the Ottoman troops over the rural area, so that they could be easily eliminated and the objectives in the town could be captured without difficulty. A few detachments of soldiers were already dispersed in conjunction with the actual census. Besides this, a few of the shaykhs persuaded the governor to send out a number of patrols, arguing that these were necessary to maintain security during the census. As a result, the garrison in Al-Karak town was seriously depleted.

The tribes of the Western Alliance readily agreed to the plans for the revolt, as did the Bararsha, the tribes of 'Iraq village, and the semi-nomads of Al-Karak; but Husayn Pasha At-Tarawna opposed it. On the one hand, he enjoyed more power through the Ottoman administration than he would without it. On the other, he feared an overbearing ascendancy of the Majaly, such as had existed before the Ottoman reoccupation. As a result of Husayn's position, Qadr went in person to the Eastern Alliance region in order to persuade the local shaykhs and tribesmen to join in the revolt. This he did all too well. While he was haranguing an assembly of men from the Damur, Sarayra, and Tarawna, passions became highly inflamed. Three Ottoman soldiers on patrol were seen passing near by and some youths promptly mounted their horses, rode out and killed them. The date for the actual begining of the revolt was set for two days later, but this precipitous action forced the Karakis to rise immediately.

Arriving back in town, Qadr found Husayn trying to persuade the people not to rebel. He had also informed the governor of the exact date and strategy of the rising, but was not believed, owing to his known antipathy for Qadr and the Majaly. Even though all the planned forces were not present in the town, Qadr ordered the Karakis to begin hostilities at once. The main government building, the Municipality, the Ottoman Bank, and the mosque were quickly occupied and all records and official documents were destroyed. The troops within the town were quickly disposed of, although some, including the governor, were able to gain refuge in the citadel. Other Ottoman administrators were killed in their homes and offices, but a few who had been befriended by local Karakis were hidden by them. Specifically, Rafifan Al-Majaly protected some officials, as did 'Uda Al-Qasus, providing an effective insurance in case of failure. Outside the town Karakis, joined by some bedouin tribesmen, eliminated the patrols and the troops guarding the census committees and they attacked railway stations and tore up some rails. On the second day of the uprising, Tahir Bek sent Qadr, Husayn, and 'Uda a message asking them for terms of peace which he promised to fulfil. However, by this time, the leaders had lost control of events, for bedouin elements had entered the town and were sacking all stores owned by non-Karakis and generally running riot.

As soon as Samy Pasha heard of these events, he sent a large body of Ottoman soldiers to Qatrany whence they proceeded to march on Al-Karak town, passing close to the Halasa village of Hamud. Five Halasa shaykhs, including 'Uda Al-Qasus, rode out to meet them, discussed the situation, and offered to act as guides. After the Ottomans had effected an entrance to the town, during which they met only token resistance in the face of their overwhelming superiority, 'Uda Al-Qasus was able to persuade the leader of the force to treat the Christians favourably. He was told that the Christian families should mark their homes with crosses which they did, also telling many Muslim friends to do the same, and, although the agreement was at times violated, the Christians received better treatment than the Muslims. 'Uda had successfully played both ends; on the one hand, giving full and active support to the revolt, and on the other, reinsuring himself and many of his group by aiding Ottoman officials when violence was at its height, and providing guides for the main Ottoman force. Rafifan Pasha Al-Majaly also collected on his insurance, for despite the Ottomans' virtual persecution of the Majaly, he remained in Al-Karak representing the tribe's interests, and was able to gain the leadership of the Majaly and of Al-Karak during the remaining years of the Ottoman Empire.

A committee to establish guilt, assess fines, and retrieve stolen records and plunder was established, consisting mostly of Ottoman officials, but also including 'Uda Al-Qasus, Husayn At-Tarawna, and two minor Karaki shaykhs. It established a fine of £60,000 (Ottoman) of which Qadr Al-Majaly was to pay half, and half was to be split among the tribes. Moreover, throughout 1911, punitive expeditions were sent to all parts of the district, many Karakis were arrested, and some lesser leaders and common tribesmen were killed or executed. The Ottomans particularly harassed and even persecuted the Majaly to the point that many of them left the district. The remainder were in such distress that the committee gave them aid in the severe winter of 1911.

A few of the leaders of the revolt were able to remain at large until the Ottomans late in 1911 declared an amnesty for all except Qadr, and he was pardoned in 1912. Moreover, only a very small part of the fine was collected, for it was halved at the end of 1911 and cancelled in 1912. These decisions probably resulted from the Ottomans' preoccupation with the war against the Italians in Tripoli, North Africa. Further, the Karakis did gain time with regard to conscription which, in the end, never was introduced, because the Ottoman Empire was dissolved at the end of the first world war.

The Karakis did have grievances and fears which caused them to revolt, but did they actually expect that they could win against the Ottoman Empire? Why did they revolt? Three distinct reasons may be put forward. First, the Ottomans had only recently reoccupied the district; they had been in Al-Karak only seventeen years. Some of the leaders, therefore, saw no reason why Al-Karak could not revert to its former independence. Secondly, the leaders felt that conscription and selective arms confiscation could so seriously threaten their security that they had to do something. They tried peaceful means by petitioning the Waly of Damascus, but failed, and violence was all that remained in their eyes. The risings, although unsuccessful, in Jabal Druze and Jabal Hawran also influenced their decision. Thirdly, the character of

Qadr Al-Majaly was a decisive factor, for he had a degree of charisma which few could resist. If there were any doubters he was able to convince them by pure force of personality. It was he who persuaded the tribesmen of the Eastern Alliance to follow him, against the active opposition of their own paramount shaykh, Husayn At-Tarawna. Finally, the revolt should not be regarded as having any connection with Arab nationalism, of which there was little, if any, awareness in Al-Karak at that time. Its sole aim was to put an end to a newly established order and to taxation, the cohesive force behind it being the fear of conscription and the personality of Qadr Al-Majaly.

Conclusion

From the above sections a coherent picture of the dynamics of the traditional political system emerges. Self-help, the tenuous nature of authority, and the position of customs and institutions, buttressed by the force of honour to uphold them, run throughout the description at all levels of the society. The flexibility of the pyramidal segmentary structure is evident from the way in which groups at various levels oppose each other, depending on the kind of problem and what is at stake. The potential rigidity of this structure is mitigated by other traditional institutions, so that if a weak group feels that it is being persecuted, it may seek and expect to find protection from another.

Even with the introduction of the power of the central government, the traditional system, although slightly altered, maintained its balance and cohesion. In a practical sense, outside power was only gradually increased and was not heavily exercised in internal Karaki affairs until after the second world war. Thus, the vast majority of minor problems and political affairs and most of the major ones remained solely within the traditional system. The power of the central government was exercised mostly, in this respect, to keep violence from rising to major proportions, disturbing the whole or a significant part of the society. Only gradually did its power seep down to minor affairs, and even in the contemporary period it does not encompass all of these.

In another sense the central government provided new institutions which either worked parallel to the traditional political ones or provided new fields for competition. On the one hand, the state introduced and implemented a legal system which does not replace, but complements the traditional one. On the other, positions in the local and central governments and their concomitant power became political prizes and a measure of political success.

4

FABRIC OF THE CONTEMPORARY
POLITICAL SOCIETY

IN the introduction to Chapter 2, it was stated that many of the
features of the traditional political society are present in the contemporary one and thereafter those which are now defunct were
noted. In this chapter and the next, therefore, only the alterations
or changes in these features are considered, though reference is
continually made to them in order to elucidate various points and
to keep the description and analysis in perspective.

The organization of this chapter essentially follows the previous
pattern, but with an initial discussion of two major developments
in the current political society: communications and education.
After that, those new and changed groups which are examined are:
(1) tribes and semi-permanent alliances; (2) village councils and
agricultural co-operatives; (3) minority groups; (4) socio-economic
strata; (5) political parties; and (6) the formal government. In a
concluding section, the interconnections and interdependence, as
well as the conflicts and opposition, of the various politically
related groups are given, in an attempt to show the problems of
the integration of the whole contemporary society and how they
are met.

Communications and Education

The rapid growth of communications and education have both
directly and indirectly affected change and development in most
politically related groups and roles in Al-Karak. Although many
of these influences are recorded in the following section, many
more will become apparent throughout the remainder of this
chapter and the next.

(1) *Communications*. The striking increase in all forms of communication in the contemporary period, but especially in the last
ten years, has brought about many changes in the structure and
dynamics of the political system. First, because Karakis are being
modernized primarily by outside forces—or at least the process
was given its initial impetus from outside the district and is
certainly being sustained by external influences—the nature,
extent, and use of communications becomes highly significant.

Secondly, improved communications make for closer contact between all sections of the population and hence, in most senses, for a greater integration of the society. Again, the central government can now penetrate more deeply and more often into the area, strengthening its control and its influence over the course of change.

Conversely, local people, particularly the leadership group, can more readily bring their views to the offices of the central government. Finally (see pp. 37 f), easier, less expensive, and more plentiful forms of transport have considerably assisted economic development in that they have opened more competitive markets to the peasant and helped to bring more goods into the *suq* at lower prices.

Although rudimentary tracks for motor vehicles existed before the contemporary period, they were difficult and prohibitively expensive to negotiate. Starting in the 1950s, roads were graded and surfaced, opening up easy and relatively inexpensive routes to the average person. The major arteries of the district, leading to Al-Karak town from the Wady Al-Mujib, the Ghawr, and the village of Al-Mazar, were surfaced in 1956. The Qatrany road, which allows easy access to Amman and the port of Aqaba was delayed until 1965. The Majaly effectively stalled the surfacing of this route for ten years, because their major villages, Ar-Rabba and Al-Qasr, lay on the road to the Wady Al-Mujib and they feared the loss of revenues and influence. By 1968 the government had also built hard-surfaced secondary roads linking over half the district's villages to the trunk roads. The others are reached by poor-quality dirt tracks which are occasionally improved.

With the development of roads has come an increase in powered transport (see Tables 11 and 12).

TABLE 11

Buses Serving Al-Karak Town (per day)

Year	Amman	South district	North district	Ghawr	Total
1948	2	..	..	..	2
1954	6	..	..	..	6
1955	6	1	..	..	7
1956	6	1	1	..	8
1957	6	3	3	..	12
1961	6	3	3	2	14
1968	8	3	4	2	17

SOURCE: The author's own research.

TABLE 12

Taxis Serving Al-Karak Town[1]

Year	Amman	South district	North district	Total
1955	5	..	..	5
1958	30	..	..	30
1960	15	..	..	15
1963	25	2	3	30
1967	45	2	3	50
1968	65	6	6	77

SOURCE: as in Table 11.

The number of heavy transport vehicles serving and operating out of Al-Karak increased between 1960 and 1968 from 3 to 15, and that of private cars from about 15 to over 60.

Telegraph lines were originally established in the Ottoman period and a few telephones were installed during the Amirate. Over the last two decades the number of telephones has grown considerably, but is still restricted by shortage of equipment. Although statistics have only been published for the past ten years,

TABLE 13

Telephones in Al-Karak District

Year	Al-Karak town Private	Official	Rural area Private	Official	Total Private	Official
1957	57	28	16	6	73	34
1959	68	40	18	13	86	53
1961	101	33	28	17	129	50
1963	133	29	27	22	160	51
1965	n.a.	n.a.	n.a.	n.a.	*c.* 225	*c.* 60
1967	n.a.	n.a.	n.a.	n.a.	*c.* 265	*c.* 60

SOURCE: *Stat. Yb. 1957–67.*

these show more than a threefold increase. Postal services have also notably improved. Mail is delivered from Amman once a day, and over half of the villages have their own post offices, all of which are subsidiaries of the central office in the town of Al-Karak.

[1] In 1958 a man from Amman established a taxi company in Al-Karak, but it failed two years later. The increase in 1968 is directly attributable to the 1967 Arab-Israeli war. Many West Bank Jordanians fled to the East Bank and some of the taxi drivers brought their taxis to Al-Karak. The new competition brought down the tariff from Amman to Al-Karak by 13 per cent.

In the contemporary period, the mass media, radio, and press have become generally available and their public is increasing. Radios are now found in at least one out of two homes in the district. Official figures indicate the nature of the increase since 1957:

TABLE 14

Licensed Radios by Registration Centre (Al-Karak District)

	Al-Karak town	Ar-Rabba	Al-Mazar	Total
1957	767	..	..	767
1959	791	..	..	791
1961	1032	..	..	1,032
1963	939	92	182	1,213
1965	1684	123	248	2,055

SOURCE: *Stat. Yb. 1957–65.*

In the 1960s inexpensive transistors came on the market, making the radio available to virtually everyone. According to best estimates for 1968, more than 5,000 sets were in use among the 8,400 families in the district. In 1968 television sets were making their appearance, and by the end of the year more than fifty aerials could be counted on top of the houses. These sets can pick up stations from Amman, Damascus, and Israel, but the radios have the whole of the Arab world open to them, along with the B.B.C., Moscow, and the Voice of America. Newspapers and journals are available in one Karaki shop which derives most of its income from their distribution. About 300 copies of *Ad-Dustur*, an Amman daily, and 150 of *Al-'Anwar*, a Beirut daily, are sold per day. *An-Nahar*, another Beirut daily, and *Al-'Ahram*, the most influential Cairo daily, are also available, with daily sales of 5–10 copies each. In addition, a few professional people subscribe to European newspapers and journals. Nearly all the newspapers are sold in the town with only a few going to each of the major villages. The average newspaper is read by three or four people, making the effective readership much larger than the number of copies sold. However, potential circulation and readership is severely limited by the low literacy rate.

The use of these new and increased forms of communication varies from group to group. The lower stratum travels by bus to Al-Karak town and Amman for major shopping, visiting relatives, dealing with officials, and occasionally for taking goods to market. Peasants, individually, in groups, or through agricultural co-operatives, hire lorries to take their grain and other bulk products to all the markets in Jordan. Taxis, being more expensive, are mainly used by members of the middle and upper strata, who can now travel more frequently to their villages or the town as well as Amman, and maintain more intensive and extensive contacts in business, with the government, and with relatives and friends. Many of the educated middle stratum have also taken advantage of this greater mobility to earn university degrees in Damascus, thereby improving their level of learning and knowledge of the world outside Al-Karak and Jordan.

The distribution of telephones reveals an interesting pattern which is the result of a variety of factors. Merchants of both 'foreign' and Karaki origin possess the largest number of telephones. Many of these instruments are open to public use, often

TABLE 15

Listed Telephones by Group in Al-Karak Town
(Percentages for 1965)

	Home	Home-office (shop)	Office (shop)	Total
'Foreign' merchants	3	11	26	40
Professionals	2	1	3	6
Eastern Alliance	8	3	6	17
Western Alliance	22	8	7	37
Muslim	(16)	(2)	(1)	(19)
Christian	(6)	(6)	(6)	(18)
Total	35	23	42	100

SOURCE: local telephone directory

upon the payment of a small fee, but the high percentage also reflects both a greater tendency on the part of this group to accept modern tools and their relatively higher affluence as compared with the balance of the population. The predominance of the Western over the Eastern Alliance directly relates to the greater political power of the former. The assistant secretary of the Ministry of Communications in Amman is from the Halasa tribe (Christian, Western Alliance) and the local director of communications for the governorate of Al-Karak is a Majaly. Consequently, in practical terms, the members of the Western Alliance are given first preference in the allocation of the restricted number of telephones. Finally, the consumption of the information media follows a pattern related to stratification and education. Newspaper readership is limited to the literate segment of the population and increases with the higher level of education. Radio does not suffer from this limitation; but the lower stratum tends to listen more frequently to Quranic readings and traditional music, while the middle and upper strata prefer modern Arabic music, news, and various forms of propaganda. The latter group then finds itself in the position of a broker, explaining events and ideas to the lower stratum and the lesser-educated. Thus, communication by word of mouth still holds a primary place among information media.

(2) *Education*. Due to its earlier limitations in scope, only in recent years has education directly affected a large proportion of Al-Karak's population. Before the Ottoman reoccupation, instruction was in the hands of missionary schools and a very few religious shaykhs. In the 1890s the Ottomans established a primary school for boys, and during the Amirate government schools were slowly developed in the district, but the missionary schools continued to provide most of the formal education. Since the second world war and especially in the last ten years, the district has experienced a rapid expansion of schools, teachers, and pupils. Most villages now have a primary school or one within easy walking distance. Lower secondary schools exist in the major areas, and upper secondary schools in Al-Karak town and in the villages of Ar-Rabba and Al-Mazar. However, there is a definite favouritism in the location of schools which follows the traditional political power relations of the various tribal groups. Thus, the plateau tribes have the highest density of schools in proportion to their population; the tribes of the Bararsha alliance and 'Iraq village come next; the semi-sedentary tribes of the north and south come third; and the Ghawarna, the exploited and discriminated against people of the Ghawr, have the least. In connection with the schools, the government has set up a savings co-operative for the pupils and in the town of Al-Karak it supports a social and sports club for them. The Boy Scouts organization is also promoted through the school system.

Besides the standard government schools, a number of special educational institutions should be mentioned. In Ar-Rabba the government runs an agricultural secondary school for boys from the south of Jordan. In the 1950s the Muslim Brotherhood established a primary school, but this has lapsed into a pre-primary school for boys and girls. In 1965 the former head of the local Communist Party opened a school for students of all ages and both sexes. The original intention was to cater for both advanced and slow pupils, but in practice most of those attending the school are of the latter category. Of the missionary schools, only the Roman

Catholic primary one remains, and, following the tradition of the area, it is attended by both Christians and Muslims. Most Karakis concede that it maintains the highest educational standards in the district and, significantly, all the members of professions send their children to it. Finally, a small proportion of the population receives some education outside Al-Karak. A few families, mostly Christians, send their children to private secondary schools in Amman. Also, an increasing number of students are attending the universities in Amman, Cairo, Beirut, and Damascus. The majority attend the latter either as full-time students or by correspondence, travelling to the university once or twice a year for examinations.

TABLE 16

Persons with 4 or more years of Formal Education: Percentage of Age Group for Al-Karak District, 1961

	15 years of age and over	15–19 years of age
Males	24·0	58·5
Females	5·6	15·9

SOURCE: Lorenz and Dakhgan, pp. 317, 336.

The growth of education in the district and town may be demonstrated in more concrete terms. In the district, at a rudimentary level, the proportion of the population receiving formal instruction has more than doubled (see Table 16). In the town, education has reached many more individuals, which reflects differing attitudes towards formal instruction between rural and

TABLE 17

Percentage of Persons aged 15–19 with 4 or more years of Formal Education: Urban and Rural Classification, 1961

	Males	Females
Al-Karak district	58·5	15·9
Al-Karak town	86·4	60·9
Rural Al-Karak	54·3	8·5

SOURCE: ibid., p. 336.

urban populations as well as the availability of schools (see Table 17). Finally, Table 18 underlines the increased emphasis on post-primary education. For example, over one-quarter of those aged

15–18 were attending school in 1961, while of those aged 15 and over, less than one-quarter attended school for four years (cf. Table 16). The proportion of children continuing at the secondary level was much higher in 1968, for, since the above figures were compiled, lower secondary schools have been built in most major areas and higher secondary schools have been established in the villages of Ar-Rabba and Al-Mazar.

TABLE 18

School Attendance: Percentage of Age Group for Al-Karak District, 1961

	5–9	10–14	15–18	19–24	5–24
Males	38·7	70·2	28·7	4·5	39·7
Females	16·6	26·4	7·0	0·6	14·0

SOURCE: Lorenz and Dakhgan, p. 330.

Corresponding to the growth in education is a broad change in attitude towards its value. Before the contemporary period and even continuing into the 1950s, most of the population spurned the schools. Ten years ago there were classrooms with teachers, but very few students. But today overcrowding of the schools is common as a high proportion of the pupils clamour for an education. All strata and groups of the population see the desirability and necessity of formal instruction and attempt to send their children to school if it is economically possible. Even in the case of women, the statistics indicate a significant increase, for fewer people now feel it is shameful for them to attend school, and undoubtedly the percentage would be much higher if more girls' schools were established. At present the ratio of boys' to girls' schools is approximately 2 : 1, and the ratio of teachers for the respective schools 3 : 1.[1] Finally, although all the figures in absolute terms are relatively low in proportion to the population, they show a very great increase in education over a short period. This trend continues, with new schools being opened each year in all areas of the district.

Although the quality of the education received in Al-Karak is developing and improving, the standard is at present fairly low. First, the teachers often do not know their subjects well and pass on their own limitations to their pupils. In the district, 54 per cent

[1] Min. of Education, *Al-taqrir al-sanawi 'an al-ta'alim fi madarisiha* (1967), p. 41.

of the teachers have attended school only to the secondary level or below it; 40 per cent have a degree from the one-year teachers' college in Amman or have attended a university for a year or two; and only 6 per cent have university degrees.[1] Secondly, learning by rote, repetition, and blind faith in the word of the textbooks are the rule. Rarely are the young people encouraged to question or challenge their material or teachers. Finally, the International Bank for Reconstruction and Development's economic study of Jordan in 1955 (pp. 27–8) emphasized the need for more practical training in the schools at the primary level, and even more so at the secondary. It argued that not only would school enrolment grow considerably, especially at the higher level, but the economy would also benefit. This criticism continues to hold good; for the Arabic language, history, and English still take up much of a pupil's time, while more practical and relevant industrial and commercial training is neither required nor emphasized. Secondary schools have, however, started to offer agricultural courses. In conclusion, it should be stated that the school system is very much in a state of transition and suffers from rapid growth and development, leaving many of the current problems to be settled in the future.

The development of education, as will be seen throughout this chapter and the next, has had definite social and political consequences. The central government has used the schools to create a sense of identity in the individual as a Jordanian and an Arab, as well as for social development and economic advancement. The various political parties have propagated their opinions and ideologies through the teachers among their members. It is the schools as much as any other force which have created the educated middle stratum, a group with significantly different social and political attitudes from the remainder of the population. Looking at education from another standpoint, it is a new field for political manœuvring: MPs promise new schools in return for votes, and political patronage is often involved in obtaining new or better teaching posts and administrative positions.

Tribes and Semi-permanent Alliances

In the contemporary period, the tribe is still the most important social political group in Al-Karak, but, relatively, it has lost power to new or changed groups in the area. Although the primary loyalty of the individual is still to his extended family and tribe, today other political groups, the village, the educated middle stratum, and the Kingdom of Jordan, compete for this loyalty and are partially

[1] Ibid., p. 135.

successful. Also, political competition no longer occurs mostly within and between tribes, but is now equally concerned with influence in the central government and its benefits. Because these are all related to developments in the other segments of the society, they are discussed below as each of these groups is presented or in the conclusion. A few basic points may, however, give an idea of the present status of the tribes and alliances.

Changes in the tribal residential pattern, although slight, are not without significance. Most of the population remains in its traditional tribal localities, but many individual families are now found in other tribes' territories. Agricultural labourers move freely from one area to another without having to seek a patron-protector beforehand. Teachers are often assigned to villages occupied by other tribes than their own and occasionally to that of a former adversary. Many of the new landowners from the plateau maintain residences in the Ghawr. In the town, tribal residence is much more mixed than in the rural area (cf. map on p. 58). It is no longer considered necessary to live among members of one's own tribe; people prefer to look for decent housing and pleasant neighbours irrespective of tribe. As a result, although tribal residence lines are followed to some extent in the town primarily because of property ownership, they have lost their former political meaning. The pattern began to change when the security imposed by the state allowed people to live in or go to any section of the district or town without fear. More importantly, the 'foreign' merchants and artisans who are not members of the local tribes, and the educated middle stratum which disregards tribal ties more than any other social group constitute an increasingly large part of the population, especially in the town. Equally, the rapid growth in the town's inhabitants, from 3,000 in 1948 to approximately 9,000 in 1968, has caused a serious housing shortage, resulting in families taking up residence wherever possible.

The direction of political demands has altered, changing the political position of the tribes and alliances in society, but maintaining definite functions for them. They are for example no longer the sole participants in important disputes. If one should arise, they may be called into play and do respond. State security has, however, largely replaced their function in this respect, for when a dispute is capable of becoming large enough to call in the residual tribal forces, the police or the army usually intervenes. In the fields of employment, credit, welfare, and services the tribe has equally lost its primary role, but has become the principal group through which the Karakis approach the government. Although in most cases there is more than one means of access and influence, the intervention of a tribal group on behalf of one of its members is the most common. When an average tribesman is seeking government aid, he usually works through one of his tribal leaders. Also, a tribal group or an alliance often applies pressure as a whole on the government for the development of its area. Finally, in representative bodies, the tribes and alliances retain their paramount roles. The municipal council of Al-Karak town continues to reflect the relative power positions of the tribes and minority groups in the town and district. Also, in electoral campaigns, the candidates for seats in the national parliament join together in electoral lists, sharing their respective support from tribes and alliances.

Village Councils and Agricultural Co-operatives

During the past eighty years, most of the Karakis changed from a semi-sedentary to a sedentary people, subsequently increasing the importance of the areas of permanent residence, the villages. Although the villagers certainly retain strong tribal identity and loyalty, the village as a whole has gained substantial significance for them. The continual common residence and traditional co-operation which is somewhat an extension of the pattern in the former encampments has contributed to this. What is much more important is that, with the development of the country, new demands have emerged for basic public services such as water, sanitation, roads, education, and agricultural advice and credit. In order to realize these demands, the villagers have often felt the need to co-operate more closely, either in putting their demands through the tribal leaders to the government, or by establishing with the aid and permission of the central government new institutions such as schools, health dispensaries, village councils, and agricultural co-operatives. The latter two are the principal concern here.

In 1954 the central government set up a programme to establish councils in all Jordanian villages. The project has been slow in coming to fruition in the whole of the country, and equally so in Al-Karak district where, in 1968, there were no more than ten village councils. These bodies consist of the local mukhtars plus 5–9 members elected by the villagers. From this group, the governor appoints a president and other officers, but, in practice, he usually accepts the wishes of the council. No one receives salaries, but a paid clerk may be provided by the government to keep records. For the village the basic advantages of having a council are ensuring a measure of local control over its own development and the retention of a large part of the locally collected taxes for its own use, as well as the ability to borrow money and to seek advice and other aid from the government for its projects. Otherwise the central government collects the taxes and spends them in the rural area as it wishes without regard to their origin. A village council has the right, for example, to improve roads, to establish a water supply, to build schools, to regulate construction, to control sanitary arrangements, and to plant and protect trees. While a local council may initiate such projects and spend taxes and borrowed money on them, the governor must be kept informed about all business and he has a right of veto.

The effectiveness of a local council depends on the industriousness of its president and the condition of local political forces. If the president sought the position solely for prestige, which is frequently the case, the council usually falls into indolence. However, if a strong, active man gains the position and enjoys the at least passive support of the government, he can often carry forward productive development schemes. Most villages have their internal political divisions which may aid or harm the workings of a council. If these divisions are relatively friendly, the competition can often spur on developments, but if they are acrimonious, they may so seriously divide the village and council that nothing is accomplished. Amicable rivalry and competition between villages has also contributed considerably towards creating better roads, schools, and reafforestation. On another level, if a local leader who is firmly opposed by a district leader obtains the presidency of a council, the district leader may put such pressure on the governor and central government that the village council president is either stopped in anything he wishes to accomplish or is dismissed.

Apart from village councils, the basic programme for agricultural co-operatives was set up in 1952 by the Co-operative Institute, an agency of the central government. The local branches, which have increased steadily from 4 in 1953 to 29 in 1968, are jointly controlled by the local membership and the central institute. The members elect a governing committee which, in turn, chooses its own president, secretary, and treasurer. The Co-operative Institute gives advice, and has the right to exercise control over the branch's finances whenever it considers this to be necessary. The funds are derived from four sources: shares purchased by the members, members' savings, interest paid on loans, and the Co-operative Institute's resources. The individual co-operatives lend money to their members for various purposes, e.g. irrigation projects, curing sick animals, land clearing and improvement. Because there have been numerous cases of individuals borrowing money and then using it for bride prices and weddings, the central institute demands that money be lent only for specifically defined projects, and it carries out periodical inspections to ensure that the funds are being employed properly. The local branches may also carry out joint programmes or projects, such as co-operative buying of seeds, fertilizers, and agricultural implements, or amalgamating small, inefficient landholdings and making them productive.

Both at the local and central levels, the tribal leaders, who were also often the usurers, resisted the formation of the co-operatives, for they feared, and rightly so, a loss of political control as well as of financial benefit. As each new branch was established, they attempted, often successfully, to gain control over it. The local administration of the Co-operative Institute has, however, been able to educate the members of the local branches with regard to the desired functions and purposes of the co-operatives and they, in turn, have eventually wrested control for themselves. Similarly, these same tribal leaders continually put pressure on the central government to curtail the co-operative programme in Al-Karak, and, as a result, the local office of the Co-operative Institute is seriously understaffed. But the two Karakis who run the office are both energetic and highly dedicated and the extent of the co-operative programme's success is due to their efforts.

Despite the limited number of village councils and co-operatives and only rudimentary government aid, the villages have definitely experienced a measure of change as regards economic development and the nature of their politics. The availability of various forms of communication has contributed by opening markets and facilitating access to the government. The new schools have also given a few of the essential tools of modernity to at least a small percentage of the population. Further, it is quite often through the teachers in the villages that the peasants and local leaders hear about, and even apply for, the new institutions and government programmes. From another point of view, these changes can be divisive, creating groups opposed to each other. The new co-operatives often antagonize the traditional elements, especially the leaders who do not want their established position altered.

Minority Groups

In the contemporary period, four major changes have taken place with regard to the minority groups in Al-Karak. Most of the Armenians have left the district for better economic opportunities elsewhere. A number of Damascenes and Hebronis have emigrated from the town, owing to the new, more highly competitive group which has moved in. Since 1948 refugee Ghazawi merchants and artisans have largely taken over the *suq*, and Palestinian peasants and bedouin have established themselves in the rural area.

(1) *Ghazawis.* The Ghazawis of Al-Karak, who originate from Bi'r Saba' and the Ghaza region of south-west Palestine, came to Transjordan as refugees during and after the 1948 Arab–Israeli War. A few families originally chose Al-Karak because they had relatives in the area who offered them help. The rest came after hearing of its economic opportunities from those who were already established. As a group they are similar to the Hebronis and

TABLE 19

Ghazawis in Al-Karak Town

Year	Individuals	Families
1949	15	3
1954	75	15
1960	425	85
1968	600	133

Damascenes, but being newcomers they have little political power. Although they are the majority in the *suq*, their commercial and civic interests are represented in the municipal council by the older, more established minorities. They do, however, have their own mukhtar, indicating that the government recognizes their separate existence.

The Ghazawis have integrated into the local society better than other Palestinians in Transjordan. This is because there are few of them, and also because they come mostly from Bi'r Saba', one of the less-developed areas of Palestine, so that there is less contrast in style of living and customs between Karakis and Ghazawis than in other areas of Jordan where East Bankers and Palestinians have mixed. There were and are, however, a number of strains. First, the older generations, who can remember life in Palestine, identify with their original homes and continually talk and dream of returning. Only part of the younger generation, which has made the effort to do so, has identified with Al-Karak. Further, the Ghazawis tend to think of themselves as culturally superior, and criticize the Karakis for being less developed. Nor have the Karakis always made the Ghazawis feel welcome. In 1951 when King Abdullah was assassinated by a Palestinian, the Karakis rioted against the few Ghazawi families, forcing them to remain in their homes for six days until the police decided to restore order. Also, in the 1950s, local people openly criticized the refugees for leaving their lands and country and wondered why they came and imposed themselves on Al-Karak. Moreover, because the Karakis have traditionally considered commercial activity to be shameful, the Ghazawis are looked down upon. In the 1960s they were rarely criticized to their face, but they certainly were in their absence. This attitude eventually becomes known, making them realize that they are still not entirely welcome or accepted. They have also had problems with the central government. In the 1950s they were not allowed to attend the public schools. As a result many of their children went to the Muslim Brotherhood primary school and the few who wished to continue their education had to bribe their way into local secondary schools. Also, because they are not Karakis by origin, they are not eligible for the free grain the Karakis receive through the Jordanian government. It took a two-year struggle for them to be able to obtain a share of the allotment assigned to the Palestinians. As regards government employment, with equal qualifications they are always hired last. In conclusion, although the group has contributed considerably to the economic development in the area through making the *suq* much more competitive, it does not enjoy the same level of integration as the other commercial minority groups.

(2) *Palestinian Peasants and Bedouin.* Three groups of Palestinian peasants and bedouin refugees came to Al-Karak after 1948. The Bustanjy, a peasant group from the Hebron area, settled in the Majaly region in the village of Al-Manshiya and another group of Hebroni peasants, the 'Abu Nuwas, live in the predominantly Tarawna village of Al-Mazar. In addition, a few sections of a Negev bedouin tribe, the 'Azazma, winter in the Ghawr and move to the plateau in the summer. Each of these groups leads a separate, inward-looking life, maintaining only economic contacts with the Karakis. Originally, the peasants mostly farmed Karaki land under *murabi'* contracts, but today most of them either cultivate small plots which they have purchased or obtain honourable share-cropping arrangements with Karaki landowners. The 'Azazma tribesmen maintain themselves by raising goats and sheep and selling their produce. It is known that they keep in touch with members of their own tribe still in Israel and, as a result, they are suspected of spying. In sum, the Palestinian peasants and bedouin have no direct political significance. Their most important contribution is perhaps to serve as a constant reminder of the Palestine problem.

Socio-economic Strata

Socio-economic stratification has taken on much more political meaning in the contemporary period than previously. In Chapter 2 it was stated that, traditionally, strata certainly existed, but that they did not form coherent groups with any distinct identity. In the last two decades, concomitant with the general change in the political society, they have become increasingly important and have developed in varying degrees some common identity among their respective members. Further, the strata are more flexible and variegated, and, with certain limitations, social mobility is becoming more common. This process of change is very much in a state of flux and the directions it will take are as yet unknown, but certain beginnings may be discerned, especially as regards the educated middle stratum. It should be emphasized that this discussion only covers stratification in Al-Karak and is not intended to be necessarily representative for the whole of Jordan or even another district.

Within the town and district of Al-Karak, four basically different strata may be identified, each with its own characteristics, definition of membership, criteria for joining, and distinctive relationships with the other strata and the society as a whole.

TABLE 20

*Estimated Percentage of the Population in the
Various Strata*

Stratum	Al-Karak district	Al-Karak town
Lower	87	35
Traditional middle	5	25
Educated middle	5	30
Upper	3	10
Total	100	100

Table 20 gives a rough approximation of the relative sizes of Al-Karak's strata, based on statistics of population, occupation distribution, landholding, and education, as well as general observations. The greatest unknown is the position of women, particularly as regards the educated middle stratum. They receive far less formal education than men (see pp. 117–18). Very few are employed except as teachers and many of these are not Karakis. But at the risk of distortion, and because a man's wife and children are usually considered to follow him in upward mobility, they are counted as members of his stratum.

Considering the district as a whole, the large majority of the population falls into the lower stratum, the peasant farmers and labourers. The two middle strata are much smaller and are composed of medium-sized landholders, merchants, and artisans for the traditional one, and teachers, civil servants, and a few professional people for the educated one. The upper stratum consists of large landholders, some of whom are also traditionally oriented political leaders and tribal *qadis*. The relative difference in size of the strata in the town as compared with the district is striking. The figure for the urban lower stratum is small because few active farmers live outside the villages and, owing to the lack of industry, only a limited number of labourers can find employment in the town. That the middle strata form over half of the population underlines the urban character of Al-Karak town, which is both the business and administrative centre. Further, owners of medium-sized landholdings often find it a comfortable place to live in, and many of the district's teachers commute from it daily to the villages to which they are assigned. Finally, much of the upper stratum lives there, for the sake of social and political contact among the leaders and with the government.

(1) *Lower Stratum.* Nearly all of the population remains in the lower stratum, mostly living as peasants, working their own land or that of others. Of all the strata, membership in this one is the most ascriptive; one inherits it from one's family and for the most part unquestioningly accepts it. The stratum is noteworthy for its lack of corporateness and very little sense of common identity. The family, tribal section, tribe, and increasingly the village, are the focuses of loyalty and identity. In a different sense, when a plateau Karaki speaks of the peasantry, he means the peasants of the plateau tribes and does not include the tribes of the periphery. In his mind, the semi-sedentary tribes, the tribes of the Bararsha and 'Iraq village, and still more so the Ghawarna, are automatically in a separate and inferior category, although he calls them peasants too.

Returning to the identity or awareness of being a peasant and a member of a group, a discernible change is taking place. In former days the peasant did realize that he was poorer than the members of the other strata and was subject to the set relationships of a social inferior, but he was cognizant of his position in a passive, completely accepting manner. However, this attitude is changing to one of active, questioning awareness. This alteration in status perception may be attributed to education, which is increasingly available to all segments of the population, to the village teachers who advocate 'socialist' ideals or 'social justice' in their classrooms, and to the few government programmes, e.g. the agricultural co-operatives, which have aided the peasant. This active awareness is a newly fledged but growing phenomenon.

In the town, a new segment of the lower stratum has come into being, the urban labourer. Because of the desire for more income and the growing rural unemployment and underemployment, many peasants seek other than agricultural work, especially in the less active agricultural season. They may be seen improving roads, constructing houses and buildings in the district, and performing day-labour tasks in the town. Some, especially those without land or close relatives, have migrated permanently to the town, seeking unskilled jobs in construction, in the *suq*, or with the government. These men and their immediate families are distant from their extended families and tribal associations, and have much less identity with them than their village counterparts of the lower stratum. While the peasant associates primarily with relatives in his village and the occasional informal groups which gather around a local leader, the urban labourer does not have these associations available. Rather, he sits in the local café, sipping endless cups of tea and playing cards. Or he joins informal groups which meet outside shops in the *suq*, where he also drinks tea and exchanges local information. Also, in addition to being in the communications centre of the district where he is subject to the current thought of all Karakis and Arab politics in general, he can see greater contrasts of wealth and living style than does the rural member of the lower stratum. These influences, plus those affecting the rural peasant, make him more aware of his relative ranking in the whole society.

The contacts between the lower stratum and the others are governed by all the vertical groups and relationships of the society, with its members always occupying the inferior position: common tribesman, sharecropper, manual labourer, client, and member of an informal group gathered around a local leader. In a daily sense, the peasant, or more often the urban labourer, is reminded of his lower position through performing small expected services for the members of the middle and upper strata. Although the mass of the peasantry remains within its group, a few individuals have attempted with a measure of success to move into one of the middle strata. Sons of peasants who have gone beyond the primary level of formal instruction now count themselves as members of the educated middle stratum. Less frequently, a peasant gains upward mobility through opening a shop in his village and then moving to the town, or by industriously cultivating his land and eventually becoming a member of the traditional middle stratum.

(2) *Traditional Middle Stratum.* The individuals of the traditional middle stratum, although divided into two distinctive groups by differences of occupation and origin, share a number of similar

characteristics. Membership is delimited by one's mode of livelihood, subsequent income, and living style, which are substantially
higher than the subsistence level of the peasant. In the contemporary period, most still become members of this stratum
because of their family and their father's position, but more and
more are entering it, either peasants gaining wealth through
farming or commerce or sons of the upper stratum who have not
kept up the required standards. Movement away from this stratum
is also common. As a body, its members have a high regard for
learning and, as a result, have supported their sons and even some
of their daughters in the pursuit of education.

The two sections of this stratum, the middle-sized landowners
and those involved in commerce, hold similar political views and
attitudes, a basically conservative approach which helps them to
maintain their given position. Their common outlook does not,
however, produce a sense of common identity as an entire group or
in sections. Kinship, tribal, and informal groups crossing strata
lines are the social entities with which the members of the traditional middle stratum identify themselves.

(3) *Upper Stratum.* The upper stratum of Al-Karak, which holds
the top economic position and most of the indigenous political
power in the district, consists of major landowners and traditionally
oriented leaders. Only a few of the older generation of this group
cannot read or write, while all those fifty years old or younger have
at least a rudimentary command of the new skills required in a
changing society. Those who manage their land and do not aspire
to other positions live mostly in the villages or the town, while
others, those who wield political power, maintain houses in both.
The Karakis who occupy positions high up in the Jordanian
government, either in civil or military posts, usually live in Amman,
but the wealthiest have houses and even large country estates in
the district. Except for a few, their daily overt living style in type
of house, food, and dress varies little from that of the traditional
middle stratum. The general lack of conspicuous consumption
may partly be ascribed to the definite limitations on wealth and the
uncertainties of agriculture, with the resulting fear of overspending.
Social customs do not condone or honour a continual or flam-
boyant show of wealth. People with political and social pretensions
do, however, openly display their wealth on feast days, weddings,
and special occasions, when they provide elaborate meals and festivi-
ties for relatives and friends of all strata and give food to the poor.

Membership is much less ascriptive or limited to a person's
birth than is ordinarily thought by the local population and outside
observers. The sole heir of a member of the stratum is virtually

assured of a position in it, but, usually, heirs are numerous, so that a man is forced to supplement his given wealth or to exercise leadership qualities in order to maintain his membership. Usually the sons of these men retain a tenuous hold on the fringes of the upper stratum or move into one of the middle strata, either by accepting a moderate inheritance and not trying to improve upon it or by staying at school beyond the primary level and becoming members of the educated middle stratum.

Although tribal and traditional group loyalties remain strong in the upper stratum, increasing identity among its members as a group is observable. They associate together in many informal groups and work out methods of co-operation in order to achieve their own individual ends and to protect and buttress their mutual position in society. Traditionally, the major leaders of the various tribes kept up a measure of contact with each other, but in the contemporary period this has become more extensive and intensive, continually crossing the vertical groups of society.

The relations between the upper stratum and the others, especially the lower, are marked by increasing distance. Members of the educated middle stratum, because of its changed attitudes and outlook, a more rationalistic approach to life, are further separated from the traditional upper stratum than were their fathers. Again, the central government has replaced many of the functions of the tribes and, correspondingly, of their leaders. Although the lower and middle strata may still work through the tribal leadership to obtain welfare and services, the source of aid is no longer this group, but the central government. This stratum, then, in a sense has become an intermediary, a considerably different position from that before the contemporary period. The basis of its power is no longer solely in Al-Karak but partly depends upon the patronage of the forces in Amman, which again weakens its relations with the mass of the society.

(4) *The Educated Middle Stratum.* The educated middle stratum is both a new basic group in Al-Karak's political society and a key to the change which is taking place in the district. Because this study is only of a small town and its district, the educated middle stratum is mostly composed of less well-educated men who fill middle- and lower-level civil-service posts and teaching positions. But this group, this lower-level educated élite, is supremely important, for through it the majority of the elements of change, the government's programmes, the new political ideas, and education, are translated day by day to the bulk of society. This stratum is then the key to social communication between the élites in Amman and elsewhere and the mass of society. It is therefore necessary to

examine in detail its composition and recruitment, its degree of self-identity and corporateness, its attitudes and relationships with others.

In Al-Karak the educated middle stratum consists of those who have attained a higher level of education, six or more years of schooling, and who use modern skills in pursuit of their livelihood. Its members are mostly teachers and civil servants, with a few members of the professions: doctors, lawyers, and engineers. Reflecting the growth of formal education in the district, the stratum is made up of young men in their twenties, thirties, and a few in their forties or older. The vast majority live in the town out of preference and for the sake of their jobs. Further, because of the definite occupational limits in Al-Karak, members of this group emigrate to Amman or Zirqa' more frequently than members of the other strata.

Recruitment into this stratum is from all the other strata of Al-Karak. The sons of the upper and middle strata often attain higher levels of education and move from their father's group to the new one. Also, the members of the lower stratum have used it as a means of upward mobility. The very newness and expanding nature of this stratum is especially attractive to the members of the lower and middle strata. However, even at the low level of development which Al-Karak has reached, limitations in employment for the educated exist, but so far the government has been willing to overstaff its offices, hiring most of those who reach the higher stages of education.

The educated men have formed a very definite mutual identity and a measure of corporateness through a few formal and informal sub-groups. Although family and tribal associations certainly retain importance for these men, the bonds have weakened to varying degrees, allowing other relationships to gain a strong hold. First, it should be noted that these men have been brought up considerably differently from former generations. They have associated much more intensively over protracted periods of time with people who are not members of their family, tribe, or village. This new pattern started in the schools, especially in secondary school, for the pupils have to leave their villages and live in Al-Karak town or more recently in Ar-Rabba or Al-Mazar. Secondly, for the vast majority, their mature lives are spent in the town, where they live next to members of other tribes, work with men of all segments of the society, and buy daily in the *suq* from a merchant of non-Karaki origins. Consequently, the nature of their lives calls for association with individuals not of their traditional social groups. Further, their occupations and social desires throw them with members of their own stratum. Thus, the sustained contact, extensive social intercourse, and similar shared values and approaches to life have created among them a sense of common identity.

Corporateness is not a characteristic of the whole of the educated middle stratum, but it is a characteristic of a number of its sub-groups which derive their members solely from among the educated and express their interests. (Political parties could appropriately be included here, but because of their distinctive qualities they are treated in the following section.) For example, the government employees' co-operative, which was founded in 1957 under the auspices and with the aid of the Co-operative Institute, maintains a membership of about sixty. Through this co-operative, government employees can save money and earn higher interest than the bank rates, or they can borrow cheaply for building a house, continuing education, a wedding, or other extraordinary expenditures. Like the agricultural co-operatives, members elect a governing committee which in turn chooses its own officers. The Co-operative Institute provides funds, audits the accounts, and has the right of financial control, but has never found this necessary owing to the responsible nature of the members.

Local branches of the Red Crescent Society and the Blood Bank gather members solely from the professionals; other people in Al-Karak are not made to feel welcome. These are essentially service organizations for the benefit of the town and district, but the members also use them for social gatherings. In addition, a rising young professional man uses these organizations as stepping-stones to higher positions. The Cultural and Sports Club, locally referred to as the *nady* (club), is the most important social centre for the educated middle stratum. The principal activities are card playing, backgammon, chess, table tennis, and an occasional football match. Although by regulation anyone may join, in practice the members come only from the educated stratum; others would feel ill at ease. The members tend to divide internally into three groups, low-level government employees, teachers and middle-level employees, and professionals. However, this is not a strict division and there is considerable contact between the substrata. The members are strongly attached to the principle of 'one man, one vote', for whenever a disagreement arises or an election of officers is needed, the issue at hand is invariably decided by ballot. All accept this method unhesitatingly and no voice challenging its appropriateness or honesty is heard.

These formal organizations, together with school associations, also lead to numerous informal groups based on the educated middle stratum. Doctors meet together two to three times monthly for a meal and drinking in a pleasant valley below Al-Karak town. Groups of from four to eight young men, regardless of traditional affiliation, meet regularly to drink tea, to discuss ideas and events, and to play cards or chess. Some of these occasionally join forces in the local coffee house, but keep themselves strictly apart from other than minimal contact with the lower stratum there. Another form of these associations consists in a number of younger men gathering around an older man with higher qualifications and a measure of success in a particular pursuit: a school principal, former army officer, lawyer, doctor, religious *qadi*. Most of these older men are joined by the educated of all traditional groups, but if the individual is one of the less successful, he only attracts educated members from his own tribe.

With the waning importance of the traditional groups for the educated of Al-Karak, these new formal and informal associations fill a void. They replace to some extent the traditional identity and loyalties with new ones based on different criteria: education, occupation, and general outlook on life. There is no one organization that expresses the interests and fills the needs of the whole stratum, which makes it impossible to argue that the stratum is corporate; it is rather the numerous sub-groups which have common activities and organization. The fragmentation of the stratum expresses the different sub-interests and social and political views of its members. Negatively, if larger, more active organizations were formed, they would probably be broken up by the government, as happened with the political parties, cf. p. 136. Finally, it should be stressed that family and tribe are by no means entirely forsaken by the educated. Some still maintain their strongest social contacts with them, while others condemn the nature of these institutions in one breath, but in the next praise their own family or tribe for its individual historical qualities and greater advancement in modern skills. Thus, identity and loyalty, depending on the individual, is in the process of change and adjustment for the educated élite of Al-Karak.

The educated men suffer from a considerable degree of frustration and disillusionment arising from their relations with other groups and their own limitations. At the primary level, many feel hampered by residual family obligations in terms of finance, emotion, and obedience. More importantly, the traditional forms of political power are seen by them as unjust and immoral; only the rule of modern law and a central government founded on the principles of social justice are acceptable to them. In real terms, they are disillusioned by the continual contravention of their rationalistic rules and achievement orientation. For instance, on the local level they are often forced to work through the traditional political structure to obtain advancement in their occupations or, at times, even their first posts. Further, they see the educated élite gaining complete political control in neighbouring countries like Syria, Iraq, and Egypt, and, in turn, feel cheated that Jordan remains a kingdom with strong tribal influences. However, the very education which has created this stratum has aroused false expectations and, because of its quality, limits the advancement of its members. The rapid increase in the number of educated men and of the lower-level government positions which they occupy is not matched by correspondingly greater opportunities in higher upward mobility, for the middle and top civil-service posts based on achievement or on political appointment have not expanded proportionately. These men are also held back by the quality of their primary and secondary education, and those who go beyond this level mostly attend Damascus University,[1] which for the majority is little more than a continuation of it. But, on the whole, they overvalue their education, because they are convinced that anything attained with such strain and sacrifice must be of high quality. They do not realize its true value in the market for jobs and advancement. In sum, most of the educated élite are disenchanted with the restrictions and nature of the present social political system, but are bound by and dependent on them, as well as being handicapped by their own inadequacy.

Despite these frustrations and limitations, these men occupy a privileged position in Al-Karak and recognize it as such. For the most part, they have experienced upward mobility and thus live better economically and have higher status than their fathers. In comparison with the mass of Al-Karak, they are financially well off. Their living standard is equal or superior to that of the traditional middle stratum and is not much below that of the majority of the upper stratum. Also, because of their education and their positions with the source of ultimate power, the government, they are respected and treated with deference.

The educated middle stratum is also the most important group as regards change and social communication. It staffs the expanded bureaucracy and translates the government's daily work and development programmes into reality for the people. Its interpretation and application is the key to how the government's activities are seen by and affect the large majority of society. Its members are the teachers who impart the skills they possess to an in-

---

[1] Very much to the credit of this group, a high proportion is continually seeking to better itself. Many take outside degrees from Damascus, travelling once or twice a year to the university for their examinations, all the while holding jobs in the government bureaucracy or in the schools.

creasingly large segment of the population, skills which are necessary for a changing society. As instructors and individuals, they communicate new ideas to their pupils and others; they teach them to question the political order and suggest alternatives. Most importantly, it is the educated middle stratum which is in a position to close the gap in social communication between the élite in Amman and the majority of the people. On one level, they wish to do this, namely, to implement the programmes which lead to change and to teach the children new skills. On another level, many of them have no desire to encourage the current political system and to close the gap between the mass of the people and the political leaders in Amman or Al-Karak whom they consider to be corrupt and outdated. Rather, they express their dissatisfaction with them and certainly contribute to a widening gap in social communication.

Political Parties[1]

Branches of various Jordanian and inter-Arab political parties were formed in Al-Karak in the 1950s. By the mid-1960s, except for the Muslim Brotherhood, they had disappeared. In this section, first, the local history and nature of each party is discussed and, secondly, more general information on membership, activities, and governmental and local response is presented.

The parochial Jordanian parties were primarily conservative in outlook, supported the monarchy, and advocated little more than limited social reform, extended welfare services, and economic development. Those with noted Karaki members were the National Union Party, the Party of the Nation, the Arab Constitutional Party, and the National Socialist Party (Mady and Musa, pp. 597, 600–1). The first three were associations of traditional élites and did not attempt to gain broad membership, but the last, the party of Haza' Al-Majaly, did establish branches in the major towns of the kingdom and gathered a limited membership, especially from the traditional middle stratum. In terms of Al-Karak's politics, these parties had little significance; they do, however, indicate that Karakis were actively involved in Amman's political affairs.

The Karaki branch of the Muslim Brotherhood was founded in 1946 and quickly gathered a substantial following, about 300 in 1950 and 500 in 1954. By 1955, however, it started to lose its members to the other inter-Arab parties. Membership consisted mostly of Muslims of the traditional middle stratum, both merchants and landowners, plus a few students, civil servants, and

[1] On the political parties' programmes, following, and activities in the Kingdom of Jordan, see Abidi, pp. 191–212.

peasants. The school established by the Brotherhood has already been mentioned (p. 116). It is the only party which carries on open activities today and which still has a substantial, though much reduced, following. About fifty members meet periodically in the school under the leadership of the current Muslim *qadi.*

In reaction against the religious nature of the Muslim Brotherhood, the local lay Christian leaders formed study groups between 1946 and 1951. These were designed to further the Christian identity of their members and of all the Christians in Al-Karak. They were entirely a local response and had no connection with similar organizations in Amman or Jerusalem. They died with the establishment of the other inter-Arab parties in Al-Karak, for the Christians could equally well use the new parties as a counterpoise to the Muslim Brotherhood.

The Karaki branch of the Ba'th Party was formed secretly in 1951 by teachers who studied in Damascus and by 1954 it had gathered a membership of 400–500. It functioned openly from 1954 through 1957, after which it continued with curtailed and clandestine activities until 1963, by which time it was largely eliminated by the government. It retains a few secretly active members today with a larger number of sympathizers. Its membership was drawn almost entirely from the educated middle stratum and the pupils in the secondary schools. In terms of religion, proportionately more Christians joined it, because of their higher standard of education and their opposition to the Muslim Brotherhood.

The Communist Party followed a similar pattern of growth and decline to that of the Ba'th. It was formed in 1951, remained active until the late 1950s, and was successfully suppressed by the government in the early 1960s. The party was founded and run by men of the professional class returning from universities in Cairo, Damascus, and Beirut, where they had learned their Marxism from British, American, and French books on the subject. Its membership never exceeded 280 in the district and was composed of teachers, civil servants, and symbolic urban labourers. Although there were Muslim members, the Christians dominated the party as regards both leadership and following.

The Arab Nationalist Party and the Islamic Party of Liberation both attempted to establish branches in Al-Karak, but they gained only a handful of members because, as they started later than the others, most people who were interested in such activities were already committed.

To recruit members and sympathizers, the parties utilized the schools, propaganda, and traditional social groups. The three major parties, the Ba'th, the Communist Party, and the Muslim Brotherhood, all had members in the schools who indoctrinated their pupils. These joined or sympathized out of belief in the political arguments, respect for their teachers, conformity to the actions of fellow students, and even in the pursuit of good school marks. The parties carried on active propaganda and recruiting efforts in the town through the printed word, newspapers and broadsides, and public and secret meetings. They also took their message to the countryside, but only the Muslim Brotherhood enrolled peasant members. The others limited their efforts to explaining their ideas and trying to obtain sympathizers. Finally, traditional group ties considerably influenced party membership. An educated man joined a party, then brought in members of his extended family and they, in turn, sought out members of their tribal section or tribe, appealing to traditional loyalty more than ideology.

The parties also organized public demonstrations at the times of the negotiations for the Baghdad Pact, the 1956 Israeli–Egyptian war, the proclamation of the Eisenhower Doctrine, and the 1957 abortive coup d'état. During the demonstrations the various parties at times co-operated in attacking the government, voicing a common desire or opinion, but at others they clashed with each other. At the start of a demonstration, the pupils marched out of school and, joined by others, assembled at the bottom of the *suq*, which rapidly shut down. Then by different routes or together, the parties' adherents and people from the street, urban labourers and shopkeepers, marched to the main government building at the head of the *suq*. There, they formed up in their separate groups and shouted their slogans. Usually, they remained peaceful, but occasionally violence would break out, forcing the government to call in the police and even the army.

The central government responded to the political challenge by outlawing the parties and imprisoning their leaders and members. In all, over 200 Karakis have been in prison for varying lengths of time for their political activities. Most were only detained for a matter of weeks or months, intensively questioned, and often subjected to physical torture. Then they were released after giving an undertaking not to continue their activities. The remainder were given prison sentences of 1–13 years, the communists receiving the longer terms. After these party activists regained their freedom, they were treated relatively well. This pattern continues today and almost all of those who were involved are now working for the government as civil servants and teachers. Through this continual repression and subsequent generous treatment, the government has been able to stamp out all effective party activity in Al-Karak with the exception of the Muslim Brotherhood which it condones.

The local traditionally oriented leadership was opposed to the parties and their activities, but remained passive in its opposition. It was not sympathetic to these groups, for they advocated a readjustment or overthrow of the social order in which it enjoyed a prominent role, and they actively challenged this role by attracting many of the traditional leaders' own followers. Therefore, the traditional leaders backed the king and the government,[1] whose support they, in turn, needed. On the other hand, if they were to maintain their position with the people in Al-Karak, they could not afford to abdicate completely to the government, allowing it to arrest and hold Karaki sons. Thus, when a Karaki, especially the son of a leader or noted person, was imprisoned, they often, though reluctantly, felt forced to use their influence with the government for his release.

The following short comparison may help to illustrate the treatment of party members, and their subsequent roles in society, as well as the continuing importance of tribal relations. Two youths, each around twenty years old, were detained by the government in the late 1950s for being members of the Ba'th Party. One was the son of a shaykh of an important Karaki tribe which has relatively good relations with the Majaly. Immediately upon his arrest, his father went to one of the top Majaly leaders in Al-Karak and asked him to use his influence to have the young man released. Using his family and tribal connections in Amman, the Majaly leader was able to have the youth out of prison by the next day. In subsequent years, through family connections and his own ability, this former Ba'th Party member rose to be head of a local-government department and has become a significant middle-level leader in his own right. The other young man was a member of quite a small tribe in the district. Although his uncle was head of this group, he did not have sufficient power to obtain his nephew's speedy release. This youth received the usual treatment and was kept in prison for a month. Since his release, he has been teaching in government schools in distant, undesirable parts of the district.

Although the parties are quiescent in Al-Karak today, they had a very significant influence on the society during their period of activity. First, they politically educated a segment of the youth, the educated middle stratum, and parts of the other groups, giving them a new point of view on social and political relationships and on how to change them. Today, many of the former members

---

[1] Al-Karak provided two ministers who were directly involved in fighting the parties. Haza' Al-Majaly was many times Prime Minister and actively promoted the Baghdad Pact. Falah Al-Madadha eight times occupied the position of Minister of the Interior, the ministry most responsible for repressing the parties. Many other Karakis filled other positions high up in the central government.

remain politically aware and are often sympathetic to the views of the party with which they were associated. Secondly the parties helped to undermine the authority and power of the traditional local leadership. Their ideologies and programmes were opposed to the established order, but, besides this, new leaders with a non-traditional base gained the active loyalty of many Karakis, particularly the young and the educated middle stratum. This, plus the expansion of the government, tended to lessen the hold of the traditional leaders over the rest of society as well as over party supporters. Thirdly, the political parties helped to bring Al-Karak much further into the mainstream of modern Arab political thought and activities.

Formal Government

The purpose of this section is to bring the basic outline of the local and central governments, which was given in Chapter 2 (pp. 71–3), up to date, by showing developments in the contemporary period.

(1) *Municipal Government in Al-Karak Town.* The legal rights, limitations, and sources of finance of the municipality of Al-Karak town remain the same as in the traditional period. But in the past two decades, the town's population has grown rapidly and, correspondingly, the municipality has increased its expenditure (see Table 21).

TABLE 21

Revenue and Expenditure for the Municipality of Al-Karak

(JD)

Year	Revenue	Expenditure
1952	16,579	16,579
1954	n.a.	
1955/6	27,744	18,217
1957/8	n.a.	
1959/60	21,900	33,900
1061/2	40,500	36,300
1963/4	42,175	64,009
1965/6	38,600	51,900

SOURCE: *Stat. Yb. 1952–66.* The financial year was changed in 1955.

Besides this quantitative increase in services, the quality of roads, water and electricity supply, and town planning has also been improved. Because of internal conflicts and ineptitude in the municipal council, significant changes in its membership were required before these improvements could be implemented. Although the various tribes' and commercial groups' relative power positions in the town and district continue to be reflected in the council, members with a civic rather than a traditional outlook now sit on it and at times control it. The political developments which allowed this new situation to arise are described at some length in Chapter 5 (pp. 162–6).

(2) *Central Government.* The major institutions of the central government, the governor, police, army, and law courts, remain as described in Chapter 2, but their roles in the local political system have expanded and become more effective. In addition, numerous government departments have set up branches in the district, all with their offices in the town. These have multiplied the central government's influence on the life of the people by providing more services, welfare, and regulations, and also by being the chief employers in the district. As in the traditional period, the central government continues to form an integral group within the political structure of Al-Karak.

Central Government Offices in Al-Karak

Dept. of Interior*
  Office of Governor*
  Police Headquarters*
  Office for Identity Papers
  Intelligence Bureau
District Army Headquarters*
Dept. of Justice*
  Tribal Court*
  Civil Court*
  Criminal Court*
  Shari'a Court*
  Public Prosecutor*
Dept. of Public Health*
  Gen. Hospital*
  Office for Eradication of Malaria
Dept. of Communications*
  Office of Post Office & Telegraph
Dept. of Education*
Dept. of Agriculture
  Office of Veterinary Services
  Office of Reafforestation
  Office for Agric. Credit Inst.
Dept. of Public Works

Dept. of Social Affairs
  Co-operative Inst.
    (Agric. Co-operatives)
    (Student Co-operatives)
    (Government Employees' Co-operative)
  Centre for Mothers and Children
  Save the Children Fund
  Students' Social & Athletic Club
  UNRWA
  School for Adult Education
  Office for Food Supply & Price Control
Office of *'Awqaf* Inst.
Office of Land Registration
Office of Gen. Accountant
Office for Antiquities

* Departments and offices present in the traditional period.

The above list shows that in the traditional period central-government offices were confined to the basic infrastructure of the state (governor, police courts, communications), and only a few services (health and education). In the last two decades, the old offices have expanded in scope and effectiveness, but many new services have been added: agricultural aid, advice, and credit; better roads for transport; co-operatives for farmers, students, and government employees; aid for the young and mothers; welfare for the poor; social centres for students; and mechanisms for food supply and price control. Because the central government is in a developing, transitional stage, many of these offices and services only minimally reach their designed functions, but each year they improve upon their previous record.

The general problems of administering and staffing the various departments in Al-Karak are similar to those of other countries. First, it should be noted that corruption and bribery at the lower levels are not known. Most Karakis maintain that these features are common at the high levels in Amman, but do not mention them in connection with Al-Karak. On the other hand, many offices are hampered by endless, mostly useless, paperwork, much of which is never seen by a second party. Further, the complexity of obtaining a given service is usually staggering and time-consuming for the average Karaki. He is required to visit many offices, to obtain numerous signatures, and to affix stamps for each. These procedures are understood by few and actually deter many from dealing with the government.

There is definite discrimination between individuals of the different strata. As a rule, when a man from the upper or middle strata comes into an office requesting a service, it is performed readily or even expedited. The necessity of going from office to office is usually alleviated for the civil servant by means of a few telephone calls or by sending his messenger to do the busy work. However, when an average lower-stratum Karaki enters, he is often made to wait endlessly until a particular bureaucrat literally feels like doing his job. Aided by the complicated procedures stipulated by the various bureaux, the man may have to spend a day or two in pursuit of the service or perhaps be entirely frustrated.

When a government office is supposed to go to the people with a programme or a development scheme, its success is heavily dependent on the head of the office and the middle-level personnel. For example, it is commonplace for agricultural experts to go to a village, to be fêted highly, and to leave without giving any service or advice. The peasants do not know what is expected, and feel honoured to be visited by men whom they consider to be their

superiors. The officials enjoy the special treatment and many feel
no compulsion to give the stipulated service. In addition, the
departments have great difficulty in finding personnel who are
willing to live in the villages or at least continually work in them.
The educated civil servants do not want to dirty their hands or to
associate with peasants on a daily basis. Nor does the mass of the
population know what its rights are. Because of the still existing
limitation of education and communications, the average Karaki is
unaware that he can ask for and receive aid, advice, and service
from the government. This is complemented by the negative idea
that the government is solely a police force and a tax collector,
both of which the peasant has always tried to avoid. To conclude
on a positive note, many exceptions to these generalizations exist.
Some civil servants are quite efficient and actively attempt to carry
out their duties regardless of the applicant's status. A few officials
do work continually in contact with the lower stratum, e.g. the
co-operative officials mentioned above. And the peasants, often
through the medium of the local teachers, are gradually learning
their rights and opportunities.

Except in some offices, the appointment of senior officials in
the local departments is heavily influenced by local politics.
Traditionally, the positions of governor and police chief are always
filled by men from outside the district in order to ensure their
neutrality. The remainder, unless technical qualifications are
mandatory, obtain their appointments through their families, and
through their relations with traditional Karaki leaders and the
politicians in Amman. Although minimal literacy and ability are
certainly required, being a politically active son, brother, or cousin
of a tribal shaykh or member of parliament is considerably more
advantageous. This pattern may be seen in the following list of the
members of the administrative council who are also heads of
government offices (see opposite page). The list mirrors the power
balance of the tribes in Al-Karak and, equally, their political influence in Amman. Of the eight Karaki-held positions, all are
from the Western Alliance and four are from the leading Majaly
tribe. Looking at the office-holders from another viewpoint, the
politically influenced nature of the appointment does have a salu-
tary effect on a man's performance in the post. Because he is partly
dependent on local political forces for his job, he must carry out
his duties relatively competently and to the satisfaction of the
Karakis. If he does not please the leaders, or he fails to satisfy
large numbers of the common people who in turn can pressure
the leaders, those who backed his appointment may have him
dismissed.

Administrative Council in Al-Karak (1968)

Office	Origin of office-holder	Requirements for appointment
Governor	Non-Karaki	Neutrality
Police	Non-Karaki	Neutrality
Land-registration	Non-Karaki	Neutrality
Public-works	Non-Karaki	Technical
Malaria eradication	Non-Karaki	Technical
Veterinary services	Non-Karaki	Technical
Accountancy	Non-Karaki	Technical
Health	Karaki-Christian	Technical
Antiquities	Karaki-Christian	Technical & political
Food supply and price control	Karaki-Majaly	Political
Education	Karaki-Majaly	Political
Post office & telegraph	Karaki-Majaly	Political
Agricultural credits	Karaki-Majaly	Political
Social affairs	Karaki-Habashna	Political
Reafforestation	Karaki-Ma'ayta	Political
Agriculture	Tafila	Political

The educated middle stratum dominates the lower levels of the civil service. As this stratum and its relations with the government and the people have been discussed at length, only the employment pattern and methods of advancement are mentioned here. Initially, it should be noted that most of the government offices are highly overstaffed. It is not uncommon to observe two to four men doing a job that one could easily perform. This results from pressures on the government from the increasing numbers of young men with secondary education who are seeking employment. Continuing in their fathers' occupations, usually farming, is not attractive to them, and often not available because of the growing population and resulting rural underemployment. Also, the private economy of Al-Karak and Jordan is not advancing sufficiently fast to employ many educated men. As a result, they fall back on public jobs in the civil service or the schools. The government finds it desirable to take many of them on, for it does not wish large numbers of active young men to be unemployed, unhappy, and therefore dangerous to the political system. Equally, nepotism and political patronage play a role in overstaffing. Once a man gains a higher office, he usually wishes to bring in members of his extended family and tribe and to give employment to others to pay off political debts. Examining lower-level government employment in individual terms, favoured postings and advancement may also be politically influenced. A young man of an important family, but with minimal educational requirements, can obtain a position in a desired location if he wishes, while an equally well or better educated man risks being sent to a distant village. Further, if one has been involved in the political parties, a government job is usually available if one's qualifications are sufficiently strong, but the posting is invariably in unfavourable, distant locations. Though with seniority and ability much of this inconvenience may be overcome, one cannot in practice hope to reach the higher levels of the bureaucracy.

In the contemporary period, the former administrative council has been divided into two: the new administrative council, consisting solely of department heads, which was mentioned above (p. 143), and the advisory council whose members are drawn from the leadership of all the major socio-political groups of Al-Karak with the exception of the tribes of the periphery.

Advisory Council in Al-Karak (1968)

Member	Alliance	Major occupation
Governor	..	..
Duliwan Al-Majaly	Western	Al-Karak town municipal council president, *Qadi*
Kraym Al-Majaly	Western	Ar-Rabba municipal council president, landowner
Yusif Al-Habashna	Western	Landowner in the Ghawr
Faris Al-Ma'ayta	Western	*Qadi*, landowner
Dr Mahmud Al-'Alawy	Western	Doctor, civically active
Za'al Al-Burqan (Al-Halasa)	Western-Christian	Commerce, construction
Sulayman Al-'Akasha	Western-Christian	Civically active
'Abdal-Wahhab At-Tarawna	Eastern	Member of parliament, *Qadi*
'Abdal-Karim At-Tarawna	Eastern	Al-Mazar municipal council president, landowner
Hajj Yahya As-Sarayra	Eastern	*Qadi*
Muhammad Zayn 'Abu Al-Faylat	Hebron Origin	Commerce, construction, civically active
Three members from Tafila		

Although it reflects power relations in the district, it is more balanced in its representation than the administrative council, because it is appointed by the governor. The council is designed to advise the governor on the needs of the governorate of Al-Karak and to provide a forum for the local leaders to hear the intentions of the government.

In conclusion, the changes which have been wrought in the formal government in the past twenty years are profound. From the rudimentary structure of providing minimal order, law courts, and a few services the government has expanded into a much larger institution. Further, it has become Al-Karak's largest employer, significantly of the educated middle stratum. As in the traditional period, its structure and functions are intertwined with the local society, yet it retains a special position, for it is ultimately controlled from Amman.

Changes in the Structure of the Whole Political Society

The structure of the whole political society in Al-Karak has altered with the changes in its structural groups and the addition of new ones. Some new socio-political relationships have been formed, while older ones have either adjusted to new conditions or remained essentially the same. The major themes of this section then are the weakening of some groups and the strengthening of others, and the effects of these changes on political integration. In addition, the government is increasingly central to all local political considerations, for it directly and indirectly affects all groups, and all groups are involved in some sense with each other through its institutions. However, it must be noted that the tribes of the periphery are, on the whole, not included in these developments, for they are only beginning to experience the influences the plateau Karakis felt two decades ago.

The most important socio-political group system in the traditional period was the pyramidal-segmentary structure of the sub-lineages through the tribal alliances. Today, this paramount position is still held by the tribal groups, but not to the same extent, for other politically related groups, especially the strata and the government, have undermined their influence and usurped their functions. First, the old strata with their increasing self-identities and the new educated middle stratum with its self-identity and partial corporateness have eroded these same qualities among the tribal groups. For example, the peasant associates with his fellow members of the lower stratum in his village, co-operative, and school, and, in turn, he is beginning to see himself as more like other peasants than his fellow tribesmen of other strata. Much more advanced in this process, the educated middle stratum is attempting to disassociate itself from tribal identity and influence. However, the whole population, with the exception of the educated men, still extends its primary loyalty to the pyramidal-segmentary tribal system. Secondly, not only has the central government been a major force behind this change through its activities in the area, fostering the growth of the strata and helping to strengthen them, it has also taken over many of the tribal groups' functions and added to them. However, the residual position of the tribe remains, for although demands are made to the government, they are often channelled through traditional tribal connections. The tribe has lost in one sphere, but has been able to gain in another, maintaining for itself a major role in the political society by adapting to the new situation. But the very fact that it is the government and not the tribe which is the source of benefits fundamentally changes the nature both of the groupings and of a man's loyalty and identity with them.

Approaching the tribal system from another standpoint, the establishment of an ordered, more developed Kingdom of Jordan has created new forms of political competition and a greater integration of Al-Karak as a whole. Thanks to the government's ability to stem successfully any potential trouble before it escalates, there has been no major civil disturbance since the *Hawshat al-Babur* of 1921. Also, in former days, the district of Al-Karak was the largest meaningful political entity that the Karakis knew and in terms of which they competed. But over the past seventy-five years, and especially in the last two decades, there has been a growing identity with Jordan as the larger political entity and Al-Karak as the sub-group. As a result, the tribal leaders and members tend to co-operate more frequently and readily to promote the general interests of the district in the Kingdom of Jordan. In addition, the form of political competition has changed from one of sometimes violent struggle amongst themselves and occasional raids on non-Karaki tribes, to largely peaceful competition for local leadership, influence in the central government, and the material benefits of both.

Of the socio-economic strata, the educated middle stratum has contributed the most to creating a new division in Al-Karak's society, but it is also tied to that society and is a key to a changed form of integration. Each of the strata, to a greater or less extent, cuts across the traditional vertical groups, the tribal system and patron-client relationships, and forms its own separate divisions, but with the exception of the educated middle stratum, they have little self-identity and no corporateness. The educated men, however, do form a distinguishable corporate group which differs from the rest of society by its education, its occupations, and its changed, more rational, non-traditional view of political and social relationships. It is a product of the change which has taken place in Al-Karak, but it also contributes significantly to bridging the gap between itself and the rest of society. Further, its members are the sons of the other strata, and through their extended families have intimate contact with and influence on them. On the other hand, a large proportion of its active members oppose the altered traditional political system in Al-Karak and Amman. This was dramatically demonstrated by the activity of the political parties in the area in the 1950s and early 1960s, and is still apparent today in their thinking. However, by a judicious balance of force and generous treatment, the government and the local leaders have persuaded the educated men at least to give up active opposition to the established order and to aid in the running of the government bureaucracy, and, at most, to participate in politics on the terms of the established system, thus undermining the divisive force of the educated middle stratum.

The central government, through its greatly expanded activity and institutions in Al-Karak, provides a new theatre and aim for political competition. It brings most groups together through its integral relations with society, and by people solving disputes within its structure and competing peacefully for its offices and benefits. In another sense, it directly and indirectly provides numerous institutions in which the various social political groups meet, conduct business with each other, and make decisions. The most notable of these are the councils and committees which are either government bodies or officially sponsored and promoted. The councils and committees listed on p. 148 do not only provide means for the leaders of the various groups to meet and deal with each other; most are also designed to serve the community, and to express its opinions, all of which contributes to social integration.

As a final note, it should be stated that this chapter is primarily concerned with the people of the plateau and not those of the periphery: the semi-sedentary tribesmen of the north and south, the men of 'Iraq village and the Bararsha alliance, and, particularly, the dark-skinned Ghawarna. Relations between the latter and the plateau tribes and groups have scarcely altered since the traditional period, and they have experienced very little internal change. Except for a rare individual, they have no members in the educated middle stratum, they have no seats on any of the councils, and very few are employed by the government other than as enlisted soldiers. As a body, although they are progressing minimally, they have been left out of most of the new developments in Al-Karak.

Councils and Committees in Al-Karak, 1968

Name	Membership[1]
Municipal council, Al-Karak town	Tribes, commercial groups, increasing numbers of civically active men
Municipal councils, 'Ay, Ar-Rabba, & Al-Mazar	Tribes & tribal sections of villages
Village councils	Tribes & tribal sections of villages
Ctees of agricultural co-operatives	Tribes & tribal sections of villages, increasingly of lower stratum
Advisory council	Tribes, tribal alliances, commercial groups, & educated middle stratum
Administrative council	Gov. dept. heads: non-Karakis & Karakis
Ctee of Agricultural Credit Inst.	Tribal & commercial groups, & educated middle stratum
Ctee of Govt. Employees' Co-operative	Educated middle stratum
Chamber of Commerce	Merchants, artisans, contractors of traditional middle stratum predominantly 'foreign' origin, but also Karaki tribes
Ctee for Red Crescent Society	Professionals of educated middle stratum
Ctee for Blood Bank	Professionals of educated middle stratum
Ctee for Boy Scouts Club	Upper, traditional, & educated middle strata

[1] Recorded solely by group, although the individual members are usually the leaders of these groups.

5

DYNAMICS OF THE CONTEMPORARY
POLITICAL SOCIETY

THE purpose of this chapter is to investigate the dynamics of the
contemporary political system in four stages which complement
the discussion of the traditional dynamics in Chapter 3. First, the
concepts of legitimacy, authority, and power are considered in
relation to Al-Karak's new and changed social groups and to the
political setting as a whole. Secondly, it is necessary to look at the
criteria for acquiring and maintaining leadership roles which have
altered with the developments in the area's political structure. In
this section, special consideration is given to the various adjust-
ments in status and its meaning, traditionally oriented leaders, the
continuing prominent role of the Majaly, and the leadership of
the educated middle stratum. Thirdly, continuity and change
in methods of settling disputes is noted, with emphasis on the
increased involvement of the central government. Fourthly, in
order to demonstrate the contemporary political dynamics in
concrete terms, a number of selected examples are given which
reflect the development of the last two decades as well as residual
traditional influences.

Legitimacy, Authority, and Power in the Contemporary Period

It was argued in Chapter 3 that traditional politics in Al-Karak
was a balance between self-help and the exercise of authoritative
decisions, complied with out of expediency or traditional inertia
rather than legitimacy. In the contemporary period, this argument
continues to hold good for much of the population, but more must
be added. Legitimacy, authority, and power in the last two decades
are best examined from two points of view: the efforts of the
Kingdom of Jordan to establish a sense of the legitimate authority
of the king, state, and government, and the corresponding receptivity of the socio-economic strata to these efforts. Receptivity is
discussed only in terms of the various strata because there is no
clear breakdown into different attitudes among the other social
groups. Furthermore, this approach brings out the problem of
change as it relates to the questions of legitimacy, authority, and
power.

The central government works for, and has created the beginnings of, a sense of the legitimacy of the political system and the monarchy, but its approach is inconsistent, and at times apparently self-defeating. Its purpose is to promote loyalty to the king, the institution of the monarchy, and the laws and basic constitution of the kingdom. To that end both new and old symbols are utilized. The king and his circle carry out a continual public relations programme designed to show him as caring and working for his people, as an active leader of the state and nation, and as the legitimate inheritor of the throne from a former legitimate king. Next, a façade of parliamentary democracy proclaims that the laws of the country come from the will of the people. But, because of the high level of corruption and electoral fraud, very few believe parliament to be representative. In Al-Karak, it is seen partly as a forum in which the kingdom's opinions may be aired, but much more as a servant of King Husayn and his circle. Members of parliament are respected, not because they have been elected, but because they have a strong local power base and, by being in Amman, have the ear of the government. What does more to create a sense of populistic legitimacy in the system are the very actions of the government. The desires and needs of the people, however inadequately, slowly, and at times corruptly, are being met. Some Karakis believe that the government and some of its officials are executing the civil and criminal law codes and providing welfare, education, and a basic economic infrastructure for the benefit of the people—not just for the state and the throne. Further, the king and the central government work closely with the traditional shaykhs, apparently in an attempt to absorb some of their traditional authority and turn it into legitimacy. Periodically, the king convokes a meeting of all the major shaykhs of the country and requests an expression of solidarity with his conduct in office and with government policy. The government also delegates some authority to the shaykhs, e.g. in traditional legal work, aids them in their local leadership positions, and, in return, demands their support for the regime.

The contradictions in this approach to creating legitimacy are twofold. First, because parliament, the symbol of democracy, is non-representative, it becomes solely an expression of political power, and can therefore do very little to establish a sense of democratic legitimate authority. Secondly, the combination of traditional and modern systems of political authority, i.e. tribal and state, creates confusion as to where authority is supposed to lie. The average Karaki does not know where his first loyalty outside his extended family should go, for it is difficult for him to distinguish where the shaykhs' authority ends and where that of the state begins. For the educated, this conflict takes a different form. In the schools, the pupils are taught loyalty to the king and the institutions of the state, but they see the shaykhs receiving authority which they are led to believe should be in the hands of others.

Turning to the strata, the lower stratum retains the traditional view, a balance of self-help and authority based on tradition, but within this group there is a developing sense of the legitimacy of the king. The regime's efforts to build up the monarchy and use the authority of the shaykhs has forged an embryonic feeling of loyalty to the king, but this is still a tenuous concept and is certainly not articulated in the peasant's mind. Much more significant for the average tribesman in daily life is the use or potential use of power and the traditional manner of accommodation between opposing forces. Equally, the state retains its image as a police force and tax collector; the peasant still views the power of the government as a force which must be reckoned with rather than a legitimate form of authority. He also continues to think of the shaykhs as mediators and arbitrators, men with traditional authority, but who are more remote nowadays because many owe their power partially to the government rather than solely to their political ability and standing in relation to the people.

The landholders and pre-1948 'foreigners' of the traditional middle stratum and the members of the upper stratum accept the authority and some of the legitimacy of the regime. From a negative standpoint, they know that they cannot move back in time to an independent Al-Karak and they do not want a social revolution in which they might lose their lands and positions. More positively, they are intimately related to the system, possess power within it, and benefit from it. As a result, they respect the given system, support it, and even extend it some legitimacy. This feeling does not go very deep, however, because of their recent historical experience: no one type of government has ruled in the area long enough to develop a sense of permanency in their eyes. Consequently, although they would lament the passing of the present kingdom, they would quickly attempt to accommodate themselves to any new power which established control in the district.

Finally, the educated middle stratum is divided into two groups: those who believe in the present political system, wishing only to reform it, and those who feel that a fundamental social and political revolution is the only answer. The former echo what they were taught in school, namely, that the state and the king are working for the good of the people and that it is the will of the people which is being implemented. They argue that the population voluntarily obeys the laws of the state out of respect for legitimate authority and not out of fear of the ultimate power of the army. This group certainly complains about inefficiency, lack of opportunity, and corruption at the higher levels; but it sees development and reform as the cure for these ills. The members of the revolutionary segment of this stratum do not agree. To them the current political system, the monarchy, and the institutions of the state are unacceptable and certainly not legitimate. As for the traditional local leaders, neither segment of the educated middle stratum considers them to be legitimate. They are followed only out of loyalty to the state on the part of the reforming group and fear of sanctions on the part of the other.

In sum, legitimate authority is sought by the state in various and seemingly contradictory ways. The government finds this necessary in order to reach all sections of the population; but many people are confused and antagonized by these conflicting approaches, and this tends to undermine any sense of legitimacy. In times of crisis, especially in defeat as in the 1967 Arab–Israeli war, these weaknesses and stresses in so newly established a state become more apparent, with inevitable effects on the already limited sense of legitimacy.

Leadership

With the changes in the contemporary period, some aspects of attaining and maintaining leadership roles have altered, while others have remained essentially the same. To investigate these developments, status will first be dealt with, and then the many types of leadership roles, including traditional leaders at various levels, the continued predominant role of the Majaly, the limited opportunities open to non-original Karakis, and the leadership of the educated middle stratum.

(1) *Status.* In comparison with the traditional period, status has become more diversified and ambiguous, and less closely related to one's kinship group. Some alterations have occurred in each of the categories: 'ascriptive', 'ascriptive and achievement', and 'achievement' described on pp. 78–80. For the first, no essential internal change has taken place, but its importance as a whole has diminished with the growth of the other two. As regards 'ascriptive and achievement', the sub-category of occupation has altered considerably with the appearance of new modes of livelihood and with changed popular attitudes. The new ranking from highest to lowest status would be: professional class; middle-sized landholders; army officers; teachers; civil servants; substantial

merchants; small landholders; merchants and artisans; soldiers; poor farmers; urban day labourers. Finally, under the category of 'achievement', two changes should be noted. First, the requirement that a man must prove his bravery is better defined in a negative sense. Bravery does not have to be demonstrated, but cowardice is certainly very degrading and condemned by society. Secondly, a new sub-category for learning must be added, because individuals with secondary-school diplomas, and particularly with university and professional degrees, enjoy high status and are treated with deference.

With the addition of more achievement-oriented status variables, a man's rank in relation to his fellow men has become more flexible and ambiguous. Once an individual moves out of the purely traditional norms, he has more control over his own destiny; he has more opportunity to overcome his ascriptive limitations and to gain higher status through achievement. With this increased flexibility, a new ambiguity in status recognition has also appeared. To compare the achievement of high status through traditional methods or more modern ones is difficult. Nor do members of the different strata take the same view of status. The educated middle stratum, for example, does not consider the ascriptive criteria as important as the lower stratum does. With the developments of the contemporary period, status takes on a different complexion— more stress on achievement, giving it greater elasticity, and a new differentiation between traditional and modern outlooks, making it more equivocal.

(2) *Traditionally Oriented Leadership.* The requirements for attaining and maintaining tribal-related leadership positions remain substantially the same as in the traditional period, but with the addition of minimal education and an ability to deal with the central government. Consequently, the emphasis on inheriting these roles or, at least, being closely related to a late leader, retains its importance, as does the necessity of having some wealth and distributing it properly. Settling disputes equitably and being the key person in marriage arrangements continues to be essential for maintaining one's position, but to demonstrate physical courage and prowess is no longer so. Although the central government entered the local political system before the first world war, it only minimally influenced the higher leadership. But because of its expansion over the last twenty years, all effective leaders must co-operate with it to some extent in order to obtain for themselves and their followers the benefits which it offers. Negatively, if a leader continually challenges the government or goes against its wishes, it can and often does undermine his position by cutting off

benefits and denying him all official posts. Men who attain high official posts become increasingly dependent on the regime, for it only appoints those whom it knows to be co-operative and loyal. On the other hand, thanks to so many of its sons occupying such positions both in the district and in Amman, Al-Karak and its traditional leaders exercise considerable influence over the government. These men are in a position to influence considerably the programmes of the government and to intervene on behalf of their fellow Karaki leaders.

(3) *Lower-level Traditionally Oriented Leaders.* The presence of the central government has permitted the development of two kinds of lower-level leaders. The first traditionally oriented type derives his power primarily from the government and only barely meets the older prerequisites for leadership. He gives presents to the appropriate officials, does favours for them, and perhaps attains the position of mukhtar. Members of this leader's group are then forced to work through him when they need to deal with the government, and he thus creates debts and a power base. Men of the second type carry on the earlier traditions, attaining and exercising their positions in the time-honoured manner. The central government, unless it feels that the man is particularly recalcitrant, endeavours to work through him. In turn, the man's group uses him as a means of access to the government. As in the traditional period, these lower-level leaders maintain relationships with the higher-level leaders and it is quite often through these that they, especially leaders of the second type, establish contacts with the central-government bureaucracy.

The followers of a lower-level leader expect new services from him besides the traditional ones of maintaining the honour of the tribe, settling disputes, and arranging marriages. The development of the area has created new expectations which can usually only be realized through the central government. The following of this type of leader is drawn almost entirely from the lower stratum. The traditional and upper strata have their own contacts with the central government. The educated middle stratum holds aloof from the traditionally oriented leadership in most spheres, except at times with regard to disputes and obtaining employment; and its members are sometimes under pressure from it as regards marriage arrangements.

(4) *Middle-level Traditionally Oriented Leaders.* Distinctly different kinds of men with quite varied qualifications are found in middle-level leadership roles. First, a number of men in their sixties or above, who established their positions before Al-Karak experienced considerable change, continue to enjoy high status and

authority in the contemporary period. For the most part, these men have successfully adapted themselves to the developments of the last two decades and are able to work well with the central government and to keep their traditional contacts with the lower-level leaders and the lower stratum. Next, most of the leaders in their forties or fifties have some secondary education, but maintain the semblance of traditional ways and try to emulate their fathers. They usually have substantial landholdings and occasionally occupy middle-level civil-service posts, their appointments being based entirely on politics rather than merit. Because they cultivate their influence in or within the government and keep their hold over lower-level leaders and to some extent over the lower stratum, they are able to maintain strong positions.

In addition, some relatively well-educated men in their thirties and a few in their forties co-operate with the established power group and maintain many of the traditional forms, but also use their talents to promote gradual change within Al-Karak. These men usually come from important families, often the top tribal shaykh's family, but are the second and third sons. Some were active in the revolutionary political parties in the 1950s, but dropped their youthful idealism for the potentials of authoritative roles in society. They are invariably high- or middle-level civil servants in Al-Karak or Amman, or officers in the army. As regards social relationships, they balance their contacts between the educated middle stratum and the other strata with more emphasis on the latter. They act as informal dispute settlers, establish reputations for generosity, and generally follow some of the traditional criteria for leadership. They are thus in a strong position as regards both the government and the various indigenous social groups. Officials seek their help in dealing with the public, and Karakis in matters concerning the government. As intermediaries or brokers they are ideally placed to create and pay off debts, enhancing their claim to leadership. Conflicts can often arise between their loyalty to their local followers and the government, but the success of these leaders lies in working out compromises which please all parties concerned.

(5) *Upper-level Traditionally Oriented Leaders.* Acquiring and maintaining top leadership roles follows a pattern similar to that of the middle level, but the men who fill these positions have more ability in all spheres. The commanding figures of the traditional period, such as Rafifan Pasha Al-Majaly and Husayn Pasha At-Tarawna, have mostly died, but the few who survive very definitely retain their power positions. For example, although the mayor of Al-Karak town, the ninety-year-old brother of Rafifan, is not very

active, he still has major influence in the political decisions of the
town and district. Most of the younger men, besides having close
relations with their tribes and alliances, are important officials in
the government: secretaries and ministers, colonels and generals,
and MPs.

(6) *Sustained Special Position of the Majaly.* As in the traditional
period, the Majaly continues to be the strongest tribe in Al-Karak.
As a group, the members of the tribe maintain more of the traditional symbols than do the other tribes, which, in turn, give them
a greater sense of mutual pride. Its leadership nurtures the
traditionally strong relations with the Christians and the Ma'ayta
and continues to dominate the tribes of the Ghawr, 'Iraq village,
and the Bararsha alliance. As regards the general change in Al-
Karak, proportionately fewer members of this tribe complete
secondary school or attend university. As a result, the Majaly
produces relatively fewer members of the educated middle stratum
and virtually none of its radicals. Nor are there many of the Majaly
in the lower civil-service posts, though the tribe is certainly well
represented in the higher appointments which go by politics rather
than merit. Because of the tribe's loyalty to the regime, it is
favoured in the army, many high-ranking officers coming from its
membership. As in the former period, the Majaly continues to
enjoy exceptional leadership. After the death of Rafifan, Haza'
Al-Majaly rose to prominence. He worked closely with the young
King Husayn and the royal circle in the 1950s, and was many times
prime minister. During this period, he kept actively in touch with
his tribe and Al-Karak, aiding his tribesmen and his extended
family with government loans, equipment, and public and private
funds. But he was assassinated in 1960, and no leader of equal
calibre has yet appeared.

(7) *Limited Access to Leadership in a Tribal Society—the Case of
Muhammad Zayn.* The opportunities for advancement to the
higher levels of leadership continue in the contemporary period
to be limited to members of the established Karaki tribes, but men
of 'foreign' origins may gain substantial, though restricted power.
An example of this pattern is Muhammad Zayn, a fifty-five-year-
old Muslim, whose father came from Hebron. His extensive and
varied activities in various branches of commerce have made him
the wealthiest businessman in Al-Karak as well as the largest
private employer. His interests, which are quite diversified, include:
a rock-crushing works 1 km from Al-Karak town, a bus company,
the largest Karaki-based construction company, concessions for
many brands of cigarettes and technical equipment, a petrol
station, and a good deal of farm land. He is also heavily involved in

non-commercial fields. The Hebronis and, in a larger sense, all the merchants and artisans of 'foreign' origin recognize him as their leader and principal dispute settler. A very devout man, he went on the Hajj ten years ago and takes an active part in the local committee for the *'Awqaf* institution which, incidentally, helps him to win some quite substantial construction contracts. In civic affairs he has been, or currently is: vice-president and member of the municipal council of Al-Karak town, member of the governor's advisory council, member of the committees for the Agricultural Credit Institute, the *'Awqaf* institution, the Red Crescent Society, and the Boy Scouts Club, also founder and president of the Chamber of Commerce and Industry. All these offices show that the Karakis are willing to co-operate with and honour a man who is engaged in commerce and is not a member of one of the established tribes. Equally, the central government, particularly the governor, recognizes his standing by appointing him to many of its councils and committees. Had it not been for his birth, however, given his personality and energy Muhammad Zayn could have become mayor of the town or an MP. Even though the native-born Karakis accept 'foreign' merchants more readily than in the traditional period, the public still sets definite limits on how far they may advance in politics.

(8) *Leadership of the Educated Middle Stratum.* Although much of the educated middle stratum dislikes the traditional leadership, it has not yet been able to form a coherent one of its own. Rather, its leaders may be divided into four categories which are not in themselves mutually exclusive. First, some of the educated men who work completely within the traditional political system and who maintain only sporadic relations with this stratum, attempt to contribute in a minimal way to reform and social advancement. In a minor sense, then, they are furthering the interests of the educated middle stratum, but cannot be reckoned among its leaders. Secondly, a few men who co-operate with the established powers consciously work for many of the ideals of the educated middle stratum. They are mostly professional men who obtain appointments on the various government councils and committees and, through these positions, exercise what influence they can for the improvement of the material well-being of all Karakis and for change in the district. Thirdly, as was mentioned in Chapter 4, successful older men attract informal groups over whom they exercise some influence. Although they contribute to and help clarify the thinking of their followers, in the larger political setting they possess scarcely any influence, with the exception of those who sit on councils and committees. Finally, the former leaders of

the now quiescent political parties experienced real, though brief, political power. They attracted a following through their ideas, teacher-pupil relationships, kinship connections, and occasional financial inducements. In co-operation with their counterparts in all areas of Jordan, they challenged the government, caused sustained crises throughout the mid-1950s, and brought about some changes in policy. By their command of the loyalty of a significant portion of the active Karakis, they helped undermine the traditional leadership. In sum, the leaders of this stratum are dependent on the fractured nature of its sub-groupings, and, except for the brief ascendancy of the party leaders, none have possessed power comparable with the traditional leaders of the district.

Dispute-settling in the Contemporary Period

The traditional reliance on self-help and the tribal *qadis* continues to be the most common method of settling disputes. The population has not yet generally accepted the power of the police as a substitute for its dependence on the potential use of force. This may be attributed to the residual fear of any dealings with the government, ignorance that the police are required to enforce the laws equally and without prejudice, and the consideration that a man is intricately connected with his family and lineage and in turn must call upon the members of the relevant group for help in order to maintain his and their honour. When a man or group does request aid from the police, this body represents an extension of the self-help system, that is, another form of counterforce against one's opponents.

The choice of a court system has become less simple. The government prefers to adjudicate solely within its own courts disputes over registered land, disagreements about written contracts, and public offences which do not involve the rights of private individuals. In cases of physical injury and death, crimes of honour, and rival tribal territorial claims, it continues to emphasize the traditional legal system even though it increasingly exercises the public right by bringing the accused to its own courts. It promotes the tribal courts because it recognizes that as mechanisms of social control they are still the most effective for solving disputes and preventing or healing social rifts, and because it wishes to buttress the position of the tribal leaders who give the regime considerable support. As in the traditional period, most disputes never reach formal tribal or modern courts, but are settled through local intermediaries. For those that do, the average Karaki attempts to choose the court where he feels he will obtain the most favourable settlement.

In cases involving the state against a number of men, the defendants usually try to arrange things so that no one is punished. The following example also illustrates some of the preceding remarks about leadership. After a number of street lamps had been broken, the municipality asked the police to investigate. The fathers of the boys responsible for the damage gathered together, suppressed the evidence, and threw the blame on a child of five who could not possibly have been responsible. Nevertheless, the child's father, a very poor baker's helper, was asked to pay the fine, a small sum, but one which he could ill afford. He appealed to the secretary of the municipality, a man whom he did not know personally. The secretary, a man in his mid-thirties and the younger brother of a highly respected former MP, often helps to solve problems which Karakis have with the government and, conversely, government officials often come to him for aid in many affairs. Upon hearing the story and seeing how destitute the man was, the secretary rang up the police and explained that the child obviously could not have broken the lamps; he even lowered the child's age to four in support of his argument. As a result, the police dropped the charge. This shows that, although the authorities may not always believe the contrived stories, they are often powerless to decide otherwise for lack of accurate evidence.

The next example illustrates the continuing importance of the relatively traditional methods of solving disputes, the position of a middle-level leader, and the often minimal role of the police. It also brings into the picture the Ghazawis and their somewhat sensitive relations with the native-born Karakis.

On a sidewalk next to one of the major streets in town, a shopkeeper offers tea and coffee and provides chairs for people. The owner of an adjacent electrical shop was offended one day when a man placed his seat in front of that shop to join a small group (all members of the same tribe) who were drinking tea next door. The ensuing argument quickly became a shouting match. When the offended shopkeeper said that the group was blocking his shop on purpose because he was a Ghazawi, a Palestinian refugee, all the tea-drinkers began shouting. They declared that it was neither here nor there whether a person was a Palestinian or not, and that it was *'ayb* (shameful) to think or say such a thing. Finally, the electrical shopkeeper declared that he could not conduct business under such conditions, closed his shop, and left.

About five minutes later, another argument was started some ten yards down the street as a direct result of the above altercation. Another Ghazawi shopkeeper was complaining that Bulbul, a Ghazawi who serves tea and coffee and brings stools anywhere one wants, was blocking his store. Within a couple of minutes, the two were exchanging blows, but were quickly separated by people who had been watching the quarrel. However, Bulbul kept arguing with a policeman who had been walking by and was eventually taken to the police station.

Bulbul was the favourite among the crowd because, although poor and without family in Al-Karak, he works hard, moves fast (hence his name, Bulbul means nightingale in Arabic), and is always friendly. About fifteen minutes after he was taken away, he came back striding fast as usual. The police had merely let him calm down and asked him to move his chairs a yard further down the sidewalk.

After another five minutes, the owner of the electrical shop drove up in the car of 'Abu Hasan, a thirty-five-year-old middle-level leader, director of a local-government department, and also a member of the same tribe as the group which was accused of blocking the doorway of the electrical shop. 'Abu Hasan had heard of the argument, sought out the shopkeeper, and asked him to come with him so that the dispute could be solved. At length 'Abu Hasan was able to get him to sit down with the tea-drinking group. Tea was ordered for all from Bulbul, to the accompaniment of jocular and admiring comments on that popular character from the bystanders. After much discussion, some of it quite voluble, 'Abu Hasan succeeded in pacifying both parties, and all soon went their separate ways.

Many other minor disputes of this sort were solved in the same way: quickly and efficiently. It is important to do this as early as possible to prevent them from building up and disrupting society. Bulbul's case was a simple one because of the relatively equal backgrounds of the two individuals and the lack of serious charges or countercharges. The other case, however, might have caused very strained relations between the Ghazawis and the relevant Karaki tribe. It was very much to the credit of 'Abu Hasan that he intervened almost immediately and amicably settled the affair. Such action helps to build up a man's personal stature in the town and district as an effective dispute-settler and a fair-minded leader.

Political Dynamics in the Villages, the Town, and the District

(1) *Municipal Councils in the Villages.* In the large villages of 'Ay and Al-Mazar, quite active political struggles, each with similar patterns, have centred on their recently established municipal councils. In 'Ay, a number of small tribes which traditionally had been ruled by more powerful ones in the village attempted to gain the presidency of the municipal council in 1966. In the election,

neither side won a clear majority and in the ensuing negotiations both were adamant in their claim to the council's top office. Unable to resolve their differences, their hostility increased until it spilled into the streets, with members of the rival tribes throwing stones and eventually shooting at each other. The governor of Al-Karak arrived the same day with a detachment of soldiers. He remained in the village for twenty days, but could not persuade either side to compromise. He then appointed a special committee with himself as president to run the municipality. In the 1967 parliamentary elections, 'Abdal-Wahhab At-Tarawna, one of the successful candidates, turned the dispute into a campaign issue. Seeking the support of the traditionally dominant leaders in 'Ay, he declared that, if he won, he would have the council reconstituted and their man named as its president. After he was elected, he fulfilled his promise, but within six months, the losing faction felt itself oppressed and violence again flared up in the streets. The governor returned with another detachment of soldiers and set up a new special committee with himself as president to conduct municipal affairs.

In Al-Mazar, the Qatawna and the Nuwaysa have always been dominated by the Tarawna. However, because they are the second largest group in the village, the Qatawna felt that they had a right to the presidency of the municipal council in some form of rotation. The consent of the Tarawna not being forthcoming, the Qatawna's anger grew. Over and above these emotions, the Qatawna vociferously objected to a project formulated by the president of the council, 'Abdal-Karim At-Tarawna, and his supporters to open a new street which would mean tearing down a few Qatawna houses. Rancour turned to violence when King Husayn visited the district in 1968. The municipal council had decided to provide a large lunch for the officers of the king's guard, but it failed to do so. The Qatawna accused the Tarawna of destroying the honour of the municipality and of the village as well. As in 'Ay, the opposing sides started throwing rocks at each other, forcing the local police to call in reinforcements from Al-Karak town. The governor used his office to try to re-establish good feeling between the two tribes, but, finding this impossible, he dissolved the council and replaced it by a special committee with himself at its head.

In both 'Ay and Al-Mazar, the disputes were caused by similar forces related to the change which is taking place in the district. The traditional minor alliances are breaking down, for they have lost part of their *raison d'être*. With no outside force to unite them, they have split into their basic tribal groups. In addition, the traditionally dominant tribes are being challenged by those whom they had ruled. Some members of the educated middle stratum like to explain this in terms of class struggle. The protagonists, however, see it solely as a struggle for political power among the tribes. With the establishment of municipal councils in the villages, new objects for political competition were created. Whoever controls the council and its presidency is in a very obvious way recognized as the leader of the village. Not only does the winner enjoy the symbols of the office, but he also has very real legal control over village affairs. He has the commanding voice in designing projects, hiring men, and the disbursement of funds. Previously, rival shaykhs claimed superiority, but unless one could persuade his opponent's followers to turn to him, there was little he could do to prove his claim. But the president and members of a council possess recognized symbols of power and control material benefits. Disputes degenerating into violence indicate that the villagers have not yet adjusted themselves to these new forms of competition.

(2) *The Municipal Council in Al-Karak Town.* Change and development throughout Al-Karak have profoundly affected the membership and activity of the municipal council of Al-Karak town. The council suffers from three distinct types of problem: the growth of its population from 3,000 in 1960 to 9,000 in 1968; the citizen's lack of confidence and co-operation; and the increasing disparity between the qualifications required for becoming a member and for executing its changing functions.

The average inhabitant of the town has virtually no sense of civic pride or inclination to co-operate with its authorities. The municipality's attempts to enforce building codes and thereby give the town a semblance of order meet with continual public resistance. It has difficulty in extracting payment for electricity, water, and other services from many of the local families. It is totally unable to persuade the average Karaki to help keep the streets clean. Though many complain about municipal inactivity and inefficiency, when an energetic, efficient man does gain temporary control, few are ready to co-operate actively with him. These attitudes reflect the earlier lack of a civic tradition and the inability of the municipality and council to create a sense of pride in the town.

With only occasional breaks, the membership of the municipal council continues to be dominated by the traditional political forces of Al-Karak. As in the former period, it corresponds to the power balance in the town and district, with a majority of members from the Western Alliance, both Muslims and Christians, one or two from the town's minority commercial groups, and one from the Eastern Alliance. The actual choice of members is usually made not by town-wide elections, but by private negotiations among the various political leaders. The Jordanian statute on municipal law provides that if the number of candidates equals the number of seats on the body, they shall be considered duly elected.[1] Thus, for example, when the last council was formed, forty men entered their names as candidates, but the town leaders and the governor met, worked out a compromise between all sides, and obtained the withdrawal of all but the required number to fill the council. The two most powerful voices in these election agreements are those of Duliwan Pasha Al-Majaly and, increasingly, of the governor. Duliwan Pasha is the perennial president of the council and a major power in the Majaly tribe. Because of his long, respected service to the country, the king places much confidence in him. As a result, he wields considerable influence which he uses to maintain the traditional balance in the council. The governor may legally intervene in many of the affairs of the municipality and in recent years he has felt it necessary to exercise this right with regard both to the selection of the council and to its operations.

The predominance of traditional methods and criteria for choosing municipal council members in the contemporary period has caused distinct difficulties in meeting the changing demands of the town's rapidly growing population. In any political system, there is invariably a difference between the qualities a man must have to win the political support of others in order to gain a specific office, and those necessary for efficiently carrying out its defined duties. In Al-Karak town, this problem has become acute. Because the council members who are chosen on the basis of tribal leadership think and compete almost solely in terms of tribal politics and traditional prestige, and because the nature of traditional tribal relations has little in common with civic co-operation, construction, and development, these men tend to have minimal aptitude and are usually ill-equipped to do the work of councillors. The new demands of an increased population cause frequent internal disputes which stalemate its activities and often end in its dissolution. Consequently, although the legal term of a council is four years, the average since 1950 has only been two.

From 1962 through 1968 the municipal council's membership and some of its activities were as follows. In 1962 a new council, chosen by the traditional methods of compromise, was made up as below, (p. 164). With only three men interested in civic progress, the council proceeded in its usual inactive manner with considerable internal bickering and divisiveness. In the spring of 1964, a flash flood cut

[1] *Majmu'at al-qawanin wa al-'anthima fi al-Mamlaka al-'Urduniyya al-Hashimiyya*, iii. 267, Law no. 29, 1955.

Municipal Council 1962–4

Name	Alliance or origin	Qualifications
Duliwan Al-Majaly	Western	Tribal leader
'Ibrahim Al-Madadha	Western	Tribal leader
'Ahmad Al-'Asasfa	Western	Civically active & tribal leader
Khalaf Al-Ma'ayta	Western	Tribal leader
'Ahmad As-Su'ub	Eastern	Tribal leader
Muhammad Zayn 'Abu Al-Faylat	Hebroni	Civically active[1]
Tuma As-Suyagh	Western-Christian	Tribal leader
Ghasan Al-'Amarin	Western-Christian	Civically active
'Isa Al-Kuwalit	Western-Christian	Tribal leader

the water supply to Al-Karak, forcing drastic rationing of what little water was brought in by army truck. The municipal council, split as it was, took no action until finally the three civically active men resigned, causing its dissolution. At this juncture, the governor intervened and appointed a special committee to run the municipality. It was composed of the following members:

Special Committee 1964–6

Name	Alliance or origin	Qualifications
Duliwan Al-Majaly	Western	Tribal leader
'Abdal-Wahhab At-Tarawna	Eastern	Tribal leader, former MP, civically active
Sulayman Al-'Akasha	Western-Christian	Civically active
Muhammad Zayn 'Abu Al-Faylat	Hebroni	Civically active
Yusif Al-Habashna	Western	Tribal leader

As may be seen from the above list, the governor created the usual tribal balance but at the same time ensured control by civically minded men. 'Abdal-Wahhab At-Tarawna and Sulayman Al-'Akasha did most of the work with steady support from Muhammad Zayn. Yusif Al-Habashna attempted to block most projects while Duliwan Al-Majaly, an octogenarian, merely looked on. The committee quickly re-established the water supply and then reorganized the whole system which had been set up in 1927. Under the old system, water was delivered only to given points in each quarter of the town, but by 1966, over 85 per cent of the houses

[1] Cf. pp. 156–7.

had their own supply. The municipality's administrative staff was increased threefold, making services more readily available and more efficient. Long-needed streets were opened and surfaced and the municipal library was expanded. In two years, many neglected needs were met.

In 1966, a new municipal council was chosen through traditional negotiations, but also with strong intervention by the governor.

Municipal Council 1966

Name	Alliance or origin	Qualifications
Duliwan Al-Majaly	Western	Tribal leader
Dr Mahmud Al-'Alawy	Western	Civically active, educated middle stratum co-operating with the establishment
Mahmud As-Su'ub	Eastern	Tribal leader
Mahmud Al-Habashna	Western	Tribal leader
Yasin Al-Mahadin	Western	Civically active
Muhammad Zayn 'Abu Al-Faylat	Hebroni	Civically active
Mikha'il Ash-Sharayha	Western-Christian	Civically active
Sulayman Al-'Akasha	Western-Christian	Civically active
Tuma As-Suyagh	Western-Christian	Tribal leader
'Abdal-Wahhab At-Tarawna[1]	Eastern	Civically active

The tribal balance was kept, but civically active members were in the majority. However, one of these died and 'Abdal-Wahhab At-Tarawna resigned when he was elected to parliament in 1967, leaving the body equally divided between the two groups. Although conditions have not degenerated to the level of 1964, by 1968 with the loss of the two active members and the frequent absence of the governor from the district, the remaining civically minded members were complaining of inactivity and thinking of having the council replaced by another special committee.

Apart from showing the disparity between the qualities required for *becoming* and for *serving as* a councillor, this example also indicates three other tendencies. The role of the central government through the office of the governor is becoming increasingly crucial in the conduct of local politics, especially when they relate to the new institutions and changing demands. Equally, the

---

[1] Specially appointed by the governor in order to keep the balance strongly in favour of the civically active men and to take advantage of his energetic leadership.

governor is pushing the direction of politics towards reform which is exemplified by his forcing a balance in the council in favour of the civically active. Finally, these same men, the progressivists, are becoming dependent in practice and in their thinking on the intervention of the government to obtain their desires. Thus, in 1954 and 1964 the governor set up special committees to reform the municipality of Al-Karak town and in 1968 with the degeneration of the regular council, the civic activists again started to pressure him to intervene.

(3) *Parliamentary Elections.* Although this section is mainly concerned with the 1967 election, a list of the district's members since the institution of direct elections in 1947 will help to establish a broader view and a time perspective.

Karaki Members of Parliament

Year	Western Alliance	Christian	Eastern Alliance
1947	Ma'arak Al-Majaly Faris Al-Ma'ayta	Khalil Al-'Amarin	..
1950	'Attallah Al-Majaly	Hany Al-'Akasha	'Ahmad At-Tarawna
1951	Haza' Al-Majaly	Juris Al-Halasa	'Ahmad At-Tarawna
1954	Haza' Al-Majaly	Saba Al-'Akasha	'Ahmad At-Tarawna
1956	Salah Al-Majaly 'Imran Al-Ma'ayta	Saba Al-'Akasha	..
1961[1]	Salah Al-Majaly 'Imran Al-Ma'ayta	Salah Al-Burqan	'Abdal-Wahhab At-Tarawna
1963	Salah Al-Majaly 'Imran Al-Ma'ayta	Saba Al-'Akasha	Salah As-Sahaymat
1967	'Abdal-Wahhab Al-Majaly 'Imran Al-Ma'ayta	Saba Al-'Akasha	'Abdal-Wahhab At-Tarawna

The balance continues to be weighted heavily in favour of the Western Alliance, but the Eastern Alliance has been able to win a seat more often that it did in the traditional period. Al-Karak's increased quota of MPs in 1961 aided in this, for now the Majaly, the two major alliances, and the Christians may each have a seat. In two elections agreements were reached for the withdrawal of all opposition candidates, but in most cases there was competition. The most recent of these, in 1967, illustrates both the general methods and forces which come into play in choosing MPs and the incipient strength of the educated middle stratum.

On 15 April 1967 a nation-wide parliamentary election took place. In Al-Karak the results of the balloting were:

[1] Additional MP awarded to district in 1961.

Parliamentary Election of 1967 in the District of Al-Karak

	Candidate	Votes
Successful:	'Abdal-Wahhab Al-Majaly	21,682
	Saba Al-'Akasha	21,146
	'Abdal-Wahhab At-Tarawna	20,769
	'Imran Al-Ma'ayta	15,750
Unsuccessful:	'Aly Al-Ma'ayta	9,148
	Mahmud Al-Habashna	8,479
	Muhammad As-Sahaymat	9,269
	'Ibrahim Al-Mahadin	4,562
	Jamil Az-Zurayqat	8,442

SOURCE: Min. of Information and Culture.

Before we look at the election manœuvring, a background sketch of each of the candidates will be given to elucidate the subsequent discussion as well as to contribute to the earlier section on leadership.

'Abdal-Wahhab Al-Majaly, son of a middle-level shaykh, is from the village of Al-Qasr, not from Ar-Rabba, the village of the major Majaly leaders of the past hundred years. He is a substantial landholder in the district, but derives most of his power from his connections with the central government. He served in sub-ministerial posts in the 1950s and 1960s and was a cabinet minister before becoming an MP. He spends most of his time in Amman and is not often seen in Al-Karak. Because of his strong position with the government, however, he is able to offer and deliver patronage readily.

Saba Al-'Akasha, a Christian and son of a lesser shaykh, has been an MP since 1954 except for the years 1961–3. Using the close relations between his tribe and the Majaly, he originally gained his position with the aid of Haza' Al-Majaly. In subsequent years he has become a favourite with the government, but is also popular with a good many of the Christians.

'Abdal-Wahhab At-Tarawna, eldest son of Husayn Pasha, took over his father's position as leader of the Tarawna and Eastern Alliance, but, in contrast to the late Pasha, he attempts to co-operate with the government and the king, despite their sustained favouritism for the Majaly. He is a large landholder and, as a result of his role as shaykh of the Eastern Alliance and his experience with his father, is a recognized tribal *qadi*. Although he was an MP from 1961 to 1963, he gave way to Salah As-Sahaymat in the next election because he preferred to spend more time on tribal affairs. He was appointed a member of the special committee to run the municipality of Al-Karak town from 1964 to 1966 and was very energetic and popular in this role (cf. pp. 164 f.). In comparison with the other successful candidates, he spends much more of his time in the district and town and consequently is more in touch with the people.

'Imran Al-Ma'ayta, son of a middle-level shaykh, has been in parliament since 1956. He holds a great deal of land and owns a beautiful estate in the Wady 'Ibn Hamad. His original election was obtained primarily through wealth and, since then, he has become known as a staunch supporter of the king and the government. He does not enjoy the popularity of the other successful candidates, mostly because of his colourless personality. Consequently, he ensures election by means of a generous spread of wealth and patronage.

'Aly Al-Ma'ayta is the paternal nephew of Faris Al-Ma'ayta, the late shaykh of the Ma'ayta. Because Faris's sons were known for their profligacy and irresponsibility, and because 'Aly had worked with him for years, upon his death in early 1968 'Aly was declared shaykh of the tribe despite his being a cripple and an illiterate. He enjoys moderate landholdings and is a respected *qadi*. In his tribe and the district, he has considerable popularity and prides himself on working for his people down to the least important and poorest individual. He also possesses a certain prestige on account of his outspoken nature and it is commonly said in the area that he even talks back to the king. He became a candidate in 1967 with the blessing of Faris Al-Ma'ayta, for they both felt that the people deserved a true, not a totally arranged, election, and that the established candidates should have some competition.

Mahmud Al-Habashna, an elderly shaykh of the tribe, has moderate landholdings and is a noted *qadi*. He lives in Al-Karak town and has been a member of the municipal council. He enjoys moderate prestige and has a reputation for honesty, but is limited by his membership of one of the weaker tribes. Like 'Aly Al-Ma'ayta, he entered the campaign in order to ensure a contested election.

Muhammad As-Sahaymat,[1] son of a late shaykh of the Damur and member of the consultative council of Transjordan in the traditional period, is a former director of the Intelligence Bureau of the Ministry of the Interior, a powerful position in Jordan. According to Karaki sources, he was dismissed after a few years

---

[1] Sahaymat is an attached tribe of the Damur (Ghasasna, Eastern Alliance). The Damur is made up mostly of a series of closely attached tribes, most of which are considered to be related by blood. As a result, important shaykhs and occasionally head shaykhs of the Damur come from these sub-groups.

in the post because of his independence and strong will. The position of Director of the Intelligence Bureau automatically creates fear and awe in the mind of the average Karaki, and dislike on the part of a large portion of the educated middle stratum. Muhammad has only a limited popularity among the Damur, owing to his reputedly high-handed dealings with them while in office and his favouritism in the distribution of patronage.

'Ibrahim Al-Mahadin, son of a minor shaykh, was the representative of the educated middle stratum in the 1967 elections. One of his brothers is known to have participated in the 1957 abortive coup led by 'Aly 'Abu Nuwwar, but is now chief of the engineering department of the municipality of Amman. Another brother is a noted attorney in Amman. In the 1950s and early 1960s, 'Ibrahim was an artillery officer in the army and, soon after the coup attempt, was sent to the United States for advanced training. He resigned his commission in 1962 and took a correspondence course in law at the University of Damascus, receiving his degree in 1966. Subsequently, he practised law in Al-Karak, but in 1968 he took a post on the legal staff of the Ministry of the Interior, Office of Public Security. He is popular with the educated middle stratum and often has a group of young men around him. He is equally respected by the established Karaki leaders, for he is willing to work with them and his views are reformist rather than radical. He entered the election campaign not only for the reasons of 'Aly Al-Ma'ayta and Mahmud Al-Habashna, but also because he wished to test and demonstrate the strength of a non-traditional candidate in the district.

Jamil Az-Zurayqat, son of a landholder, is a trained engineer, but lives mostly off income from agricultural land. He is little known and entered the campaign in order to take advantage of the votes of those who did not wish to support the established candidates.

As a rule, candidates for parliament enter into agreements with each other to campaign as a group and to exchange various kinds of support. In 1967 the four successful candidates were all united on one ticket. 'Abdal-Wahhab Al-Majaly contributed support from the Majaly, and their traditional clients, the Bararsha and the Ghawarna, and considerable strength among the Batush, the Bany Hamida, and the 'Amr. 'Imran Al-Ma'ayta added the bulk of the Muslim section of the Western Alliance and Saba Al-'Akasha assured Christian support. The Eastern Alliance votes and those of part of the Bararsha were supplied by 'Abdal-Wahhab At-Tarawna. With the exception of the latter, each candidate also had the strong, active backing of the central government which contributed to their funds and made their election promises more credible. Although 'Abdal-Wahhab At-Tarawna did not have the support of the government, neither did he have it against him. The other three candidates chose him as the fourth member because he balanced the ticket for the major alliances and enjoyed considerable popularity in the town and district. 'Aly-Al-Ma'ayta and Mahmud Al-Habashna also joined forces. Originally, they called upon 'Ibrahim Al-Mahadin to become the third Muslim, but upon his refusal, they formed a ticket with Muhammad As-Sahaymat. The remaining men stood as independents.

Other forms of negotiation also took place at high levels. Before the election of 'Abdal-Wahhab Al-Majaly, the MPs and major leaders of the Majaly had always come from the village of Ar-Rabba, specifically from the Yusif section and recently from Muhammad's lineage.[1] Having obtained the blessing of the regime in Amman, 'Abdal-Wahhab decided to take advantage of the current void in strong Majaly leadership and break this tradition. His meeting with Duliwan Al-Majaly and the other Ar-Rabba leaders was reported to have been acrimonious, ending at last in grudging agreement because of the government's attitude, the tradition of the Majaly to stand as a whole, and its strong support for the regime. In addition, the candidates attempted to persuade their opponents to step out of the campaign. 'Abdal-Wahhab At-Tarawna approached Muhammad As-Sahaymat, but he met with no success, for Muhammad thought he had earned the post by his services to the country. It is also locally believed that Saba Al-'Akasha offered to pay Jamil Az-Zurayqat 1,500 dinars to withdraw in his favour. The successful ticket as a whole tried to persuade 'Ibrahim Al-Mahadin not to stand, offering him the position of assistant secretary in any ministry of his choice. He refused because he had stated publicly that he would be a candidate and therefore did not want to go back on his word. Equally, he wanted to provide at least some competition and to test the strength of the reform vote. No one approached 'Aly Al-Ma'ayta, for all knew his reputation for honesty and being outspoken.

The actual campaign process involved all politically related groups in the district. The candidates delivered public speeches mostly in praise of their own virtues, past services, and promises for the future. Frequently, they participated in the mutual cursing and considerable invective which occasionally degenerated into fighting among their supporters. More importantly, they visited all the middle-level and many of the low-level leaders from whom

---

[1] Some of the names which have been frequently mentioned in this study are: Qadr, Rafifan, Duliwan, Salah, and Haza'.

they gathered support by various means. Promises to have schools built and roads improved and to secure positions in the bureaucracy and the army for their followers were the most common form of patronage. At times, village leaders extracted help in their local power struggles, e.g. 'Abdal-Wahhab At-Tarawna promised the traditionally dominant tribes in 'Ay that he would have the local municipal council re-established with their man as president. Direct cash payments for votes were also not uncommon. The candidates who enjoyed the favour of the regime were in the best position to fulfil their pledges for government action or jobs and the lower-level leaders realized this. As a result, these local leaders mostly supported the successful ticket, but the few who did not want to for traditional or personal reasons were in a dilemma. For example, although 'Ibrahim Al-Mahadin sought out these village leaders and was very favourably received by many of them, he could not elicit their support because they in turn needed to meet the demands of their followers. Consequently, apart from the educated middle stratum, he obtained the votes of only half of his own tribe and 'A'jam alliance (Shamayla and Madadha) and of a section of the Bararsha. Equally, the losing ticket was able to rely only upon the traditional loyalty of their own tribes or sections of them.

Not only did the candidates of the successful ticket make promises of material support and jobs, but they also used covert threats. They took advantage of the strong economic control the plateau tribes have over some of the people of the periphery and over all the Ghawarna. They also reminded recalcitrant local leaders that they had it in their power to cut off some government welfare and services. Because they have appointees and allies in significant positions throughout the civil service in Al-Karak and Amman, as well as in such other posts as head of the local bank, their reminders carried great weight.

At all levels the voting process was not very honest or legal, but reflected the relative power positions of the candidates. Initially, it should be noted that in 1967 there were 38,128 legally registered voters,[1] whereas, given the population of the district, there could not possibly be more than 10,000.[2] Virtually three out of four 'legally registered' voters did not exist. The total number of votes

---

[1] Figure supplied by Min. of Information and Culture.

[2] Official statistics give the 1966 population of Al-Karak district as 54,006, of which only males, eighteen years of age and over, may vote. The number of children under eighteen accounts for not less than 60 per cent of the population (figure extrapolated from: Dept. of Stat., *Population and labour force in the agricultural sector, 1967* (1968), p. 42). This leaves 21,602 adults of whom only half are males, totalling only 10,801 possible voters. Also, in the 1967 elections, members of the armed forces and police of whom there are a substantial number in Al-Karak, could not vote.

cast in the election is not available, but official sources indicate that the candidates on the winning ticket averaged around 19,800 votes and those on the losing ticket around 8,900, a total of 28,700, almost three times the number of males eighteen years old and over who actually live in the district.

On election day, the police were ubiquitous and for the most part aided the local village leaders who are the key men in turning out the excessive vote. In the actual balloting, these men used various classical 'illegal' techniques: (1) having or encouraging certain men to vote a number of times; (2) buying votes; (3) physically assaulting recalcitrants; and (4) stuffing the ballot boxes or replacing them with others. Where a local man had complete control, by employing these methods he provided votes equivalent to the number of all men, women, and children of the village for his candidates. In some villages, because of a split within the leadership, village quarters and even tribal sections were allowed to vote for opposing candidates, so as not to cause a serious local crisis. In a very few rural localities, the voter's choice was up to the individual, but each man still voted two or three times. In Al-Karak town, less than half of the votes were dictated by the leaders, the balance of the population, which is made up of the two middle and upper strata, voted as they wished.

In conclusion, the election, won by the government-supported ticket, benefited Al-Karak in many ways. Much more was forthcoming in the way of patronage and promises from a contested election than if matters had been settled solely by negotiation and no balloting had taken place. More money changed hands and more was filtered down to the lowest levels. More commitments for material aid and employment were elicited and these pledges are currently in the process of being fulfilled. As for the successful candidates, they gained or regained their positions, collected on past political debts owed to them by local leaders, and made new ones for themselves. 'Ibrahim Al-Mahadin proved that a substantial minority is willing to back a reforming candidate and had the satisfaction of defeating all other contenders in Al-Karak town. Turning to more general observations, it may be noted that to be a successful candidate, one must have: (1) strong connections with the central government or, at least, friendly relations with it and the assurance that it will not favour one's opponent; (2) considerable funds derived from local or government sources; (3) enough acumen to gather the active support of the local leaders; and (4) membership of a balanced ticket. Finally, the dynamics of selecting members of parliament brings all the politically related groups and leaders into the political process.

Conclusion

The dynamics of contemporary Karaki politics is marked by change and by continuity with the past. Part of the population now thinks of the Kingdom of Jordan in terms of legitimate authority, but the majority, although it has the beginnings of a sense of loyalty for the king, continues to conduct its affairs in terms of self-help and traditional authority. Whole new forms of leadership based on the new and altered social groups have come into being, but the traditionally oriented patterns or alterations thereof maintain their paramountcy. Balancing tradition and change, political activity has taken on many variations. Disputes arise and are settled entirely as they were a hundred years ago, while others result from written contracts and are adjudicated in government courts using contemporary codes of law. Tribes struggle for control of new political institutions such as municipal councils, and political party leaders recruit followers partly by expounding ideas of social justice and revolution. Although influences for change first reached Al-Karak before the Ottoman reoccupation and increased during the Amirate, the district has at present reached a much more advanced stage of transition in which traditional and modern political forces either mesh or conflict continuously with each other.

6

CONCLUSION: CHANGE AND INTEGRATION IN THE POLITICAL SYSTEM

CHANGE in Al-Karak has resulted in a number of cleavages in the socio-political system, for example: the increasing distance between the socio-economic strata, the differences between the educated and uneducated, the more rapid development of the town in contrast to the rural area, the distinction between modern and traditional outlooks or approaches to life, and the growing division between rulers and ruled. Although these features may all be observed solely within Al-Karak district, in another way they exist just as much between Amman and the district, with Al-Karak town in an intermediary position. The intention here then is to bring the major themes of this study together by outlining these gaps which have been mentioned either directly or indirectly in the body of the study and by indicating if and how they are being bridged.

The increased meaning and differentiation of the various socio-economic strata is perhaps the most significant local social development in Al-Karak during the contemporary period. The educated middle stratum has drawn away from the mass of the population in terms of education, occupation, and approach to life; also, its members express disapproval of the traditional political system, wishing either to reform it or radically to alter it through a social revolution. As a result of changed economic relationships, the waning role of the tribe, and the broader functions of the central government, to a varying extent the local leaders and other members of the upper stratum no longer have the same close contacts with the common tribesman as in the traditional period. The gap in education which is related to the developments in stratification may be viewed in three fundamental ways. The simplest difference is between the literate and the illiterate which largely corresponds to the younger and older generations combined with economic opportunities. Equally important, the minimally literate who have received formal instruction for four years or less are greatly outdistanced by those who continued to the secondary level. Another qualitative difference exists between these two groups and those who have professional or university degrees. The modern versus traditional outlooks or approaches to life are reflected in the various strata and educational levels. The educated middle stratum, in contrast with the rest of the population, tends to adopt a more rationalistic view, while the younger elements of the traditionally oriented leadership group partially accept this even though they conform to many of the older norms.

Because people who possess modern skills or have significant political power overwhelmingly tend to live in the town, the widening gap between the urban and rural areas mirrors in a large measure the stratification and educational divisions. This distinction may also be seen in the two possible analytical approaches to this study. On the one hand, it would not have been feasible to investigate the traditional town by itself because of its integral relationship with the district. On the other, as a result of the developments of the last two decades, it would have been possible to look at the town separately in the post-1950 period, but owing to the persistence of the traditional structure this would not have been true to the system.

Finally, the establishment and growth of the central government have created entirely new cleavages between the nation-state and the province. Amman is now a major source of authority and power; no longer are these political goals only in the hands of Karakis as was the case before the Ottoman reoccupation or predominantly so as during the Amirate. The members of the lower stratum and many of the middle and upper strata have little sense of identity with the bureaucracy, regime, business, and social life in Amman. Consequently, all the gaps which exist within the district exist on a far greater scale between the district and Amman.

Both consciously and unconsciously, attempts from numerous directions are being made to temper these divisions, creating the beginnings of a new political integration. The tribal structure is used by new forces to meet the residual traditionalism of the majority of the population. Recognizing the value of this mechanism for social control, the central government works through the tribal leaders and *qadis* in many kinds of disputes and in affairs involving the tribes or tribal groups as units. Although the pyramidal-segmentary structure has noticeably lost power and functions to other groups, it still provides valuable institutions for contact between the strata. Even though many of the educated middle stratum express disdain for the tribes, this group is intricately connected with them through kinship ties which in turn allow for sustained contact between the two sides. Traditionally oriented leaders connect the regime in Amman with their local constituencies. These men are more remote from their followers than previously, but, as was demonstrated in the example of the 1967 parliamentary elections, they take them into consideration in their political actions.

The government is fostering numerous development programmes; co-operatives, communications, education, the provision of welfare and credit, which are specifically designed to close the social and economic gaps. Just in the last decade, most of Al-Karak's children started to receive at least a rudimentary education. The majority of the population now has access to the mass media through the radio and may take advantage of inexpensive transport. Although progress is slow, the peasantry is being helped in its attempt to raise itself above the level of economic subsistence. The government has also created or promotes formal councils and committees on which many of the groups of the society have mutual contact which they otherwise would not have. As a result of these activities, the various segments of the society are being brought closer together and are becoming more actively and questioningly aware of each other and their relative positions.

The process of eliminating these cleavages, which are not mutually exclusive, raises the problem of the structure of government in political and organizational terms. At the highest levels in Amman, two types of élite may be defined. Some are largely traditional in orientation, while others favour slow reform, or promote and work for rapid, but not revolutionary change. Almost all desire economic development in Jordan and most, at the least, evolutionary social change. The traditionally oriented élites maintain their relationships with the people through the tribal structure. Because they only want minimal development, it is sufficient for their purposes. Although many of the more modern élite have this structure open to them as well, it does not meet their requirements because of its inherently conservative character. This group may exercise sporadic influence through the mass media and occasional trips to the small towns and rural areas, but it cannot implement its policies in this way. For the regular execution of government business, these élites must fall back on the bureaucracy. As in any bureaucracy, they must work through many stages before their programmes and the daily exercise of government business reach the population. At the bottom are the lesser-educated men, the lower-level civil servants and teachers, who apply day by day the policies of the top élite. It is through their eyes and actions that the broad mass actually sees what the élite in Amman initiated. Thus, the educated middle stratum which has been discussed at length and brought into this study many times is one of the major keys to the whole process of change. Modernization certainly cannot come about without the entire chain of people, resources, institutions, and actions, but in the context of a small town and district this group holds the crucial position.

Approaching the question of integration from another point of view, the Karakis do have a role in establishing the course of the government's actions and this central body is an integral part of Al-Karak's political structure. That the central government has considerable independent power is not denied, but the local Karakis, either individually or as members of the town's government offices, advisory councils, and committees, do exercise significant influence. When a few individuals wish to proceed along particular lines which require by law the agreement of the central government, they may jointly present a plan for acceptance or rejection and then apply pressure from many directions to have it approved. Equally important are the Karakis in Amman in middle- and high-level posts, especially those who are there as a result of local political patronage. These men are in strategic positions from which they can influence programmes and government operations for the benefit of their Karaki constituents. Consequently, the central government should be seen as a group within the structure, for it not only acts upon others, but is also acted upon by them. Although it holds a superior position thanks to its control of the ultimate power of the state, it is another group, albeit one of a different nature, within the political system.

Politics in Al-Karak, the town and district, no longer retains its unitary character, dominated solely by what has been termed the traditional system. In the contemporary period, considerable differences in terms of stratification, education, orientation towards life, and relations between rulers and ruled have developed. Numerous mechanisms are being used in order to close these gaps and to create a transformed political integration. At the same time, much of the population continues to employ traditional methods or slightly altered forms of them in the course of their daily lives.

APPENDICES

1. *Tribal Names and Villages of Residence*[1]

Tribe	Villages
'Abid	Sakka
'Adayla*	'Amiqa, 'Um Hamat, Thaniyya, Zuhum, Mahna
'Aghwat	Baqi'
'Alawy*	Buwab
'Akasha*	'Adr, Samakiyya, Majdalin
'Amr*	'Abu Taraba, Mughayyir, 'Ariha
'Aybasat	Simra
'Ayyubiyin*	Sayl Al-Karak
Bany Hamida	'Imra', Safra, Faqu'
Baqa'in*	'Adr
Bashabsha*	Mahay
Basirawiyya	Faqu'
Batush	Tayyaba
Bayayda	Madin
Buwaliz*	
Damur*	Mashayrfa, Mahna, Ghawayr
Faraya	Jadayda
Habashna*	Rakin, Bithan, Mazra'a
Haddadin*	
Hajazin*	'Adr, Majdalin, Samakiyya
Halasa*	Hamud
Hataybat	'Iraq
Jabur*	Jid'a Al-Jabur
Jalamda	Madin
Kafawy	Jadayda
Karakiyya*	Mahna
Kharasha	Jahr, 'Um Sarara, Majra, Mahayr, 'Um Al-Hatathir, Dararja, Khawfa
Khata	'Iraq
Madadha*	'Ifranj, Hayy
Madanat*	'Adr, Lujun
Mahadin*	'Azra, Simra, 'Ifranj, 'Aynun
Majaly*	Rabba, Qasr, Yarut, Murud, 'Asal, Thara'
Masanat*	
Masarwa	Jad'a Al-Sayayda
Mbaydin*	Thaniyya, Madin
Mu'asafa	Murud, Hawwiyya
Mu'ayta*	'Adr, Batir, Mumya', Lujun

[1] Starred tribes have members in Al-Karak town. Although some of the village names are written with 'Al-', the usage is inconsistent.

Tribe	Villages
Muwajda*	'Iraq
Nu'aymat*	That Ras, 'Ayna, Shaqir
Nuwaysa*	Mazar, Rajm Al-'Alanda
Qadah	Mahay
Qarum	Jadayda
Qatawna*	Mazar, Rajm Al-'Alanda
Qaysiyya	Rabba, 'Ifranj
Sahaymat*	Ghawayr, Mahna
Sarayra*	Mu'ta, Sul, Hashimiyya
Sayayda	Jad'a Al-Sayayda
Shamayla*	'Ifranj, Buwab
Sharfa*	'Um Rumana, Sayl Al-Karak
Sunna'*	
Su'ub*	Mumya', Thaniyya
Suwadma	Sayl Al-Karak
Tanayshat	Baqi'
Tarawna*	Mazar, Manshiyya, Husayniyya, 'Um Hamat, 'Um Rabayr, Zuhum, Dalayqa
Thanaybat*	Jadayda
Yatma	'Iraq
Zurayqat*	Rabba

2. *Other Groups of, and around, Al-Karak*

Group	Description
'Abid al-Majaly	Former slaves of Majaly
'Abu Nuwas	Palestinian refugees
'Adwan	Tribe of the Balqa'
'Ahlaf	Ghawarna alliance gp
'A'jam	Al-Karak alliance gp
'Amarin	Halasa tribal segment
'Asasfa	Habashna tribal segment
'Awaysa	Ghawarna alliance gp
'Azazma	Bedouin tribe of Negev, refugees in Al-Karak
'Azizat	Former Karaki tribe, now in Balqa'
Bany 'Attiya	Bedouin tribe
Bany Sakhr	Bedouin tribe
Bararsha	Al-Karak alliance gp
Burqan	Halasa tribal segment
Bustanjy	Palestinian refugees
Gharaba	Al-Karak alliance gp
Ghasasna	Al-Karak alliance gp
Ghawarna	People of the Ghawr
Ghazawy	Palestinian refugees
Hawrany	Refugees from Hawran
Hijaya	Bedouin tribe
Huwaytat	Bedouin tribe

Group	Description
'Imamiyya	Al-Karak alliance gp
'Iraq Alliance	Al-Karak alliance gp
Khanazira	Ghawarna alliance gp
Khaza'y	Traditional iron-smiths
Kuwalit	Baqa'in tribal section
Mihlaf	Ghawarna alliance gp
Qasus	Halasa tribal section
Qum Al-Hawsh	Al-Karak alliance gp
Ruwala	Bedouin tribe
Sharaqa	Al-Karak alliance gp
Shawarib	Halasa tribal section
Suyagh	Madanat tribal section

3. *Arabic Terms and Phrases*

Term or phrase	Meaning
'Ahl	Residential family.
'A'ila	Extended family, residential family.
'Alim	'One who knows', one who looks after the interests of the other side in a *bin'amma* treaty.
'Aqid	Raid leader.
'Ashira	Tribe, bedouin tribal section.
'Atwa ad-dam	Guarantee that no member of the killer's *khamsa* will be killed during the *fawrat ad-dam* period.
'Atwa lidifa'	Guarantee that no one of the killer's *khamsa* will be killed outside the district.
'Awlad fulan	Children of so and so, subsection (lineage) of a tribe.
'Ayal fulan	Children of so and so, subsection (lineage) of a tribe.
'Ayb	Shameful, disgraceful.
Ba'ir an-nawm	'Camel of sleep' paid by 5th generation of killer's *khamsa* to stay in the district.
Bayt	Physical house, man and all his sons.
Bin'amma	Negotiated treaty for defence, offence, or mutual relations.
Bisha'a	Ordeal by hot iron placed on the tongue (see p. 101).
Dakhil	'One who enters', one who seeks protection.
Dar	Physical house, man and all his sons.
Dinar, Jordanian	$2·80.
Diya	Payment in cash or kind in a killing.
Diya 'ajnabiyya	Payment for intentional killing between Karaki and non-Karaki.
Diya Muhammadiyya	Payment for accidental killing.
Dunum	1,000 sq. m.

Term or phrase	Meaning
Fakhith	Tribal section, subsection (lineage).
Fannan	Craftiness, slyness, artistry.
Fara'	Tribal section, subsection (lineage).
Farq	Tribal section.
Fawrat ad-dam	'Outburst of blood', period of $3\frac{1}{3}$ days when the deceased's *khamsa* may kill any member of the killer's.
Gharra	Young unmarried woman who must be given as partial payment in a killing (see p. 88).
Hamula	Tribe, tribal section.
Haqq 'am	Public right.
Haqq khas	Private or particular right.
Hawshat al-Kafawy	1921 dispute.
Hawshat al-Babur	1921 dispute.
Jaz'iyya	Criminal
Khamsa	Five-generation group involved in a killing.
Khawa	Payment for protection or service rendered.
Madaniyya	Civil.
Miry	Government land.
Mukhtar	Local representative of the government in the tribe and the tribal representative to the government.
Munahy	Judge for disputes involving blood or honour.
Murabi'	Man who works full time during the agricultural year and theoretically receives one-fourth of the crop from the land for which he is responsible.
Musha'	Periodic redistribution of land.
Mushahy	Judge for minor disputes.
Nady	Club.
Qabila, pl. Qaba'il	Bedouin term for tribe and tribal section.
Qadi	Judge.
Shari'a	Islamic law.
Shaykh al-masha'ikh	Shaykh of the shaykhs.
Suhba	Negotiated treaty of friendship between two groups, e.g. Al-Karak or a Karaki tribe with an outside group.
Suq	Bazaar, market place.
Tulba	Demand as partial payment in a killing for part of the guilty party's best land.
'Urf	Customary law.
'Usra	Residential family.

SELECT BIBLIOGRAPHY

I. *Works in Arabic*

'Arif, 'Arif Al-. *Al-Qada' bayn al-badu.* Jerusalem?, 1933.
'Azizat, Yusif Shwayhat Al-. *Al-'Azizat fi Madaba.* Amman, 1960?.
Dabbagh, Mustafa. *Biladna Falistin.* 1/2. Beirut, 1966.
Kilany, Faruq Al-. *Al-muhakim al-khasa fi al-'Urdun. Beirut,* 1966.
Mady, Munib Al-, and Sulayman Musa. *Tarikh al-'Urdun fi al-qarn al-'ishrin.* Amman?, 1959.
Majaly, Haza' Al-. *Mudhakkiraty.* Amman?, 1960.
Nimr, 'Ihsan Al-. *Tarikh Jabal Nablus wa al-Balqa'.* ii. Nablus, 1961.
Qasus, 'Uda Al-. *Kitab al-qada' al-badawy.* Amman, 1936.
Salman, B., *Khamsa 'a'wam fi sharqy al-'Urdun.* Jerusalem, 1929.

2. *Works in Other Languages*

Abidi, Aqil. *Jordan, a political study, 1948–57.* London, Asia Publishing House, 1965.
Antoun, R. T. Conservatism and change in the village community, *Human Organization,* 24 (Spring 1965), 4–10.
—— On the modesty of women in Arab Muslim villages; a study in the accommodation of traditions, *Amer. Anthropologist,* 70 (Aug. 1968), 671–97.
—— On the significance of names in an Arab village, *Ethnology,* 7 (Apr. 1968), 158–70.
Apter, D. E. *The politics of modernization.* Chicago UP, 1965.
Baer, G. Land tenure in the Hashemite kingdom of Jordan, *Land Economics,* 33 (Aug. 1957), 187–97.
Binder, L., National integration and political development, *Amer. Pol. Sci. R.* 58 (Sept. 1964), 622–31.
Burckhardt, J. L. *Travels in Syria and the Holy Land.* London, Murray, 1822.
Cohen, A. *Arab border villages in Israel.* Manchester UP, 1965.
Dissard, J. Les Migrations et les vicissitudes de la tribu des 'Amer, *R. biblique* (Jerusalem), 18 Jan. 1905, 410–25.
Doughty, C. M. *Travels in Arabia Deserta.* i. CUP, 1888.
Easton, D. *A framework for political analysis.* Englewood Cliffs, NJ, Prentice-Hall, 1965.
—— *A systems analysis of political life.* NY, Wiley, 1965.
Eisenstadt, S. N. *Modernization: progress and change.* Englewood Cliffs, NJ, Prentice-Hall, 1965.
Epstein, A. L. *Politics in an urban African community.* Manchester UP, 1958.
Forder, A. *In brigands' hands and Turkish prisons 1914–18.* London, Marshall, 1919.
—— *Ventures among the Arabs in desert, tent, and town.* Boston, Mass., Hartshorn, 1905.
—— *With the Arabs in tent and town.* London, Marshall, 1902.
Fortes, M., and E. E. Evans-Pritchard. *African political systems.* London, OUP, 1963.

Geertz, C., ed. *Old societies and new states.* NY, Free Press of Glencoe, 1963.

Glubb, Sir J. B. *Britain and the Arabs, a study of fifty years.* London, Hodder, 1959.

—— Economic situation of the Transjordan tribes, *J. Rl. Central Asian Soc.*, 25 (July 1938), 448–59.

—— *Handbook of the nomad, semi-nomad, semi-sedentary and sedentary tribes of Syria.* GSI(T), HQ 9th Army, 1942.

—— *The story of the Arab Legion.* London, Hodder, 1948.

Goichon, A. M. *Jordanie réelle.* 2 v. Paris, de Brouwer, 1967.

Halpern, M. *The politics of social change in the Middle East and North Africa.* Princeton UP, 1963.

Harris, G. L., and others. *Jordan.* New Haven, Conn., Human Relations Area Files, 1958.

Hill, G. *With the beduins.* London, Fisher Unwin, 1891.

IBRD. *The economic development of Jordan.* Baltimore, Johns Hopkins, 1957.

Irby, C. *Travels in Egypt and Nubia and Asia Minor during the years 1817 and 1818.* London, T. White, 1823.

Jaussen, Le P. Antonin. *Coûtumes des Arabes au pays de Moab.* Paris, Libr. d'Amérique et d'Orient Adrien Maisonneuve, 1948.

Kautsky, J. H., ed. *Political change in underdeveloped countries: nationalism and communism.* NY, Wiley, 1962.

Kirkbride, Sir A. *A crackle of thorns.* London, Murray, 1956.

Laoust, H. *Les Gouverneurs de Damas sous les Mamlouks et les premiers Ottomans 658–1156/1260–1744.* Inst. français de Damas, 1952.

Levy, M. J., Jr. *Modernization and the structure of societies.* 2 v. Princeton UP, 1966.

Libbey. W. and Franklin Hoskins. *The Jordan Valley and Petra.* i. NY, Putnam, 1905.

Lutfiyya, A. M. *Baytin, a Jordanian village.* The Hague, Mouton, 1966.

Marx, E. *Bedouin of the Negev.* Manchester UP, 1967.

Médebielle, P. *Kérak, histoire de la mission.* Jerusalem, Imp. du Patriarcat Latin, 1961.

Merrill, S. *East of the Jordan.* London, Bentley, 1881.

Murphey, R. F., and L. Kasdan. The structure of parallel cousin marriage, *Amer. Anthropologist*, 61 (Feb. 1959), 17–29.

Musil, A. *The manners and customs of the Rwala Bedouin.* NY, Amer. Geog. Soc., 1928.

Parsons, T. An analytical approach to the theory of social stratification, *Amer. J. Sociol.* 45 (May 1940), 841–62.

—— *The social system.* London, Routledge, 1951.

Patai, R. *The Kingdom of Jordan.* Princeton UP, 1958.

Peake, F. *History and tribes of Jordan.* Miami UP, 1958 (First publ. Arabic 1935?).

—— Transjordan, *J. Rl. Central Asian Soc.*, 26 (July 1939), 375–96.

Peters, E. The proliferation of segments in the lineages of the Bedouin of Cyrenaica, *J. Rl. Anthrop. Inst.* 90 (Jan.–June 1960), 29–53.

Polk, W. R. *The United States and the Arab world.* Harvard UP, 1965.

Saulcy, F. de. *Voyage autour de la Mer morte.* i. Paris, Gide & Baudry, 1853.

Seton, C. R. W. ed. *Legislation of Transjordan, 1918–1930.* London, Crown Agents, 1931?.

Shwadran, B. *Jordan, a state of tension*. NY, Council for Middle Eastern Affairs, 1959.
Shils, E. *Political development in the new states*. The Hague, Mouton, 1968.
Smith, M. G., Segmentary lineage systems, *J. Rl. Anthrop. Inst.* 86 (July–Dec. 1956). 39–80.
Stirling, P. *Turkish village*. London, Nicolson, 1965.
Sweet, L. E. *Tell Toqaan: a Syrian village*. Ann Arbor, Michigan UP, 1960.
Szyliowicz, J. S. *Political change in rural Turkey, Erdemli*. The Hague, Mouton, 1966.
Tristram, H. B. *The land of Moab*. London, Murray, 1873. ·
Vatikiotis, P. J. *Politics and the military in Jordan*. London, Cass, 1967.
Wallerstein, I., ed. *Social change, the colonial situation*. NY, Wiley, 1966.
Weber, Max. *From Max Weber*. ed. and tr. by H. H. Gerth and C. Wright Mills. London, Routledge, 1948.
—— *The theory of social and economic organization*. ed. and tr. by A. M. Henderson and T. Parsons. NY, Free Press, 1964.
Williams, J. R. *The youth of Haouch El Harimi: a Lebanese village*. Harvard UP, 1968.
Wiseman, H. V. *Political systems*. London, Routledge, 1966.

3. *Jordanian Official Publications (all publ. in Amman)*

Dept. of Stat. *1953 census of agriculture*. 1953.
—— *Al-dirasa al-sina'iyya li'am 1965*. 1967.
—— *First census of population and housing*. 1964. 4 v.
—— *'Ihsa'at al-masakin li'am 1952*. 1952.
—— *Population and internal migration*. 1967.
—— *Population and labour force in the agricultural sector, 1967*. 1968.
—— *Statistical yearbooks*. 1950–67.
Min. Ed. *Al-taqrir al-sinawi 'an al-ta'alim fi madarisiha*. 1967.
Min. Interior. *Regional planning in Jordan*, by V. Lorenz and A. Dakhgan, ii/3. 1967.

4. *Unpublished Material*

'Daftar qararat al-majlis al-balady fi al-Karak' (Journal of the resolutions of Al-Karak municipal council). 1951–66.
Mahadin, Dawi' Al-. 'Al-Karak'. Arabic MS. written at the American University of Beirut. 1963.
Qasus, 'Uda Al-. 'Memoirs'. MS written in mid-1920s.
Public Record Office. F.O., 195. Damascus Consul, 1890–1913, C.O. 733, Palestine 1921–4; C.O. 831, Transjordan, 1925–37.

INDEX

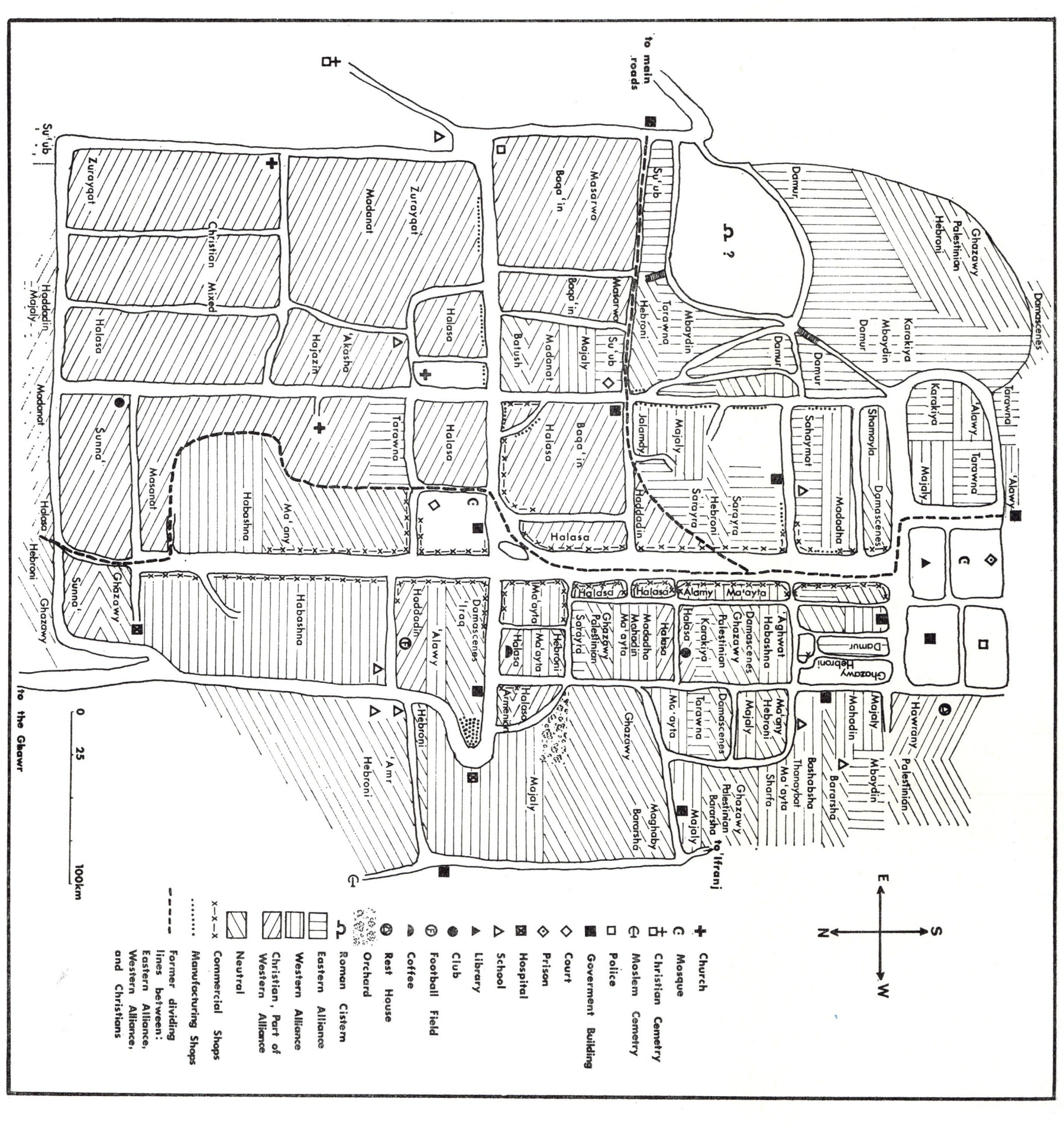

6. AL-KARAK TOWN CITADEL

Church +
Mosque (
Christian Cemetery (
Moslem Cemetery ✝
Goverment Building ▢
Police ☐
Court ◇
Prison ◇
Hospital ▨
School △
Library ▲
Club ●
Football Field ⊕
Coffee ▲
Rest House ⚲
Orchard 🗘
Roman Cistern ⊙
Eastern Alliance ▨
Western Alliance ▧
Christian, Part of
Western Alliance ▨
Neutral ▢
Commercial Shops ▨
Manufacturing Shops ▨
Former dividing
lines between: – – –
Eastern Alliance, ·······
Western Alliance,
and Christians x–x–x